personal typewriting

FOR JUNIOR HIGH SCHOOLS

THIRD EDITION

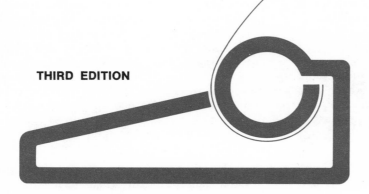

S. J. WANOUS Professor of Education
University of California, Los Angeles

BERLE HAGGBLADE Professor of Office Administration
Chairman, Office Administration Department
Fresno State College

Copyright © 1971
by South-Western Publishing Co.
Cincinnati, Ohio

Standard Book Number: 0-538-20680-2
Library of Congress Catalog Card Number: 78-142721

8 H 8

Published by

T68 **SOUTH-WESTERN PUBLISHING CO.**

Cincinnati   Chicago   Dallas   New Rochelle, N.Y.   Burlingame, Calif.   Brighton, England

Preface

In writing the Third Edition of PERSONAL TYPEWRITING for Junior High Schools, the authors were guided by the following goals:

1. To produce a book well within the ability range and interests of junior high school students for a course of either one or two semesters.

2. To include drills and other aids of the kind and number needed to develop a level of basic skill sufficiently high to permit students to forget their machines in order to handle problem copy.

3. To include in the book a variety of problems dealing essentially with the production of personal and school papers.

4. To provide problems on business letters and other common business forms in order to orient the students to vocational typing.

5. To include instruction and drills on basic English and writing as a means of helping the students to "write on the typewriter."

6. To build into the book a number of features which would enable the teacher to adapt it to the individual needs of his students.

7. To enable students satisfactorily completing the junior high school course to continue with advanced work in vocational typewriting.

Junior High School Level. This book was written especially for junior high school students. In the keyboard sections, only two new keys are covered in a lesson. Keyboard drills concentrate on only one new key at a time. The keys taught are reviewed vigorously and frequently.

The drill and timed writing copy is easy in the early lessons and advances in gradual stages until copy of average difficulty is used. The topics covered in skill-building and problem copy are geared to the interests and experiences of junior high school learners.

The materials in the book on capitalization, punctuation, outlines, footnotes, book reviews, and other school papers were correlated with similar materials in language arts books for the junior high school grades.

Basic Skill. The view is firmly held that personal-typing students must learn to type so well that they can forget the machine in order to focus their attention on the wording and form of the papers they must prepare. To this end, technique drills with goals to be achieved are included in almost every lesson. Speed and control aids are generously spaced throughout the entire book. The copy appears in print, rough draft, and script in order to enable students to develop typing skill under realistic conditions.

Personal and School Papers. Once an acceptable level of basic skill has been developed, the book covers the form and preparation of personal notes, personal business letters, themes, outlines, book reviews, speech notes, class notes, minutes of meetings, agenda, and other personal papers. The students type first from model copy containing detailed reminders. Later they type from unarranged copy.

Composing on the Typewriter. The development of composing skill on the typewriter is a major aim of this book. Short composing drills are started in Lesson 36, after the students have fixed desirable technique patterns. These drills lead gradually to the composing of letters and short papers.

Organization of the Book. The book contains 150 lessons—enough for a two-semester course. The first 75 lessons cover skill development and basic problems. The second 75 lessons review materials covered in the first 75 lessons and present advanced work. In the first half of the book, for example, themes without footnotes are covered. In the second half the students type longer themes with footnotes and bibliographies. Extra-credit problems and alternate suggestions for composing activities are included to accommodate students with varying needs.

New Features of the Third Edition. Type size has been increased, making the copy easier to read and comprehend. The illustrations are larger and more prominent. This applies to the forms the students type as well as to stroking illustrations.

All punctuation drills and complex forms have been moved to the second half of the book in order to give the lessons better balance in the development of new materials.

The amount of graded paragraph copy provided for skill building and measurement has been increased by about thirty percent in order to give the student a maximum of fresh copy on which to develop basic skill.

Acknowledgements. Many teachers and students have helped the authors in collecting, organizing, and writing the materials for this book. We acknowledge their invaluable contributions and express sincere appreciation for their aid and encouragement.

S. J. Wanous • Berle Haggblade

Contents

Operating Parts of the Typewriter

All typewriters have similar parts. These parts are identified in the four segments of a typewriter given below and on page v. Each segment is a composite and not an exact drawing of any one typewriter. For this reason, the exact location of a part may be slightly different from that on your typewriter, but the differences are, for the most part, few and slight.

Extra parts peculiar to your typewriter can be identified by reference to the instructional booklet prepared especially for your typewriter.

In using the illustrations below, follow the line from the number to the part. The function of each part is explained in the textbook. Learn to operate each part correctly, as it is explained to you.

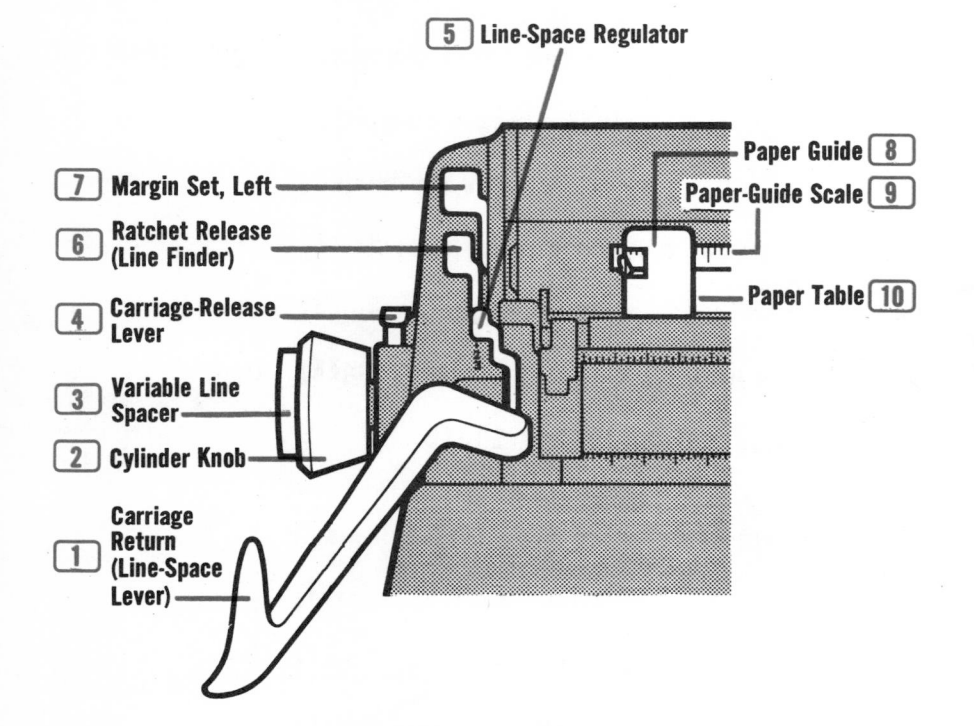

5 Line-Space Regulator

7 Margin Set, Left
6 Ratchet Release (Line Finder)
4 Carriage-Release Lever
3 Variable Line Spacer
2 Cylinder Knob
1 Carriage Return (Line-Space Lever)

Paper Guide 8
Paper-Guide Scale 9
Paper Table 10

Top Left Segment of a Typewriter

Top Right Segment of a Typewriter

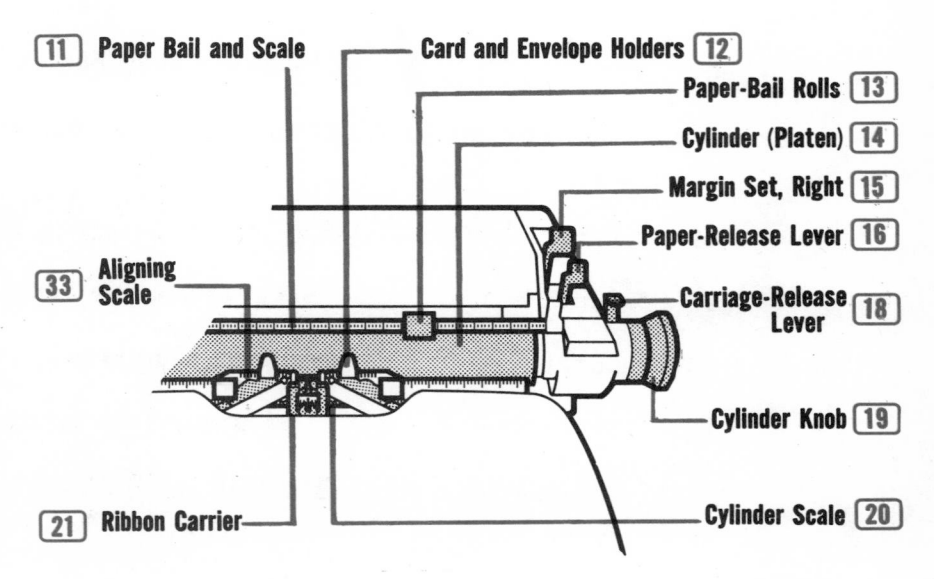

11 Paper Bail and Scale
Card and Envelope Holders 12
Paper-Bail Rolls 13
Cylinder (Platen) 14
Margin Set, Right 15
Paper-Release Lever 16
Carriage-Release Lever 18
33 Aligning Scale
Cylinder Knob 19
21 Ribbon Carrier
Cylinder Scale 20

Lower Segment of a Manual Typewriter

Backspace Key 30
Margin Release Key 25
Ribbon Control, Stencil Lock 22
Ribbon Reverse 32

Shift Key, Left 28
Shift Key, Right 26
Shift Lock, Left and Right . 29
Space Bar 27

Tab Set Key 23
Tab Clear Key 31
Tabulator Bar 24
Touch Regulator 34

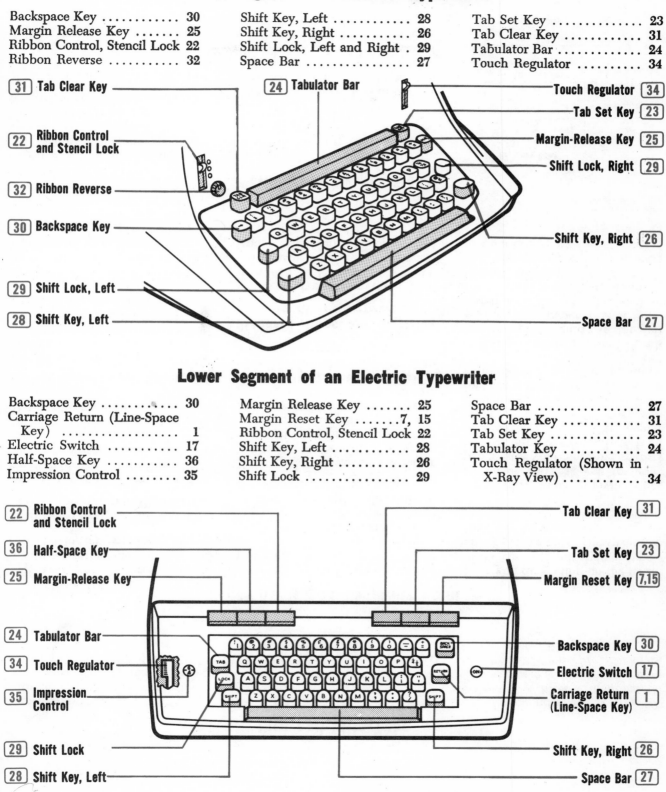

31 Tab Clear Key

24 Tabulator Bar

Touch Regulator 34

Tab Set Key 23

22 Ribbon Control and Stencil Lock

Margin-Release Key 25

32 Ribbon Reverse

Shift Lock, Right 29

30 Backspace Key

Shift Key, Right 26

29 Shift Lock, Left

28 Shift Key, Left

Space Bar 27

Lower Segment of an Electric Typewriter

Backspace Key 30
Carriage Return (Line-Space Key) 1
Electric Switch 17
Half-Space Key 36
Impression Control 35

Margin Release Key 25
Margin Reset Key 7, 15
Ribbon Control, Stencil Lock 22
Shift Key, Left 28
Shift Key, Right 26
Shift Lock 29

Space Bar 27
Tab Clear Key 31
Tab Set Key 23
Tabulator Key 24
Touch Regulator (Shown in X-Ray View) 34

22 Ribbon Control and Stencil Lock

36 Half-Space Key

25 Margin-Release Key

24 Tabulator Bar

34 Touch Regulator

35 Impression Control

29 Shift Lock

28 Shift Key, Left

Tab Clear Key 31

Tab Set Key 23

Margin Reset Key 7,15

Backspace Key 30

Electric Switch 17

Carriage Return 1 (Line-Space Key)

Shift Key, Right 26

Space Bar 27

Machine Adjustments

• *Operating a typewriter involves more than learning to stroke the keys. This page and page vii contain information regarding machine adjustments which you must know for the particular typewriter you are using.*

Pica and Elite Type

Pica:	fjfjfjfjf (10 letters)
	1 inch
Elite:	fjfjfjfjfjf (12 letters)

Some typewriters are equipped with pica type; some with elite type. Pica type is larger than elite type. Note the difference.

Typewriters are of three types in regard to setting the paper guide and arriving at the center point.

1. Royal, Olympia, and Smith-Corona "Secretarial 250" Electric

Set the paper guide on 0 on the paper guide scale. When 8½" x 11" paper is inserted with the left edge against the guide, the center-ing point will be 42 for pica and 51 for elite machines.

2. IBM Model D and Remington

The fixed centering point is 0 for both pica and elite machines. Marks on the paper guide scale aid the typist in setting the paper guide to center paper correctly.

3. Smith-Corona Nonelectric, R. C. Allen, IBM Selectric, and Underwood

You may set the margin stops for any length of line desired, such as a 50-, 60-, or 70-space line. To have equal left and right margins, take these two steps:

Step 1: Subtract half the line length from the center point of the paper. Set the left margin stop at this point.

Paper Guide and Centering Point

A variety of marks appear on the paper table or copy guide scale to aid the typist in setting the paper guide scale for automatic center-ing of 8½" x 11" paper. Marks on the paper bail scale indicate the center point of the paper.

If no marks appear on the paper bail scale to indicate the center point of the paper, insert the paper after the paper guide has been set. Add the carriage scale reading on the left edge of the paper to the reading at the right edge. Divide this sum by 2 to arrive at the center point.

Standard Directions Applying to All Typewriters

On every typewriter, there is at least one scale, usually the cyl-inder scale (No. 20), that reads from 0 at the left to 85 or more at the right, depending on the width of the carriage and style of type—either pica or elite. The spaces on this scale are matched to the spac-ing mechanism on the typewriter.

To simplify direction giving, your instructor may ask you to insert paper into your machine so that the left edge corresponds to 0 on the carriage scale. The center point on 8½" x 11" paper will then be 42 on the carriage scale for pica machines or 51 (or 50 for convenience) on elite machines.

If this procedure is adopted, ad-just the paper guide to the left edge of your paper after it is in-serted with the left edge at 0 on the carriage scale. Note the posi-tion of the paper guide. Move it to this point at the beginning of each class period.

• *The cylinder scale (No. 20) range is from 0 to about 90 on pica machines; from 0 to about 110 on elite machines.*

Setting the Margin Stops

Step 2: Add half the line length, plus 5 to 8 spaces for the end-of-line bell, to the center point. Set the right stop at this point.

The best margin balance is achieved when the right margin stop is set so the bell will ring about 3 spaces before the point at which you want the line to end.

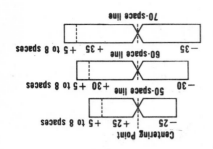

Royal Electric and Nonelectric

1. Set the left margin stop by placing your left index finger behind the left "Magic" margin control and moving it forward. Move the carriage to the desired point; return the margin control to its original position.
2. Repeat Step 1 for setting the right margin stop, using the right "Magic" margin control.

Olympia

Move the left and right margin stops to the desired positions on the scale in back of the cylinder.

Smith-Corona Electric

1. Set the left margin stop by depressing the left carriage release button and the left margin button. Move the carriage to the desired location and release the two buttons simultaneously.
2. Use the same operation to set the right margin.

IBM Selectric

Move the stops to the desired position to get the line length required.

Smith-Corona Nonelectric, R. C. Allen

1. To set the left margin stop, move the carriage to the desired point and touch the left margin button or key.
2. Repeat Step 1 for setting the right margin stop.

IBM and Underwood Electrics

1. Set the left margin stop by moving the carriage until it is against the left margin stop; depress and hold down the margin set key as you move the carriage to the desired position; then release the set key.
2. Repeat Step 1 for setting the right margin·stop.

Underwood Nonelectric

1. Move the left and right margin stops to the desired position on the front scale.
2. The margin indicators on the front scale indicate balanced margin set positions.

Remington Nonelectric and Electric

Set the left and right margin stops by moving them to the desired positions.

Clearing and Setting the Tabulator Stops

Tab Clear – To clear the tabulator mechanism, depress the tab clear key as you move the carriage its full width. To remove an individual stop without canceling other stops, tabulate to the stop, and operate the tab clear key.

- *On Smith-Corona and Olympia typewriters, the total tab clear key clears all stops at one time without moving the carriage.*

Tab Set – To set tabulator stops, move the carriage to the desired position; then depress the tab key. Repeat this operation to set as many tabulator stops as are needed.

Changing the Ribbon

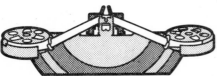

Path of the ribbon as it winds and unwinds on the two spools

- *In general, the instructions given here apply to standard and electric typewriters. Consult the manufacturer's pamphlet accompanying your machine for special instructions.*

1. Wind the used ribbon on one spool. Usually it is best to wind it on the right spool.
2. Study the route of the ribbon as you wind. Note especially how the ribbon winds and unwinds on the two spools. Note, too, how the ribbon is threaded through the ribbon-carrier mechanism.

3. Lift the right spool slightly off its hub to see if both sides are the same. Study both sides of the spool so you will replace it properly.
4. Remove the ribbon from the carrier, and remove both spools. Note how the ribbon is attached to the empty spool. The new ribbon must be attached in the same manner.
5. Fasten the new ribbon to the empty spool, and wind several inches of the new ribbon on it.
6. Place both spools on their hubs, and thread the ribbon through the carrier. Make sure the ribbon is straight.

Basic Techniques

Position of Hands

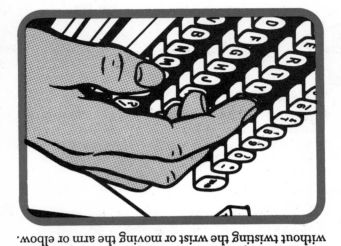

When a finger makes a reach from its home position to strike another key, the other fingers remain on or near

their home keys. Such reaches are made by the finger without twisting the wrist or moving the arm or elbow.

Don't buckle your wrists upward. Hold your wrists down near, but not resting on, the front frame of the typewriter. The forearms should form a parallel line with the slope of the keyboard.

Don't rest your fingers heavily on the home keys. Barely touch them with your fingertips. Feel the keys; don't smother them.

When typing, keep your fingers deeply curved. Girl typists must keep fingernails neatly trimmed. You can't type with long nails.

Do not permit your hands to turn over on the little fingers. Hold the hands directly over the keys. Turn the hands inward slightly to get straight strokes.

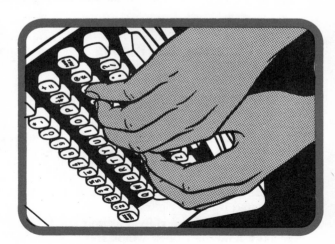

Posture

Good posture is vital in learning to type well. Given here are 10 guides of good form. Study the guides carefully. Observe them whenever you work at your typewriter.

1. Book at right of machine on bookholder or with something under top for easier reading.

2. Table free of unneeded books and papers.

3. Front frame of the typewriter even with the edge of the desk.

4. Body centered opposite the **h** key, 6 to 8 inches from front frame of typewriter.

5. Sit back in chair. Hold shoulders erect with body leaning forward slightly from waist.

6. Elbows held near the body.

7. Wrists held low with forearms parallel to the slant of the keyboard. Do not rest lower hand on frame of typewriter.

8. Your feet on the floor, one just ahead of the other.

9. Head turned toward book with eyes on copy.

10. Fingers curved and held over second row of keys.

Typing Rhythm

Strike the keys at a steady pace, without breaks or pauses. At first, you will think each letter as you type it. Later, you will think and type short, easy-to-type words and phrases as a whole. You will type longer, hard-to-type words by letters or syllables. You will combine whole word typing with letter or syllable typing into a smooth, fluent, steady rhythm.

Stroking

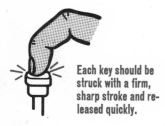

Each key should be struck with a firm, sharp stroke and released quickly.

Center the stroking action in your fingers. Keep elbows, arms, and wrists quiet as you type.

Your fingers should be deeply curved. Use quick, sharp strokes. Release the keys quickly by snapping the fingers toward the palm of the hand.

Hit the keys squarely with short, quick, straight strokes.

The finger is snapped slightly toward the palm of the hand as the key is released.

Spacing Between Words

Almost one in every five strokes is made with the space bar. To operate the space bar correctly:

1. Hold the right thumb curved under the hand just over the space bar.
2. Strike it with a quick down-and-in motion of the thumb.
3. Keep the right wrist low and quiet as you strike the bar.
4. Keep the left thumb out of the way.

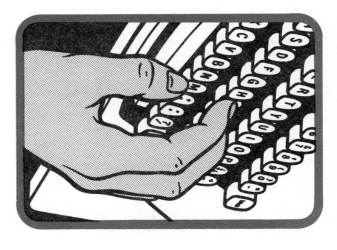

Paragraph Indentions

You will use the tabulator bar or key (No. 24) to indent for paragraphs. Find this bar or key on your typewriter. Touch lightly the tab bar (right index finger) or tab key (right little finger). Deeply curve the other fingers in making this reach.

Returning the Carriage

Manual Typewriter

Return the carriage following these steps:

1. Move the left hand, palm down, to the carriage-return lever (No. 1). Keep your right hand in home position and your eyes on the book.

2. Move the lever forward to take up the slack.

3. With the fingers bracing one another, return the carriage with a flick of the wrist.

4. Quickly return your left hand to its home position and continue typing at once.

Electric Typewriter

1. Reach the little finger of your right hand to the carriage-return key (No. 1).

2. Tap the return key quickly.

3. Quickly return the finger to its home-key position and continue typing at once.

Shift Keys

Use a one-two count:

One – Depress the shift key and hold it down.

Two – Strike the capital letter; then quickly release the shift key and return the little finger to its typing position.

Erasing and Correcting Errors

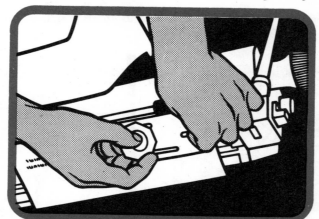

1. Move the carriage to the extreme right or left so that the eraser crumbs will not fall into the typewriter.

2. To avoid moving the paper out of alignment, turn the cylinder forward if the erasure is to be made on the upper two thirds of the paper; backward, if on the lower third of the paper.

3. To erase on the original sheet, lift the paper bail out of the way and place a 5- by 3-inch card in back of the original copy and in front of the first carbon sheet. Use an eraser shield to protect the letters that are not to be erased. Use a hard typewriter eraser. When you complete the erasure, brush the eraser crumbs away from the typewriter.

4. Move the card in front of the second carbon sheet if more than one copy is being made. Erase the errors on the carbon copy with a soft (or pencil) eraser first, then with the hard typewriter eraser used in erasing on the original copy.

5. When the error has been neatly erased on the original and all the carbon copies, reposition the carriage to the proper point, and type the correction.

Typewriter Care

Do Daily

1. Brush the dirt and dust from the typebars.
2. Keep desk free of dust, especially the area under the machine.
3. Cover the machine when it is not in use.
4. Shut off power on an electric typewriter after each use.

Do Weekly

1. Clean type faces, using approved cleaner.
2. Move the carriage to extreme end positions. With cloth moistened with oil, clean the carriage rails on each side.
3. Clean platen, feed rolls, and paper-bail rolls with cloth moistened with cleaning fluid.

Key-Location Drills for Electric Typewriters

"at" sign

Use @ for at in typing bills: 15 pins @ $10 each. The @ is the shift of 2; type @ with the s finger. Space before and after @, as follows: 14 @ $9.50. Buy 437 @ 59. Sell 703 @ 57. We sold 49 @ $5.58.

All typewriters Shift of 2 Type with s finger

"cent" sign

¢¢ jj ¢j ¢j ¢j The ¢ sign is the shift of 6: 66¢. ¢¢ ¢j ¢j ¢j¢ Strike ¢ with the right first finger. Do not space between the ¢ and a figure: 7¢; 85¢. Use ¢ in typing bills: 38 for 74¢ and 48 for 92¢.

All typewriters Shift of 6 Type with j finger

Asterisk

** kk **; kk k*k k*k The * is the shift of 8: 88*. ** kk *k *k Strike * with the right second finger. Use * for some footnotes: I read a book by Hill.* Use ** for a second footnote: I liked his poem.**

All typewriters Shift of 8 Type with k finger

Underline

;; ;_; ;_; _; _; The _ is the shift of the hyphen. _; ;_; Strike the _ with your right fourth finger. She read Irving Stone's The Agony and the Ecstasy. Hit all the keys with quick, short, sharp strokes.

All typewriters Shift of hyphen Type with ; finger

Apostrophe
Quotation marks
(Shift of ')

'; ;'; ;'; The ' is at the right of the semicolon. Strike ' with the right fourth finger: It's here. The " is the shift of the '. "I can go," he said. Use the word "can" often. "Can't" is a weak word.

All typewriters Right of ; key Type with ; finger

"equals" sign
"plus" sign
(Shift of =)

;=; ;=; ;=; =; The = is located on the fourth row. Strike = with the fourth finger. Two = 2. Z = 4. The + is the shift of =. 22 + 36 + 64 + 98 = 220. The equals sign: =; the plus sign: +; 3 + 4 = 7.

All typewriters* 4th row, right 4th finger

1 key
Exclamation point
(Shift of 1)

a1a a1a 1a The 1 key is located on the fourth row. Strike 1 with the left fourth finger. Send me 11. The ! is the shift of 1. Be quick! Hurrah! Run! Send 121 at once! Count to 11; then fire! Hurry!

All typewriters* except IBM, optional on Selectric 4th row, left 4th finger

Bracket key
([is shift of])

a]a a]a]a The] key is located on the fourth row. The [is the shift of]. Reach with [4th] finger. ;]; ;]; ;]; The] key is located on the third row. In that year [1964], he left for Paris [Illinois].

IBM 4th row, left 4th finger Olivetti-Underwood 3d row, right 4th finger

---

* Interchangeable key on the Remington.

Summary of Related Learnings

Capitalization Guides
(pp. 81, 100, 115, and 232)

Capitalize:

1. The first word of a complete sentence.
2. The first word of a quoted sentence. (Do not capitalize fragments of quotations resumed within a sentence.)
3. The pronoun I, both alone and in contractions.
4. Titles of organizations, institutions, and buildings.
5. The names of languages and numbered school subjects. The names of other courses are not capitalized.
6. Days of the week, months of the year, and holidays, but not seasons.
7. Names of rivers, oceans, and mountains.
8. North, South, etc., when they name particular parts of the country, but not when they refer to directions.
9. Names of political parties, religious groups, nationalities, and races.
10. Adjectives that come from a proper name.
11. The names of stars, planets, and constellations, except sun, moon, and earth, unless these are used with other astronomical names.
12. The title of a person when used with his name.
13. First words and all other words in titles of books, articles, periodicals, headings, and plays, except articles, conjunctions, and prepositions. NOTE: The title of a book may be underscored or typed in all capital letters.
14. The first and last words, all titles, and all proper names used in the salutation of a letter.
15. Only the first word of the complimentary close.
16. All titles appearing in the address of letters.
17. A title following the name of the dictator in the closing lines of a business letter.

Number Expression Guides

1. Even sums of money are typed without the decimal and ciphers. (52a, p. 92)
2. Type distances in figures. (53a, p. 94)
3. Type market quotations in figures. (69a, p. 119)
4. Be uniform in typing fractions: ½ and ¼, but 1/2 and 1/5. (96b, p. 162)
5. Use figures to type dates. When the day date comes before the month, use a figure and follow it with th, st, or d. (130b, p. 207)
6. Spell a number beginning a sentence even though figures may be used later in the sentence. (130b, p. 207)
7. Use figures with a.m. and p.m. Use words with o'clock. (130b, p. 207)
8. Type amounts of money, either dollars or cents, in figures. (134b, p. 216)
9. Use ¢ and @ in typing bills. (134b, p. 216)
10. Type percentages in figures. (126a, p. 201)
11. Type policy numbers without commas. (138a, p. 221)

Punctuation Guides

Apostrophe (p. 206)

1. Use an apostrophe in writing contractions.
2. It's means it is. Its, the possessive pronoun, does not take an apostrophe.
3. Use the contraction o'clock (of the clock) in writing time.
4. Add 's to form the possessive of any singular noun.
5. Add an 's to plural nouns that do not end in s.
6. If a plural noun does end in s, add only an apostrophe after the s.
7. The apostrophe denotes possession. Do not use it merely to form the plural of a noun.
8. Use 's, however, to form the plural of figures, letters, signs, and words referred to as words.
9. Add an apostrophe and s to a proper name of one syllable which ends in s to show possession.
10. Add only an apostrophe to a proper name of more than one syllable which ends in s to show possession.

Colon (p. 176)

Use a colon:

1. To introduce a list of items or expressions.
2. To separate the hours and minutes when they are expressed in figures.
3. To introduce a question or long quotation.

Comma (pp. 143 and 167)

Use a comma(s):

1. After each item in a series, except the last.
2. To separate consecutive adjectives when the and has seemingly been omitted. Do not use the comma when the adjectives do not apply equally to the noun they modify.
3. To separate a dependent clause that precedes the main clause.
4. To separate the independent parts of a compound sentence joined by and, but, for, or, neither, nor.
5. To prevent misreading or confusion.
6. To set off a direct quotation from the rest of the sentence. (Do not set off an indirect quotation from the rest of the sentence.)

7. To set off *yes, no, well, now*.
8. To set off parenthetic expressions that break the flow of a sentence. (If the parenthetic expression comes at the beginning or end of a sentence, use one comma.)
9. To set off the name of the person addressed.
10. To set off appositives. (Do not use a comma to separate two nouns, one of which identifies the other.)
11. To separate the day date from the year and the name of the city from the name of the state.

Dash and Parentheses (p. 181)

1. Use a dash to show a sudden break in thought.
2. Use a dash before the name of an author when it follows a direct quotation.
3. Use parentheses to enclose an explanation.
4. Parentheses may be used to enclose the personal title *Miss* or *Mrs.* when used with a typed name. Modern practice omits the parentheses. (47d, p. 84)

Period, Question Mark, Exclamation Point (p. 139)

1. Use a period after a statement or command.
2. Use a period after initials.
3. Use a period after most abbreviations. (Nicknames are not followed by periods.)
4. Use a question mark after a question.
5. After requests and indirect questions, use a period.
6. Use an exclamation point to express strong or sudden feeling.

Quotation Marks (p. 185)

1. Place quotation marks around the exact words of a speaker.
2. When the quotation is broken to identify the speaker, put quotation marks around each part. (If the second part of the quotation is a new sentence, use a capital letter.)
3. Do not use quotation marks with an indirect quotation.
4. Use quotation marks around the titles of articles, songs, poems, themes, short stories, plays, and the like.
5. Always place the period or comma inside the quotation mark.

Semicolon (p. 169)

Use a semicolon:

1. Between the clauses of a compound sentence when no conjunction is used. (If a conjunction is used to join the clauses, use a comma between them.)

2. Between the clauses of a compound sentence that are joined by such words as *also, however, therefore,* and *consequently*.
3. Between a series of phrases or clauses that are dependent upon a main clause.

Spacing Guides (pp. 51, 53, 59, and 132)

1. Space twice after end-of-sentence punctuation.
2. Space twice after a colon. (EXCEPTION: Do not space before or after a colon in stating time.)
3. Space once after a period that ends an abbreviation; twice if that period ends a sentence. Do not space after a period within an abbreviation.
4. Space once after a semicolon or comma.
5. Space before and after the *&* and the *@*.
6. Space between a whole number and a "made" fraction.
7. Do not space between a figure and ½, ¼, #, %, and ¢.
8. Do not space between the $ or the # and the following figure.
9. Do not space between quotation marks or parentheses and the words they enclose.
10. Do not space before or after the hyphen, the apostrophe, the dash, or the diagonal.

Word-Division Guides (p. 55)

Do not:

1. Divide words of one syllable, such as *thought, friend,* or *caught*.
2. Separate a syllable of one letter at the beginning of a word, such as *across*.
3. Separate a syllable of one or two letters at the end of a word, such as *ready, greatly,* or *greeted*.
4. Divide words of five or fewer letters, such as *also, into, duty,* or *excel*.
5. Separate a syllable that does not contain a vowel from the rest of the word, such as *wouldn't*.
6. Divide the last word on a page.

Divide:

1. Words only between syllables.
2. Hyphened compounds at the point of the hyphen; for example, *self-control*.
3. Words so that *cial, tial, cion, sion,* or *tion* are retained as a unit.
4. A word that ends in double letters after the double letters when a suffix is added, such as *fill-ing*.
5. A word in which the final consonant is doubled when a suffix is added between the double letters, such as *control-ling*.

Index

Index to Special Drills

Cycle 1 •

Learning to Operate Your Typewriter

In Cycle 1 of this book, you will learn how to type by touch. You will learn, too, how to use many of the special parts on your typewriter.

When you complete the lessons of this cycle, you will use your typewriter to type stories, themes, letters, and other personal papers.

• Unit I

Learning to Operate the Letter Keys

Know Your Typewriter

Book Placement

Place this book to the right of your typewriter on a bookholder, or put something under the top of the book. Slant it so that you can read the print easily.

Machine Parts

Find each part listed below on your typewriter. Use the illustration as an aid. Learn the names of the parts as they will be used often throughout the book.

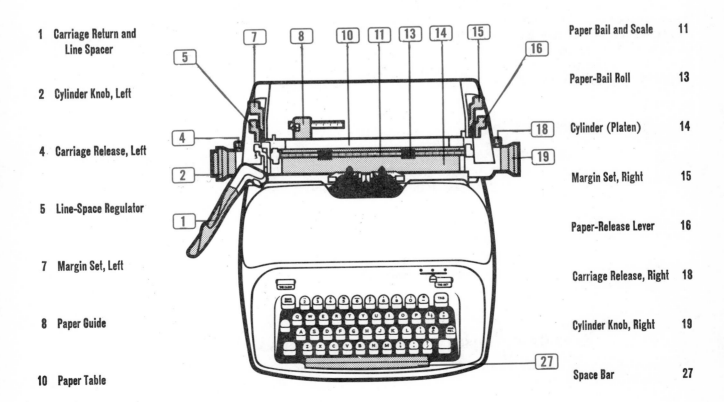

1	Carriage Return and Line Spacer	Paper Bail and Scale	11
2	Cylinder Knob, Left	Paper-Bail Roll	13
4	Carriage Release, Left	Cylinder (Platen)	14
5	Line-Space Regulator	Margin Set, Right	15
7	Margin Set, Left	Paper-Release Lever	16
8	Paper Guide	Carriage Release, Right	18
10	Paper Table	Cylinder Knob, Right	19
		Space Bar	27

150a • Keyboard Review • Each line at least three times

All letters SS   Jack gave Liza an exquisite pink flower made by his mother and sister.

Figure   During that day—May 29, 1962—the market average rose over 27 points.

Opposite hand   We refused to return to resume further talks upon hearing of the ruse.

Flowing, rhythmic stroking

Easy   I know that the majority of our problems grow smaller as time goes by.

| 1 | 2 | 3 | 4 | 5 | 6 | 7 | 8 | 9 | 10 | 11 | 12 | 13 | 14 |

150b • Timed Writings

10 minutes

Directions – Type a 1- and a 5-minute writing on 146d, page 233. Circle errors. Compute *gwam*.

150c • Problem Measurement

30 minutes

Problem 1—Interoffice Memorandum – Type the following memorandum in the form illustrated on page 227.

To: Shirley Schramm / From: Robert J. Piersol / Date: April 14, 197– / Subject: Additional Copies of Ellis Report / Please run off 35 additional copies of the Ellis Report. They are to be attached to the staff meeting minutes of April 3. I have to keep the original copy, so please do not let anything happen to it. (¶) If you do not have time to distribute this material, give Jane a call and she will get someone to help you. It would probably be a good idea to remind her that all engineers are to receive these copies, even if they were not in attendance at the last meeting. Thanks very much for your help. / (xx)

Problem 2—Invoice – Type the following invoice in the form illustrated on page 229.

Sold To The Mullennix Mart, 487 North Sixth, Lincoln, Nebraska 68520 / *Terms* 2/10, n/30 / *Date* May 15, 197– / *Our Order No.* 4258 / *Cust. Order No.* 646 / *Shipped Via* A & M Freight / *Salesman* Louis Mudge

Quantity	Description	Unit Price	Amount
1	S12-726 Transistor Tape Recorder	29.95 ea.	29.95
5	M16-107 LP Record Baskets	7.50 ea.	37.50
2 doz.	E9 1.4v Portable Radio Batteries	8.25 doz.	16.50
			83.95

150d • Extra-Credit Typing — Composing a Business Letter

Directions – Compose a letter to Mr. M. E. Minich, 35 Mesa Drive, Tempe, Arizona 85281. Your purpose is to let him know his schedule for the Management Development Program. Include in the body of your letter the table given in 148c, Problem 2, page 236. Use modified block style with mixed punctuation.

Get Ready to Type

Adjust Your Typewriter

- *The numbers in parentheses following names of machine parts are those assigned to them on pages iv, v, and 1.*

1. Paper guide (No. 8): Adjust the paper guide. The directions for adjusting it vary from machine to machine. Read the directions for your typewriter on page vi.

2. Line-space regulator (No. 5): Set the line-space regulator at "2" for double spacing.——→

3. Margin stops (Nos. 7 and 15): Set the margin stops for a 50-space line, unless this has already been done for you. The directions for setting margin stops vary from machine to machine. Read carefully the directions for your particular typewriter on pages vi and vii.

Insert Paper into Your Typewriter

1. Place typing paper to the left of and turned endwise to the typewriter.

2. Pull the paper bail (No. 11) away from the cylinder (No. 14).

3. Grasp the paper in the left hand.

4. Drop the bottom edge of the paper behind the cylinder (No. 14) and against the paper guide (No. 8). At the same time bring the right hand to the right cylinder knob (No. 19) and twirl it with a quick movement of the fingers and thumb.

5. Adjust the paper bail (No. 11) so that it holds the paper against the cylinder. If necessary, adjust the paper-bail rolls (No. 13). The paper-bail rolls should be about 2 inches from

the left and right edges of the paper.

6. If the paper needs straightening after it is inserted, release it long enough to straighten it. Use the paper-release lever (No. 16).

Check Your Position at the Typewriter

- *See page ix for a larger posture illustration.*

1. Place this book to the right of the typewriter on a book-holder, or put something under the top to raise it for easier reading.

2. Have the front of the typewriter even with the edge of the desk. Your body should be centered opposite the h key.

3. Your body should be 6 to 8 inches from the front frame of the typewriter.

4. Don't slump; sit erect. Hold your elbows near the body.

5. Have your feet on the floor, one just ahead of the other in order to give you good balance.

149b • **Building Skill on Figures and Symbols** • Each line three times 10 minutes

1   SS   I believe the booklet entitled <u>Your Career</u> is on the desk in Room #39.

2   Disney's "Wonderful World of Color" will be shown tonight at 7:30 p.m.

3   Pam Beck (who attended Fort Miller last year) will run the 220 for us.   Work for control

4   Their old Abbott & Costello films can be rented for approximately $15.

5   Only 5% of those who invested received more than 9¢ a share last year.

| 1 | 2 | 3 | 4 | 5 | 6 | 7 | 8 | 9 | 10 | 11 | 12 | 13 | 14 |

149c • **Problem Typing**   30 minutes

Problem 1—Business Letter from Script

50-space line   Date on line 18   Block style   Open punctuation   Current date   Carbon copy   Large envelope

Mr. Gordon L. Ray / 1006 Capitol Avenue / Topeka, Kansas 66634 / Dear Mr. Ray (¶) Enclosed is our refund check for $11.98 covering the purchase price of the drill you recently returned. (¶) We hope this method of handling your order meets with your approval. Please think of us again whenever you need tools or electrical equipment. / Yours very truly / Gerald Novack / Customer Service / (xx) / Enclosure

Problem 2—Interoffice Memorandum

Directions – Type the following memorandum in the form illustrated on page 227.

To: All Employees / From: Wayne Brooks, Manager / Date: February 7, 197– / Subject: Excessive Employee Absence / During the last two weeks several supervisors have brought to my attention the fact that excessive absences among staff members have been causing some work load problems in our various departments. (¶) I realize that the majority of you are most conscientious about using your sick leave only for its intended purpose. You know that each employee was hired to do a job because that particular job has to be done. If you are not here, someone else must attempt to do your work in addition to his own. Naturally, when we are considering people for promotions, we have to give a good deal of weight to past attendance records. (¶) Again, I do want to stress that the sick leave program is to be used when needed, but I want you also to be more aware of what problems continued absences cause your fellow employees and the management. I know we can count on your cooperation. / (xx)

Problem 3—Business Letter from Script

Directions – Retype the letter in Problem 1 above, making these changes: 1. Address the letter to Mr. C. E. Nelson, 41 Butler Street, Joplin, Missouri 64801. 2. Change the amount of the check to $14.95.

• Lesson 1

1a • Find the Home Keys and Space Bar

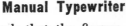

1. Place the fingers of your left hand on a s d f.

3. Take your fingers off the home keys. Replace them. Say the keys of each hand as you touch them. Repeat several times to get the "feel" of these keys.

4. Hold your right thumb over the middle of the space bar. Strike it with a quick, inward motion of your right thumb. . Keep the left thumb out of the way.

2. Place the fingers of your right hand on j k l ;.

5. Curve your fingers. Hold them very lightly over the home keys.

6. Type the line below. Say and think each letter as you strike it.

```
ff jj dd kk ss ll aa ;; fdsa jkl; fdsa jkl; fj fj
```

1b • Return the Carriage

Manual Typewriter

2. Check that the fingers of the right hand are on their home keys.

3. Move the lever forward to take up the slack.

1. Move the left hand, palm down, to the carriage-return lever (No. 1).

4. With the fingers bracing one another, return the carriage with a flick of the wrist.

5. Return your left hand at once to its home position.

Electric Typewriter

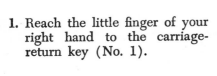

1. Reach the little finger of your right hand to the carriage-return key (No. 1).

2. Tap the return key quickly.

3. Return the finger at once to its home-key position.

148c • Problem Measurement   *30 minutes*

Problem 1—Business Letter in Rough Draft

50-space line
Date on line 18
Modified block
Blocked ¶'s
Open punctuation
Carbon copy
Large envelope

June 17, 197-

~~Mr.~~ Dr. Harry Jaskinski
The National Business ~~School~~ College
3029 Aberdeen Avenue
Madison, Wisconsin 57346

Dear ~~Mr.~~ Dr. Jasinski

On Firday, June 23, the military affairs committee ~~is~~ t will
sponsor~~ing~~ a luncheon at the Madison Country club in
one¶ honor of Col, Orville Molmen and his wife. The luncheon
#¶ ~~is plann~~ scheduled for 11:45 a.m.
Colonel Molmen, Commanding Officer at ~~Fort~~ Camp Washington, us July 1.
has been re assigned and will be leaving ~~next week~~. We
~~¶hope~~ are hoping that all community business represent-
atives and thier wiyes will join in the program. and professional brief, informal

Because tile is limited, it is necessary that we extab-s
lish a reservation deadline of June 21. Please return
your check in the enclosed envelope.
and reservation card

Sincerely yours,
Warren Montagne, Chairman
Military Affairs committee

(Add ref. initials
and enclosure
notation)

Problem 2—Table

MANAGEMENT DEVELOPMENT PROGRAM

Half sheet
Centered vertically
Double spacing
6 spaces between columns

←————Triple-space

Topic	Date	Leader
What Is Management?	September 12	Mr. Minich
Management Decision Making	October 10	Mr. Cutler
Management Communication	November 7	Mr. Lewis
Management Policy	December 12	Mr. Hendry

• Lesson 149 • *70-space line*

149a • Keyboard Review • Each line at least three times   *5 minutes*

All letters SS	The woman gave hazy explanations for both of Judge Mackey's questions.	
Figure	Approximately 1,074 girls and 875 boys were enrolled there after 1970.	Feet on the floor
Opposite hand	Mrs. Weiner held a lien against their car and later tried to seize it.	
Easy	He knew he could pay for a new bicycle with the profit from his route.	

| 1 | 2 | 3 | 4 | 5 | 6 | 7 | 8 | 9 | 10 | 11 | 12 | 13 | 14 |

1c • Home-Key Practice

Directions – Type each line with your teacher at least once.

Technique Goal – Think and say each letter as you strike it.

1   ff jj ff jj ff jj ff jj ff jj fj fj fj fj fj fj fj

2   dd kk dd kk dd kk dd kk dd kk dk dk dk dk dk dk dk

3   ss ll ss ll ss ll ss ll ss ll sl sl sl sl sl sl sl

Home keys

4   aa ;; aa ;; aa ;; aa ;; aa ;; a; a; a; a; a; a; a;

Think and say each letter

5   fj dk sl a; fj dk sl a; fj dk sl a; fj dk sl a; fj

6   fdsa jkl; fdsa jkl; fdsa jkl; fdsa jkl; fdsa jkl;

1d • Technique Builder — Stroking

Directions – Type each line once with your teacher. Type the lines a second time by yourself.

Technique Goal – Curve your fingers. Use quick, sharp strokes.

1   all all fall fall all all fall fall all fall falls

2   ad lad ad lad ad lad all a lad all a lad all a lad

3   as ask as ask as ask ask all ask all ask all ask a

Home keys

4   ask a lad; ask all lads; all ask a lad; a lad asks

Quick, sharp strokes

5   all fall; as a lad falls; all fall; as a lad falls

6   a lad; a lad falls; all lads; all lads fall; a lad

1e • Remove the Paper

1. Pull the paper bail (No. 11) out from the cylinder (No. 14).

2. Depress the paper-release lever (No. 16).

3. Remove the paper with your free hand.

4. Return the paper-release lever to its original position.

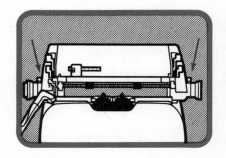

1f • Center the Carriage

Before leaving your typewriter, center the carriage. To do so, depress the right or left carriage-release lever (No. 4 or 18), and move the carriage to the approximate center of your typewriter.

Also, pick up all paper and dispose of it.

Lesson 148 · *70-space line*

148a • Keyboard Review • Each line at least three times

5 minutes

All letters	SS	Wilbur Jessup may get the bronze plaque for fixing the very old clock.
Figure		Wall Street had 16,410,000 shares of stock traded on October 29, 1929.
Weak fingers		The popular politicians followed the policy favored by their populace.
Easy		If he signed up for the class, he would have to take it eighth period.

Quiet wrists and arms

| 1 | 2 | 3 | 4 | 5 | 6 | 7 | 8 | 9 | 10 | 11 | 12 | 13 | 14 |

148b • Speed Stretcher • Use Speed Stretchers for 5-minute writings, or use each paragraph for 1-minute writings.

10 minutes

GWAM
1' 5'

All letters
¶ 1 DS
65 words
1.4 si

When a baby is born in the South Sea Islands, several new coconut   13 3 53
trees are planted to make sure that the new arrival will have enough   27 5 55
to eat in his later years. Coconuts are utilized for food in all stages   42 8 58
of growth. Many experts on food and nutrition state that nobody can   55 11 61
starve in lands in which the coconut tree grows.   65 13 63

¶ 2
68 words
1.4 si

The green nut produces clear, sweet water that is highly refresh-   13 16 66
ing. Milk from the ripe nut is considered to be as easy to digest as   27 18 68
cow's milk and nearly equal to it in food value. The meat of a half-   41 21 71
ripe coconut is used as a vegetable; that of a ripe nut, as dessert.   55 24 74
The coconut is enjoyed by millions of people as food almost daily.   68 27 77

¶ 3
68 words
1.4 si

The nut also furnishes oil for soap, lotions, candles, and oleo,   13 29 79
as well as food for cattle. The tree itself is a source of sugar, and   27 32 82
its leaves go into brooms, screens, hats, bags, and table mats. The   41 35 85
shell of the nut is made into buttons and eating utensils. Certainly   55 38 88
this tropical tree is among our most versatile and useful plants.   68 40 90

¶ 4
48 words
1.3 si

The coconut tree bears fruit in about seven years. Good trees   13 43 93
produce from eighty to one hundred nuts a year. The best yield twice   27 46 96
that many. The nuts are gathered a half dozen times yearly, providing   41 48 98

All ¶'s
1.4 si
a year-round supply for the natives.   48 50 100

| 1' | 1 | 2 | 3 | 4 | 5 | 6 | 7 | 8 | 9 | 10 | 11 | 12 | 13 | 14 |
| 5' | | | 1 | | | 2 | | | 3 | | | |

• Lesson 2

2a • Know Your Typewriter

1. As your teacher calls the parts listed on page 1, find them on your typewriter.

2. Adjust the paper guide. If necessary, read the directions for your machine on page vi.

3. Set the margin stops for a 50-space line, unless this has already been done for you. If necessary, read the directions for your typewriter on pages vi and vii.

4. Set the line-space regulator at "2" for double spacing.

5. Insert paper. Adjust the paper-bail rolls.

6. Check your position: Front of typewriter even with desk edge. Body centered opposite **h** key, 6 to 8 inches from front of typewriter. Sit erect; hold elbows near body. Feet on floor, one foot ahead of the other.

2b • Keyboard Review

Directions – Type each line once with your teacher.

Spacing Guide – Space once after a semi-colon (;) within a line.

1		ff jj dd kk ss ll aa ;; ff jj dd kk ss ll aa ;; fj
2		fj dk sl a; fj dk sl a; fj dk sl a; fj dk sl a; fj
3	Home keys	all all fall fall lad lad ask ask all fall ask lad
4		all fall; as a lad falls; all lads fall; ask a lad
5		ask a lad; ask a lad; ask all lads; as a lad falls

Think each key as you strike it

Plan for Learning New Keys

1. Find new key on keyboard chart.
2. Locate key on your typewriter.
3. Place fingers over home keys.
4. Know what finger strikes key.
5. Watch your finger as you make the reach to the new key.
6. Type each short drill twice on the same line. Be sure to use the correct finger.

2c • Location of G and U

Find **g** on the chart. Find it on your typewriter keyboard. Place your fingers over the home keys. Touch **gf** lightly without moving the other fingers from their typing position.

←——REACH TO G   REACH TO U——→

Find **u** on the chart. Find it on your typewriter keyboard. Place your fingers over the home keys. Touch **uj** lightly without moving the other fingers from their typing position.

TYPE **g** WITH THE **f** FINGER

TYPE **u** WITH THE **j** FINGER

fgf fgf gf gf lag lag lag   • Type twice on same line •   juj juj uj uj dud dud dud

• Lesson 147 • *70-space line*

147a • Keyboard Review • Each line at least three times
5 minutes

All letters SS My box was packed with five dozen jars of apple, fig, and quince jams.

Figure Our nation ranked fourth in production in 1860; we were first by 1894.

Type steadily

Double letters I succeeded in addressing all five letters in a matter of three weeks.

Easy Those girls who could work at the game were asked to sign their names.

| 1 | 2 | 3 | 4 | 5 | 6 | 7 | 8 | 9 | 10 | 11 | 12 | 13 | 14 |

147b • Building Skill on Figures and Symbols • Type each line once. Then type two 1-minute writings on each sentence.
10 minutes

1 SS In 1963, Arnold Palmer broke his own golfing record ($81,448 in 1962).

2 Many Irish males between 20 and 39 (about 66%, in fact) are bachelors.

Work for control

3 In the 1963 Grand Prix, Jimmy Clark set a lap record of 131.147 m.p.h.

| 1 | 2 | 3 | 4 | 5 | 6 | 7 | 8 | 9 | 10 | 11 | 12 | 13 | 14 |

147c • Problem Typing
30 minutes

Problem 1—Business Letter in Modified Block Style

60-space line   Date on line 18   Indented ¶'s   Modified block   Mixed punctuation   Carbon copy   Small envelope

• *The opening and closing lines of this letter are in problem form. Capitalize and punctuate them correctly.*

january 5, 197– / mr harold e lane / 1428 east chestnut avenue / atlanta georgia 30342 / dear mr lane / We appreciate very much your attendance at the recent preview showing of our latest office equipment. We were glad that such a large number of people were able to come on rather short notice. (¶) It was a real pleasure for us to explain the new 110 Series family of computers. Although it was our intention to make this first session as complete as possible, we realize there may be areas of special interest to you in which you would like more information. Should you have questions about any aspect of this system, I hope you will get in touch with your local NRA dealer. He will be happy to help you. (¶) Thanks again, Mr. Lane, for being with us. Sincerely yours / w f parker / sales representative / (xx)

Problem 2—Business Letter with Subject Line

Directions – Retype the letter in Problem 1. Add this subject line:

SUBJECT: Preview Showing of 110 Series

Problem 3—Business Letter with Attention Line

Directions – Type the letter in Problem 1 again. Omit the subject line, and address it to:

Goertzen Supply Company / 1006 Capitol Avenue / Topeka, Kansas 66634 / Attention Mr. Elvin Goertzen / Gentlemen

2d • Location Drills — G and U

Directions – Type each line once with your teacher. Type the lines a second time by yourself.

Technique Goal – Think and say each letter as you strike it.

1	g	fgf fgf fgf fgf gf gf gf gf lag lag flag flag flag
2		lad lad glad glad lag lag flag flag slag slag flag
3	u	juj juj juj juj uj uj uj uj dud dud dull dull dull
4		full full dud dud dull dull us us us fuss fuss dud

Type g with the f finger

Type u with the j finger

2e • Technique Builder — Eyes on Copy

Directions – Set the line-space regulator at "1." Type each line twice as shown.

Technique Goal – Keep your eyes on the book. Think each letter as you type.

- *To double-space between groups of lines, operate the carriage-return lever or key twice. To triple-space, operate the lever or key three times.*

1   fdsa jkl; fdsa jkl; gf uj gf uj gf uj jug jug jugs ← Single-space
    fdsa jkl; fdsa jkl; gf uj gf uj gf uj jug jug jugs ← repeated lines

2   lug lug slug slug lad lad glad glad lag lag flags;
    lug lug slug slug lad lad glad glad lag lag flags;

Double-space when you start a new line

3   us us fuss fuss dug dug; dug a jug; dug a full jug
    us us fuss fuss dug dug; dug a jug; dug a full jug

4   a lad; a jug; a lug; a jug; a flask; a glass flask
    a lad; a jug; a lug; a jug; a flask; a glass flask

Triple-space between parts ← of a lesson

2f • Fluency Practice

Directions – Type each line twice. Double-space after the second typing of a line.

Technique Goal – Use quick, sharp strokes. Release the keys instantly.

1   a lad; all lads; a lug; all lugs; a dud; all duds;

2   a full lug; a full jug; a full glass; a full flask

3   all fall; lug lugs; jug jugs; flag flags; us fuss;   Each line twice

4   dusk dusk gull gull gulls fluff fluff; a dull gull

5   a lad; a lad falls; a lad lags; a lad lugs; a lad;

Remove paper—Center carriage

GWAM
1' 5'

All letters
¶ 1 DS
44 words
1.4 si

Although there has been talk for years about moving people via   13 3 55
fast trains, monorails, or tubes, the automobile continues to reign   26 5 57
supreme. Auto makers say there may soon be as many cars in the land   40 8 60
as there are adults.   44 9 61

¶ 2
48 words
1.4 si

No one knows, of course, just what cars of tomorrow will be like.   57 11 63
The consumer might be able to buy a tiny shopping car for use around   71 14 66
town, a large cruiser to drive out on the highway, and a specialized   85 17 69
vehicle for his recreational needs.   92 18 70

¶ 3
52 words
1.4 si

Safety will be the aim of many changes in cars of the future. One   105 21 73
official predicts that warning lights to alert drivers to dangers such   120 24 76
as tires that are low on air will be common. Engineers are working on   134 27 79
rear-view devices that will be better than mirrors.   144 29 81

¶ 4
56 words
1.4 si

If the trend to more and more cars continues, there is no doubt   157 31 83
that some kind of traffic control systems will be required. Some now   171 34 86
in limited use are connected to computers that change traffic light   184 37 89
timing of the direction of traffic in freeway lanes to speed the flow   198 40 92
of cars.   200 40 92

¶ 5
60 words
1.4 si

Disposing of old cars as they wear out will also pose a massive   213 43 95
problem. About six million cars are junked every year in the United   227 45 97
States alone. Laid end to end they would stretch nearly around the   240 48 100
earth at the equator or fill an eight-lane highway bumper-to-bumper   254 51 103

All ¶'s
1.4 si

from New York to San Francisco.   260 52 104

1' | 1 | 2 | 3 | 4 | 5 | 6 | 7 | 8 | 9 | 10 | 11 | 12 | 13 | 14 |
5' | | | 1 | | | | | 2 | | | | 3 | | |

146e • **Creative Typing** • Type a short paper on how you expect to use your typing skill. Give your paper a title and type the final copy in unbound manuscript style as directed on page 95.   *10 minutes*

• Lesson 3

3a • Keyboard Review

Directions – Type each line once with your teacher. Type the lines again by yourself.

- Spacing: Double.
- Margins: 50-space line. Set the left stop 25 spaces to left of center of paper. Move the right stop to the end of the scale.

Posture Goal – Sit erect. Hold elbows near the body. Keep wrists low and quiet.

g   `fgf fgf gf gf lad glad lad glad lag slag lag flag;`

u   `juj juj uj uj lug slug lug slug jug jugs jug jugs;`   Eyes on this copy

All letters taught   `us us dusk dusk fluff fluff all fall; a flag falls`

             `a full lug; a full jug; a full flask; a full glass`

3b • Location of E and H

Find **e** on the chart. Find it on your typewriter keyboard. Place your fingers over the home keys. Touch **ed** lightly. Move the **d** finger upward and forward without moving your hand.

←—REACH TO E   REACH TO H—→

Find **h** on the chart. Find it on your typewriter keyboard. Place your fingers over the home keys. Touch **hj** lightly without moving the other fingers from their typing position.

TYPE e WITH THE d FINGER   TYPE h WITH THE j FINGER

`ded ded ed ed led led led`   • Type twice on same line •   `jhj jhj hj hj had had had`

3c • Location Drills — E and H

Directions – Type each line once with your teacher. Type the lines a second time by yourself.

Technique Goal – Snap the finger toward the palm of the hand after each stroke.

e   `ded ded ded ded ed ed ed ed led led fled fled fled`   Type e with the d finger

       `led lag led lag fled flag us use use fuse fuse use`

       `sue sue due due glue glue jade jade desk desk fell`

h   `jhj jhj jhj jhj hj hj hj hj hall hall had had half`   Type h with the j finger

       `had a half; had a half; a half lug; had a half jug`

       `ash gash lash sash flash flush hush husk shall has`

Improving Your Basic Skills — Measurement

General Directions • Lessons 146 – 150

Machine Adjustments – Follow the general directions given in earlier units of this cycle.

Erasing – Unless your teacher directs otherwise, erase and correct any errors you make.

Special Forms – Type the problems on the special forms provided in the workbook or on plain paper.

• Lesson 146

• *Use a 70-space line for all lessons in this unit.*

146a • Keyboard Review • Each line at least three times   *5 minutes*

All letters	SS	The boxer jabs a quick volley into a dazed opponent when fighting him.
Figure		We hope to hold the 1975 meetings on March 29-31 instead of April 4-6.
Balanced- and one-hand		if it is to pull, if it is to trace, if it is to join, if it is to get
Easy		To get to the top of the oak, do not merely sit on the acorn and wait.

Fingers deeply curved

| 1 | 2 | 3 | 4 | 5 | 6 | 7 | 8 | 9 | 10 | 11 | 12 | 13 | 14 |

146b • Control Builder • Type four 1-minute writings at your control rate.   *5 minutes*

DS   When our western states were young, travel across their arid lands

posed a problem. In seeking an answer, someone proposed the camel. It

**65 words
1.4 si**   could carry heavy loads, move quickly across deserts, go without water,

Type without pauses

and live on prickly pears and scrub brush. Although the beasts did

well, the railroads soon took their jobs away.

146c • Capitalization Guides — Business Letter Parts • Read the explanations; each line three times.   *5 minutes*

Line 1 – In business letters, capitalize the first and last words, all titles, and all proper names used in the salutation.

Line 2 – Capitalize only the first word of the complimentary close.

Line 3 – All titles appearing in the address should be capitalized.

Line 4 – If a title follows the name of the dictator in the closing lines of a business letter, it must be capitalized.

1	SS	Dear Sir: My dear Sir: Dear Mr. Smith: Dear Dr. Johnson: Dear Mary
2		Yours truly, Sincerely yours, Yours very truly, Cordially yours, Yours
3		Mr. John Good, Manager; Miss Ellen Day, Secretary; Mr. Ben Blue, Chief
4		John Brown, President; Fred Hill, Attorney; Mary Stone, Vice-President

Quick, firm reach to the shift key

| 1 | 2 | 3 | 4 | 5 | 6 | 7 | 8 | 9 | 10 | 11 | 12 | 13 | 14 |

3d • Technique Builder — Finger-Action Stroking

Directions – Set line-space regulator at "1."
Type each line twice.

Technique Goal – Move your fingers, not your arms or wrists.

```
1    fdsa jkl; fdsa jkl; gf uj ed ed hj hj led fled leg
2    sell sells fell fell dull dull seek seek feel feel
3    due due duel dude dude had had he he she she shell
4    flee flee gull gull sell sell shell shell had shad
5    jell jell us us use use fuse fuse sue sue had half
```

← Double-space after second typing of line

Triple-space between
← lesson parts

Reach to first row

Finger-Action Stroking

When one of your fingers reaches from its home position to strike another key, keep the other fingers near their home keys. Make the reach without raising the wrist or moving your arm or elbow.

Reach to third row

3e • Fluency Practice • Each line three times

```
1    he had; she had; he led; she led; a lad had a half
2    he led; she led; he led us; she led us; had a dull
3    he has; she has; he has a half lug; she has a full
4    a dull hue; a full glass; a full keg; she had half
```

Type without pauses

• Lesson 4

- *Spacing: Double.*
- *Margins: 50-space line.*

4a • Keyboard Review

Directions – Type each line once with your teacher.
Type the lines again by yourself.

Posture Goal – Sit back in your chair with body centered opposite **h** key.

```
e    ded ded ed ed led led fled fled sled sled sell led
h    jhj jhj hj hj had had hall hall half half held led
u    juj juj uj uj lug dug full full sue sue fuel us us
     keg jug she shall half glass; she had a dull duel;
     jell husk dusk; a full keg; a half lug; she shall;
```

Eyes on this copy

All letters taught

145b • Timed Writings • Type a 1- and a 5-minute writing on 141d, page 226. Circle errors. Compute *gwam*.

10 minutes

145c • Problem Typing

30 minutes

Problem 1—Interoffice Memorandum with Table

Directions – Type this interoffice memorandum in the form shown in 142c, page 227. Use a 60-space line. Leave 5 spaces between columns in typing the table. Double-space before and after the table. Prepare one carbon copy.

- *If necessary, see directions for arranging tables on page 109.*

To: William H. Pollard / *From*: Harry A. Raynes, Vice-President / *Date*: June 6, 197– / *Subject*: New Accounts / The following investors have purchased a Participating Agreement in the Trust Fund according to the terms set forth in our latest bulletin:

Mr. and Mrs. Jay Caffee	M329385
Mrs. Elma Hodge	E284376
Dr. Edward Reighard	E038298

As you know, the Agreement permits the making of periodic additional investments. In every case these investments mean an extension of an established program. Each investor has set his goal at $1,200. (¶) Participating Agreement Certificates should be delivered to these people as soon as the account numbers have been registered by the Trustee, First National Bank of Dallas. / (xx)

Problem 2—Table

Directions – Type the following table centered vertically on a full sheet. Triple-space between the heading and the first item; double-space the items. Leave 6 spaces between columns. Prepare one carbon copy.

- *If necessary, see directions for vertical centering on page 62.*

TRUST FUND INVESTORS, MAY 1, 197–

Miss Barbara Atwood	431 Oak Street	Odessa, Texas 79760
Mr. Ellis T. Austin	5221 Elm Avenue	Tulsa, Oklahoma 74126
Mr. Robert F. Bennett	347 Garden Way	Dallas, Texas 75252
Mr. John T. Emerson	5127 Maple Street	Ogden, Utah 84427
Mrs. Richard Helm	54 Gail Street	Taos, New Mexico 87571
Mr. Victor Jepson	1426 Linwood Drive	Phoenix, Arizona 85033
Mr. Robert F. Pietrowski	6822 Riker Street	Austin, Texas 78741
Mr. Jay Quinn	1030 Paul Avenue	Reno, Nevada 89546
Mrs. Helen F. Rohrer	78 Laurel Drive	Dallas, Texas 75239
Mr. Tony Thele	3177 Pearl Street	Tucson, Arizona 85758
Miss Judy Van Gundy	37 Shaw Drive	Tulsa, Oklahoma 74114
Mrs. Wilma Wight	1919 Long Avenue	Reno, Nevada 89562

145d • Extra-Credit Typing

Problem 1

Directions – Type the interoffice memorandum given in 142c, Problem 1, page 227. Prepare one carbon copy. Fill in the headings as follows:
To: T. A. Young / *From*: Earle J. Moore / *Date*: *May* 25, 197– / *Subject*: New Date Stamp Procedure

Problem 2

Directions – Type on a half sheet the table given in 145c, above. Center it vertically. Triple-space after the heading; single-space the items. Leave 4 spaces between columns. Prepare a carbon copy.

4b • Location of R and I

Find **r** on the chart. Find it on your ←—REACH TO R   REACH TO I—→ Find **i** on the chart. Find it on your
typewriter keyboard. Place your fingers over the home keys. Touch **rf** lightly. Move the **f** finger upward and forward without moving your hand.

Place your fingers over the home keys. Touch **ik** lightly. Raise the **j** finger slightly to give the **k** finger freedom of movement.

TYPE **r** WITH
THE **f** FINGER

TYPE **i** WITH
THE **k** FINGER

```
frf frf rf rf fur fur fur    • Type twice on same line •    kik kik ik ik did did did
```

4c • Location Drills — R and I

Directions – Type each line once with your teacher. Type the lines again by yourself.

Technique Goal – Reach to **r** and **i** without moving your hands forward. Hold the wrists low and quiet.

```
r       frf frf frf frf rf rf rf rf fur fur furs furs sure      Type r with
                                                                 the f finger
        surf surf rug rug drug drug rue rue rule rule jars

i       kik kik kik kik ik ik ik ik did did slid slid dike      Type i with
                                                                 the k finger
        dike jig jig fig fig dish dish fish fish fill fill
```

Hands turned sidewise

Straight, Direct Stroking

Do not permit your hands to turn sidewise on the little fingers. Hold the hands directly over the keys. Turn the hands in toward your thumbs slightly to get straight, direct strokes.

←——Wrong   Right——→

Hands directly over keys

4d • Technique Builder — Straight, Direct Strokes • Change to single spacing. Type each line two times.

```
1       fdsa jkl; rf rf rf ik ik ik did did dike dike ride
                                                             ←—Double-space
2       rug rug rig rig drill drill frill frill lark rifle
3       rid rid ail ail rail rails sail sail keel keel lid
4       rig rig rug rug side side rule rule jail jail sale
5       he has; she has; he had; she had; he did; he slid;
                                                             ←—Triple-space
```

144b • Typing Titles of Articles and Poems

10 minutes

Directions – 1. The first line gives the rule; the remaining lines apply it

2. Type each sentence three times; then take a 1-minute writing on each sentence.

1 ss The name of a poem, article, or play should be set in quotation marks.

2 Today, each English class will read Longfellow's "Paul Revere's Ride." — Quick carriage return

3 He saw it in Leigh White's article, "Chicago's Airport of the Future." — return

4 Joyce and Beth were lucky to get such good tickets for "My Fair Lady."

| 1 | 2 | 3 | 4 | 5 | 6 | 7 | 8 | 9 | 10 | 11 | 12 | 13 | 14 |

144c • Problem Typing

30 minutes

Problem 1—Interoffice Memorandum • As directed in 142c, page 227

To: The Staff / From: E. R. Mead, Manager / Date: November 12, 197– / Subject: Wrist Calendars / Many of you have commented about the excellent response you received from customers regarding the wrist calendars we provided as gifts last year. We are therefore planning to give these handy calendars to our regular customers and friends again this year. (¶) Please pick up your supply from Miss Johnson in Room 119. If you think you will need more than she has set aside for you, you can request extras after each employee has received his original supply. (¶) You will note that they are printed on each side for use with either a yellow or white gold watch band. / (xx)

Problem 2—Invoice • As directed in 143c, page 229

Sold to Russel & Coe, 538 East Indian Road, Fort Wayne, Indiana   46807
Terms 2/10, n/30 / *Date* December 12, 197– / *Our Order No.* 98736 /
Cust. Order No. 3749 / *Shipped Via* Union Freight / *Salesman* D. L. Bastady

Quantity	Description	Unit Price	Amount
2	M53 C-2594 Hand Mixers	15.95 ea.	31.90
10 pr.	FM-79Z Wire Cutters	4.45 pr.	44.50
8 gal.	23-60 White House Paint	8.95 gal.	71.60
			148.00

• Lesson 145 • *70-space line*

145a • Keyboard Review • Each line at least three times

5 minutes

All letters ss Elizabeth very quickly solved the sixth problem again just for Weston.

Figure Mt. McKinley, the highest point in North America, is 20,320 feet high. — Sit erect

Long reach The builders in Illinois had only a minimum of light aluminum numbers.

Easy It is usually better to keep your chin up than to stick your neck out.

| 1 | 2 | 3 | 4 | 5 | 6 | 7 | 8 | 9 | 10 | 11 | 12 | 13 | 14 |

4e • Fluency Practice

Directions – Each line three times. Double-space after the third typing of a line.

Technique Goals – Return the carriage without looking from the copy. Type at a steady pace.

1   he had a disk; she hid a dish; she had a dark dish

2   he had a red sled; he did ride; he had a hard ride

3   she had a fur; she had a real fur; she sells furs;

4   he held a safe lead; she held a shelf; he hid here

Type without stopping

• Lesson 5

- *Spacing: Double.*
- *Margins: 50-space line.*

Quick, Sharp Stroking

Strike each key with a quick, sharp stroke. Release it quickly.

Snap the finger slightly toward your palm as the key is released.

5a • Keyboard Review • Type once — then repeat

Home row   fdsa jkl; fdsa jkl; gf hj gf hj fall glad half had

r   frf frf rf rf fur fur sure sure surf surf rug drug

i   kik kik ik ik did did slid slid dike dike hid hide

Quick, sharp strokes

All letters taught   disk rush gull ride lake jail fail; she hid a sled

she had a hard sled ride; she held a real fur sale

5b • Location of C and N

Find **c** on the chart. Find it on your typewriter keyboard. Place your fingers over the home keys. Touch **cd** lightly. Hold the a finger in typing position, but let the other fingers move slightly.

←—REACH TO C   REACH TO N—→

Find **n** on the chart. Find it on your typewriter keyboard. Place your fingers over the home keys. Touch **nj** lightly without moving the other fingers from their typing position.

TYPE c WITH THE d FINGER

TYPE n WITH THE j FINGER

dcd dcd cd cd car car car   • Type twice on same line •   jnj jnj nj nj and and and

143c • Problem Typing

Problem 1—Invoice

• *An invoice is a bill. It is a printed form on which are typed the quantities and items delivered, the unit prices, the extensions, and the total. Some invoices have ruled columns; some do not.*

Directions – Type the invoice shown below. Clear your machine of tab stops; set your left margin and new tab stops at the positions indicated. Make one carbon copy. (*A form is provided in the workbook.*)

Lindquist and Larson Company

48 Katherine Avenue
Fort Wayne, Indiana 46827
Telephone (219) 748-3948

INVOICE

DATE August 5, 197–

SOLD TO Tom Willis Supply Shop
410 West Curtis Street
Terre Haute, Indiana 47836

OUR ORDER NO. 90388

CUST. ORDER NO. 1290

SHIPPED VIA Rapid Transit

TERMS 2/10, n/30

SALESMAN Robert Larson

QUANTITY	DESCRIPTION	UNIT PRICE	AMOUNT
1	S12 D-9048 12-Transistor Radio	49.95 ea.	49.95
8 rolls	E14 X-12 "3000" Speed Film	1.25 roll	10.00
5 gal.	X60 B-9093 Insecticide	2.48 gal.	12.40
			72.35

Margin — Tab — Tab — Tab (Double-space)

Invoice

Problem 2—Invoice • As directed in Problem 1

Sold To Luellen Hardware, 1393 Granada Avenue, Jackson, Mississippi 39264 / *Terms* 2/10, n/30 / *Date* June 15, 197– / *Our Order No.* 90389 / *Cust. Order No.* 2387 / *Shipped Via* National / *Salesman* Robert Larson

Quantity	*Description*	*Unit Price*	*Amount*
4	S18 B-3570 Clock Radios	22.95 ea.	91.80
2	P19 B-3257 Car-Home Coolers	49.95 ea.	99.90
12 doz.	S61 109 "Hawkeye" Golf Balls	6.35 doz.	76.20
			267.90

• Lesson 144 • *70-space line*

144a • Keyboard Review • Each line at least three times

5 minutes

All letters SS Dick's primary job was to explore the large maze even more frequently.

Figure Dan lives at 5767 North Bond Street; his telephone number is 477-8487.

Shift The game of Jai Alai originated among the Aztec Indians of old Mexico.

Easy If you type right, you will be hitting those keys as if they were hot.

Elbows in

| 1 | 2 | 3 | 4 | 5 | 6 | 7 | 8 | 9 | 10 | 11 | 12 | 13 | 14 |

5c • Location Drills — C and N

Directions – Type each line once with your teacher. Type the lines again by yourself.

Technique Goal – Strike each key with a quick, sharp stroke. Release it quickly.

c dcd dcd dcd dcd cd cd cd cd cud cud call call cake   Type c with
    lick lick sick sick such such rice lace luck cluck   the d finger

n jnj jnj jnj jnj nj nj nj nj an an and and sand end   Type n with
    land land ran ran end end lend lend sign sign send   the j finger
    fin fin find find rain rain gain gain sun sun sung

5d • Technique Builder — Quick, Sharp Stroking • Single spacing — each line twice

1 nu nu cd cd ail fail an and land and hand end lend
2 run rung sun sung sin sing fine find kind can hand
3 in inch end send ice slice sliced us dusk rush run   Quick, sharp
4 lark lack lake cake ache arch urn churn sign learn   strokes
5 an and land sand hand end send lend ail fail sails

5e • Fluency Practice • Each line three times

1 she can run; she can slide; she can run and slide;
2 he can lend; he can lend a hand; he can send a rug
3 he he; if he is here; he hid in; he hid in a field   Type steadily
4 and find; and he can find; and he can find a guide

• Lesson 6

• Spacing: Double.
• Margins: 50-space line.

6a • Keyboard Review • Type once — then repeat

n   jnj jnj nj nj an an and clan land land sun sun end
c   dcd dcd cd cd cud cud cull cull call call luck can
r, i   frf kik rf ik fur fir furl fire ride hire fir fail   Eyes on
    this copy

All letters taught   slide hail grill sure lake drake flack jack field;
    he and she can run; held a nail; lack a drill flag

Problem 2—Interoffice Memorandum – Type the following memorandum according to the directions given in Problem 1.

To: Richard Rogers, Office Manager / From: Robert Ross, General Manager / Date: July 25, 197– / Subject: Staff Meeting / Our next staff meeting will be held on Wednesday afternoon at 3:15. We shall have to meet in the committee room on the third floor because our regular committee room is being used for a sales conference. Please notify all the members in your department of the time and place. (¶) Your report will be the first item we have to consider. If you can have copies made for everyone, I think we can save quite a bit of time. Since we have a very full agenda, it looks as though the meeting will probably last until nearly 5 o'clock. / (xx)

• Lesson 143 • *70-space line*

143a • **Keyboard Review** • Each line at least three times   *5 minutes*

All letters	SS	We expected the six girls to make a quick move to Arizona before July.	
Figure		The largest fish ever caught by rod was a shark weighing 2,536 pounds.	Wrists and
Long words		The first atom bomb explosion was detonated at Alamogordo, New Mexico.	elbows still
Easy		You must have a goal in mind if you want to profit from your practice.	

| 1 | 2 | 3 | 4 | 5 | 6 | 7 | 8 | 9 | 10 | 11 | 12 | 13 | 14 |

143b • **Speed Stretcher** • Use Speed Stretchers for 5-minute writings, or use each paragraph for 1-minute writings.   *10 minutes*

G W A M
1'   5'

All letters
¶ 1
61 words
1.4 si
DS

Every summer many thousands of teenagers search for jobs in which   13 3 42
they can earn some money for a trip, a new fishing rod, or simply to   27 5 44
help out with the family budget. Getting a paycheck of your very own   41 8 47
can be fun, but there are several points that should be kept in mind   55 11 50
in obtaining summer employment.   61 12 51

¶ 2
67 words
1.4 si

Try to get employment that is in line with your career plans. In   13 15 54
that way you can gather first-hand information about your chosen career.   28 18 57
You will be able to decide whether or not you and your career make a   42 21 60
good team. It's quite important that you learn this about yourself.   56 23 62
This is not the only principle to keep in mind, however.   67 26 65

¶ 3
66 words
1.4 si

A summer job affords you a chance to learn how to work. Capi-   12 28 67
talize on that opportunity to learn how to work with others, to take   26 31 70
directions, and to put what you already know to the acid test. This   40 34 73

All ¶'s
1.4 si

is the real payoff for summer work—an opportunity to learn what is   54 36 75
expected, plus a chance to see how well you can fill the bill.   66 39 78

| 1' | 1 | 2 | 3 | 4 | 5 | 6 | 7 | 8 | 9 | 10 | 11 | 12 | 13 | 14 |
| 5' | | 1 | | | 2 | | | 3 | | | |

6b • Location of T and . (period)

Find **t** on the chart. Find it on your ←REACH TO T   REACH TO .→ Find the period on the chart. Find it typewriter keyboard. Place your fingers over the home keys. Touch **tf** lightly without moving the other fingers from their typing position.

on your typewriter keyboard. Place your fingers over the home keys. Touch **.l** lightly, lifting the little finger only enough to give freedom of movement.

TYPE **t** WITH
THE **f** FINGER

TYPE **.** WITH
THE **l** FINGER

```
ftf ftf tf tf fit fit fit    • Type twice on same line •    l.l l.l .l .l fell. fell.
```

6c • Location Drills — T and . (period)

Directions – Type each line once with your teacher. Type the lines again by yourself.

Technique Goal – Reach to the new keys without moving the hands out of position.

t
```
ftf ftf ftf ftf ftf tf tf tf it it fit fit lit lit
```
Type **t** with the **f** finger
```
lift lift the then then then stiff stiff fit it it
```
```
tan than than than hit hit jet jet let let sit sit
```
Type **.** with the **l** finger
. (period)
```
l.l l.l l.l l.l l.l .l .l .l fill. full. sell. l.l
```

6d • Shifting for Capitals — Left Shift Key

The left shift key (No. 28) is used to type capital letters with the right hand.

USE A
ONE-TWO
COUNT

One – Depress the shift key with the **a** finger. Hold it down.

Two – Strike the capital letter; then quickly release the shift key and return the **a** finger to its typing position.

Directions – Change to single spacing. Type each line two times.

Spacing Guide – Space twice after a period that ends a sentence, except when the period comes at the end of the line. When it does, return the carriage without spacing.

1
```
Hi Hi Hi Hi Hill Lue Lue Luke Hi Hill and Lue Luke
```

2
```
Jud ran.  Jud ran here.  I can see.  I can see it.
```
Space twice after period

3
```
Jill hid a lid.  Hugh had it.  I can see Lil Hill.
```

• Lesson 142 • *70-space line*

142a • Keyboard Review • Each line at least three times   5 minutes

All letters SS   My exploits as a jockey amazed quite a few after they began to arrive.

Figure-Symbol   Attendance at all their home games increased 5% between 1968 and 1971.   Wrists low

Adjacent keys   Sandra has always assumed that all necessary assistance was available.   and still

Easy   People should not blame others for a problem they bring on themselves.

| 1 | 2 | 3 | 4 | 5 | 6 | 7 | 8 | 9 | 10 | 11 | 12 | 13 | 14 |

142b • Technique Builder — Stroking • Each line twice   5 minutes

1   SS   quiz azure police apply taxes flaw hazy axe zero soap war palm was set

2   upon square zone plow lamp play flax cases quack zipper zeal possesses   Fingers

3   They politely applauded the plays. The astronauts waited on the pads.   deeply

4   Samuel soon saw that I was acquitted. His lazy pupils flunked a quiz.   curved

| 1 | 2 | 3 | 4 | 5 | 6 | 7 | 8 | 9 | 10 | 11 | 12 | 13 | 14 |

142c • Problem Typing   30 minutes

Problem 1—Interoffice Memorandum

• *The interoffice memorandum is used for correspondence between offices or departments within a company. Its chief advantage is that it can be set up quickly.*

Directions – Type the interoffice memorandum shown. Use a 60-space line.

Great Western Mortgage Service, Incorporated

1017 PACIFIC AVENUE   **TELEPHONE (206) 998-3828**   **SEATTLE, WASHINGTON 98174**

INTEROFFICE CORRESPONDENCE

		Words
Personal title omitted	**TO:** Robert E. Hampton	5
	FROM: William C. Wayne	9
	DATE: July 21, 197-	14

← ——————— Double-space

SUBJECT: New Date Stamp Procedure   21

← ——————— Triple-space

The mail room returned the attached envelope to us today with   33
a note asking that we stop using our present stamp. The one   45
made for our office should be thrown away as we have not used   58
a post office box address for several years.   67

A new stamp is being made, and we should get it next week. If   79
it is necessary for you to use the old one during the next few   92
days, just draw a line through the box number and write in our   105
street address. Please tell the others in your department to   117
follow the same procedure until you get your new stamp.   128

Reference initials   xx   129

Interoffice memorandum

6e • Technique Builder — Shift-Key Control

Directions – Each line two times. **Technique Goal –** Hold the shift key down until you strike the capital letter; then release it quickly.

1   tf .l tf .l if if it it is is the the the fit fits

2   he the then; an than thank; in thin think; at that

3   it fit fight; he the their thing; rid rides stride

4   It is here. Hal hid it. Jeff can see it. I ran.   Space twice after period

5   Jess can tell us. He can sell it. I can take it.

6   He has the right light. Jess can see it at night.

7   It is light. It is right. It is right and light.

• Lesson 7

- *Spacing: Double.*
- *Margins: 50-space line.*

7a • Keyboard Review

Directions – Type once; then repeat. **Posture Goal –** Hold shoulders erect with body leaning forward slightly from the waist.

t   tft tft tf tf the then than it fit fight lit light

Shift   Hi Hi Hill Jud Jud Judge Li Li Lil; Lil King; Lulu

. (period) l.l l.l .l .l Jud can sell. Lil can fill the jug.   Space twice after period

All letters taught   Karl said that he called at night. He can see us.

Jeff and Jack caught that large fish in June Lake.

7b • Location of V and Y

Find v on the chart. Find it on your typewriter keyboard. Place your fingers over the home keys. Touch vf lightly without moving the other fingers from their typing position.

←—REACH TO V   REACH TO Y—→

Find y on the chart. Find it on your typewriter keyboard. Place your fingers over the home keys. Touch yj lightly without moving the other fingers from their typing position.

TYPE v WITH THE f FINGER

TYPE y WITH THE j FINGER

fvf fvf vf five five five   • Type twice on same line •   jyj jyj yj yj jay jay jay

		GWAM
		1' 5'

All letters
¶ 1 DS
44 words
1.4 si

In the days before TV and the daily paper brought weather reports 13 3 55
and farm news quickly to all our homes, one household item was thought 27 5 57
to be almost as important to the good life as the Bible. That item 41 8 60
was an almanac. 44 9 61

¶ 2
48 words
1.4 si

According to one editor, city folks seem to like almanacs as much 57 11 63
as their country cousins do. He thinks this is because nearly everyone 72 14 66
has a love for the soil in him, and an almanac represents a link with 86 17 69
life on the farm of bygone days. 92 18 70

¶ 3
52 words
1.4 si

Almanac ranks have now shrunk to roughly a dozen different ones 105 21 73
from the hundreds that were printed a century ago. One that claims 118 24 76
to be among the oldest was founded at the time George Washington was 132 26 78
President. It still has its old-time cover and type style. 144 29 81

¶ 4
56 words
1.4 si

Today there are still readers who swear by almanac predictions. 157 31 83
Some like to read the choice bits of homespun philosophy, the helpful 171 34 86
household hints, and the stale jokes found in almanacs. Morticians, 185 37 89
banks, and stores of every kind give them to their best customers each 199 40 92
year. 200 40 92

¶ 5
60 words
1.4 si

At the heart of each almanac is its calendar, telling about the 213 43 95
daily rising and setting habits of the sun and moon and suggesting 226 45 97
excellent days for planting and fishing. Many of these handy guides 240 48 100
to better living come with a hole in one corner so they can be hung 254 51 103

All ¶'s
1.4 si

from a nail in the kitchen wall. 260 52 104

1' | 1 | 2 | 3 | 4 | 5 | 6 | 7 | 8 | 9 | 10 | 11 | 12 | 13 | 14 |
5' | 1 | 2 | 3 |

141e ● **Skill Comparison** ● Type a 1-minute writing on each sentence in 141a, page 225. Compare rates.   *5 minutes*

7c • Location Drills — V and Y

Directions – Type each line once with your teacher. Type the lines again by yourself.

Technique Goal – Think the letters as you type. Use quick, sharp strokes.

v   fvf fvf fvf fvf vf vf vf vf five fives lives lives   Type v with the f finger

     have have five five give give dive dive hive hives

y   jyj jyj jyj jyj yj yj yj yj jay jays lay lays slay   Type y with the j finger

     sly sly fly fly try try jay jay ray ray stay stays

     the they dry dray try tray fry fray lay slay yells

7d • Shifting for Capitals — Right Shift Key

The right shift key (No. 26) is used to type capital letters with the left hand.

USE A
ONE-TWO
COUNT

One – Depress the shift key with the ; finger. Hold it down.

Two – Strike the capital letter; then quickly release the shift key and return the ; finger to its typing position.

Directions – Change to single spacing. Type each line two times.

Spacing Guide – Remember to space twice after a period that ends a sentence (except at the end of a line).

1   Sue Sue Dick Dick; Sue and Dick; Rus Rus Rush Rush

2   Sue is here. Dick can see Sue. Gus Rush can fly.   Quick, firm reach to the shift key

3   Dick is ill. He left the ring. Rus can take Sue.

7e • Technique Builder — Shift-Key Control

Directions – Each line three times. Double-space after the third line.

Technique Goal – Hold the shift key down until you strike the capital letter; then release it quickly.

1   vf yj vf yj day day dry dry say say stay stay days

2   the they ray tray stray sly slay ray gray yet year

3   I can have. I can have a tray. He can give five.   Return without spacing after . at the end of the line

4   Jan and I can stay. Jan can stay there five days.

5   Hal and Karl are here. Jay left his sleigh there.

6   He can learn. He can gain all the skill he needs.

Typing Business Forms

General Directions • Lessons 141 – 145

Machine Adjustments – Use a 70-space line for drills and timed writings in this unit. Single-space sentences and drill lines. Double-space between groups of repeated lines. Double-space paragraph copy. It will be necessary for you to reset your margins before typing problem copy.

Erasing – Your teacher will tell you whether or not you are to erase errors on problem copy.

Special Forms – For problems, use the forms provided in the workbook or plain paper.

• Lesson 141

141a • Keyboard Review • Each line at least three times   *5 minutes*

All letters	SS	To move enough zinc for export would require buying trucks and a jeep.	
Figure		In an 1895 car race, the winner drove 53 miles in 10 hours 23 minutes.	Eyes on
Opposite hand		Dick Dark had a knack for finding all kinds of kindling on their dike.	this copy
Easy		It is true that one who does not drive his auto right may not be left.	

| 1 | 2 | 3 | 4 | 5 | 6 | 7 | 8 | 9 | 10 | 11 | 12 | 13 | 14 |

141b • Control Builder • Type four 1-minute writings at your control rate.   *5 minutes*

Words

DS   Gerbils are small rodents of Old World origin. They make fine,   13

active pets. A hamster can be an introvert, but not a gerbil. They   27

65 words
1.4 si
drink tiny amounts of water, so their cages don't need much cleaning.   41

Because of their good nature and ease of care, gerbils are in growing   55

demand for use in medical research these days, too.   65

141c • Speed Ladder Sentences   *10 minutes*

Directions – Type each sentence for 1 minute with the call of the guide at 15-, 12-, or 10-second intervals.

Technique Goal – Return the carriage quickly.

			GWAM 15" 12" 10"
1	SS	Be sure your feet are flat on the floor.	32 40 48
2		One foot should be placed ahead of the other.	36 45 54
3		Proper position of the feet will aid your balance.	40 50 60
4		Keeping your elbows close to your body will help, also.	44 55 66
5		Hold your wrists down low, just above your typewriter frame.	48 60 72
6		Keep the hands quiet; do not bound them in the air when you type.	52 65 78
7		Make quick, sharp strokes with your fingers well curved over the keys.	56 70 84

| 1 | 2 | 3 | 4 | 5 | 6 | 7 | 8 | 9 | 10 | 11 | 12 | 13 | 14 |

• Lesson 8

8a • Keyboard Review

Directions – Type once; then repeat.   Posture Goal – Wrists held low; elbows near body.

v	fvf fvf vf vf five five live live hive hive sleeve
y	jyj jyj yj yj jay jay say say stay stay yell yells

Wrists low

Shift	Gus Rus Al Sue Ruth Glen Dan and Fred; Val and Jan
All letters taught	Dan and Sue can catch the large fish in June Lake.
	Ray Kirk says I can have the five trays Sue needs.

Elbows near body

8b • Technique Builder — Stroking • Single spacing — each line at least two times

1		He had a jar. The hat is in the sun. He can run.
2	Two- and three-letter words	The lad can see us. It is in a rug. I had a gun.
3		I can get it in a day if Al can see us. It is he.

Quick, sharp strokes

4		Sue hid the red rug. The lad can hit the fat hen.
5	Three-letter words	She can get the rug and the gun. Dan hid her hat.
6		Dan and Sue hid the gun and fur. She has her hat.

Instant release

7		They left here last year. They sent the red list.
8	Four-letter words	They sent five jugs. Tell Ruth they have her car.
9		They have nine huge kegs; they sent the keys here.

Wrists low and still

10		Griff likes these signs. Frank likes large desks.
11	Five-letter words	Chuck still takes these cakes. Clara sells sleds.
12		Grace stays there. Keith fills these large tanks.

```
|   |  1  |  2  |  3  |  4  |  5  |  6  |  7  |  8  |  9  |  10  |
```

Fingers deeply curved

8c • Sentence Skill Builder

Directions – Type a 1-minute writing on the first line of each group of lines in 8b. Compute your gross words a minute (*gwam*).

In typewriting 5 strokes are counted as one word. Each line in 8b has 50 strokes, or 10 words. For each full line typed, give yourself a score of 10 words. Two full lines typed, for example, give you

20 gwam. For a partially typed line, note the scale under the sentences. Add the figure nearest the last word or letter typed to your complete sentence score. This total is your gross words a minute (gwam).

140c • Problem Typing

30 minutes

Problem 1—Business Letter in Modified Block Style

60-space line	Date on line 18	Modified block	Indented ¶'s	Mixed punctuation	Current date	Carbon copy	Large envelope

Miss Vicky Wall / 8811 West Third Street / Baltimore, Maryland 21234 / Dear Miss Wall: / Our little booklet, *How to Learn Music at Home,* is enclosed with this letter. I know you are anxious to discover how soon you can be playing the instrument of your choice. (¶) Our unique picture method is explained on pages 10 and 11. Through this new approach to learning music, you will be able to play simple melodies right from the very first day. (¶) On page 15, you will want to read about some of our most famous pupils. Many outstanding professional musicians got their start by using our methods. Even more important, however, is the fact that thousands of people from all walks of life have had their lives enriched by being able to play for their own enjoyment. (¶) I am sure you will want to fill out and mail the enrollment form that is printed on the back cover of the booklet. Your first lesson will be on its way to you the day your letter is received. / Very sincerely yours, / HOME STUDY MUSIC SCHOOL / David H. Weakley, President / (xx) / Enclosure

Problem 2—Composing a Business Letter

Directions – Compose an answer to the letter typed in Problem 1. Mention the type of instrument you wish to learn to play and state that you are enclosing your enrollment form. Use the letter style you prefer. Use your own return address.

• *With your teacher's permission, you may type the Alternate Suggestion below instead of this problem.*

Alternate Suggestion

60-space line	Date on line 18	Block style	Mixed punctuation	Carbon copy	Large envelope

September 4, 197– / Mrs. Victor Panico / 639 East Portals Drive / Greeley, Colorado 80639 / Dear Mrs. Panico: / We are planning to open a child care center for small children, ages three through five. The center will endeavor to provide a happy and wholesome schedule of activities for children during the day when their parents cannot care for them. (¶) We are hopeful that the opening date will be November 1. The facilities will operate Monday through Friday from 7 a.m. to 6 p.m. every month of the year. Fees will be $18 per week. (¶) In order to determine the need and desire for such a day care program, we should like your cooperation in completing and returning the enclosed form. If you want to be informed when the center is opened, please place a check mark in the space indicated. / Very truly yours, / CHILD CARE CENTER / Susan Cresto, Manager / (xx) / Enclosure

140d • Extra-Credit Typing

Problem 1 – Type Problem 1, page 217, in block style, open punctuation. Address the letter to Blomgren & Company (same mailing address), Attention Mr. Blomgren.

Problem 2 – Type Problem 2, page 223, in modified block style, mixed punctuation. Add an appropriate subject line.

Problem 3 – Type the problem you did not type for 140c, above.

8d • Indenting for Paragraphs

You will use the tabulator bar or key (No. 24) to indent for paragraphs. Find this bar or key on your typewriter. Touch lightly the tab bar (right index finger) or tab key (right little finger). Deeply curve the other fingers in making this reach.

Next, turn to page vii and read how to use the tab clear key (No. 31) and the tab set key (No. 23).

8e • Paragraph Typing

Directions – Set machine for a 5-space paragraph indention and double spacing. Type twice. Repeat if time permits.

Technique Goal (*Manual*) – Hold the tab bar or key down until the carriage stops.
(*Electric*) – Tap the tab key lightly and immediately return to the home position.

	Words
Tab⟶ Len Grell has a tent near June Lake. He can	9
stay at the lake all day in the fall. Al says he	19
can use his raft.	22
Tab⟶ I shall see Al at the lake in a day if he is	31
there. Al and Len can have the raft. I like the	41
clear air and sun there.	46

| 1 | 2 | 3 | 4 | 5 | 6 | 7 | 8 | 9 | 10 |

• Lesson 9

- *Spacing: Double.*
- *Margins: 50-space line.*

9a • Keyboard Review

Directions – Type once; then repeat.

Posture Goal – Sit back in chair. Eyes on copy.

t   tf tf tf fit fit hit hit sit sit kit kit trite jut

n   nj nj nj fan fan fun fun gun gun run run send send

v   vf vf vf five five dive dive give give stave stave

y   yj yj yj jay jay gay gay lay lay dry dry slay slay

Eyes on this copy

All letters taught

Jack said the craft is in the shed near the field.

Sue can have Ray shut the large gate at the track.

| 1 | 2 | 3 | 4 | 5 | 6 | 7 | 8 | 9 | 10 |

Problem 1—Business Letter with Enumerated Items

| 60-space line | Date on line 18 | Modified block | Indented ¶'s | Mixed punctuation | Current date | Carbon copy | Large envelope |

- *Indent the enumerated items 5 spaces from each margin.*
  Double-space before and after each of the items.

Mrs. Mary Miller / 3197 Cornell Drive / Flint, Michigan 48505 / Dear Mrs. Miller: / As one of our best customers, you are eligible for the Master Charge Card that is enclosed. (¶) Here are just a few of the Card's many advantages:

1. It is honored throughout the state by over 50,000 merchants.

2. It identifies you to merchants as a person of good standing.

3. There are no dues and no interest charges when you pay within 30 days.

If you wish, Mrs. Miller, you may extend your payments by paying as little as 5% of your outstanding balance or $10 each month, whichever is greater. (¶) Your signature on the back of the Card is sufficient. Need we say more? Cordially yours, / Robert Pengilly / Sales Representative / (xx) / Enclosure

Problem 2—Business Letter in Rough Draft

50-space line
Date on line 18
Block style
Open punctuation
Carbon copy
Large envelope

May 12, 196—

Miss Chris ^tina Twiggs, President
Future Business Leaders ℗o america
East^ Alisal High School
Bismarck, (N. Dak.) 58543 *spell out*
Dear Miss^ Twiggs⊙

shall We ~~will~~ be glad to have you^r ~~club visit~~ *group tour* our plant. ^We's *It is a pleasure*
for us ~~like~~ to meet young poeple who are intrested in business.

The month of ^May ~~April~~ is full on^our sch edule. If it will ~~can~~
shall be convenient for your to plan your vist for ~~May we~~ June,
~~will~~ look forward to seeing you thàn. ¶Please fill out
enclosed the^ schedule card indicatnig which date your prefer.

very
Yours^ truly
(xx) Elaine Smith, Secretary
^Enclosure

We can handle up to 35 visitors without making special arrangements. If your group will be larger, please indicate this on the card.

• Lesson 140 • *70-space line*

| All letters | SS | A judge watched Max very quickly analyze bad checks the forger passed. |

Figure — Mrs. Brock told the seventh grade students to add 5/6, 19/30, and 2/3.

Left-hand weak fingers — What size quilts do you have? Sally saw six dozen square zinc plates.

Easy — A few of the rogues had thrown rocks at the big signs outside of town.

Feet on the floor

| 1 | 2 | 3 | 4 | 5 | 6 | 7 | 8 | 9 | 10 | 11 | 12 | 13 | 14 |

9b • Location of B and O

Find **b** on the chart. Find it on your typewriter keyboard. Place your fingers over the home keys. Touch **bf** lightly, allowing your **d** and **s** fingers to move slightly to give freedom of action.

←— REACH TO B   REACH TO O —→

Find **o** on the chart. Find it on your typewriter keyboard. Place your fingers over the home keys. Touch **ol** lightly without moving the other fingers from their typing position.

TYPE b WITH
THE f FINGER

TYPE o WITH
THE l FINGER

fbf fbf bf bf fib fib fib   • Type twice on same line •   lol lol ol ol old old old

9c • Location Drills — B and O

Directions – Type each line once with your teacher. Type the lines again by yourself.

Technique Goals – Reach to the new keys with your fingers. Keep your wrists and elbows low.

1 b fbf fbf fbf fbf bf bf bf bf buff buff job job jobs   Type b with the f finger

2   bug bug both both rob rob bold bold ball ball fobs

3   bus bus by by buy buy but but hub hub lab lab burn

4 o lol lol lol lol ol ol ol ol old old fold fold cold   Type o with the l finger

5   so so to to do do of of of log log loss loss go go

9d • Technique Builder — Wrists Low and Steady

Directions – Change to single spacing. Type each line two times.

Technique Goal – Curve your fingers; not your wrists. Hold your wrists low and steady.

1   ol bf ol bf old sold cold bold hold loss lost gold

2   cold could should bond bound found ground so sound   Curve your fingers

3   by buy bug but rub rubs rob robs bid bids birds by

4   to do; to do the; to go; to go to the; to go there

5   if you; if you do; if you do so; if you can do the   Wrists and elbows still

6   Be there. I can be there. Bill could not buy it.

7   They can buy it all right. They can buy it there.

| 1 | 2 | 3 | 4 | 5 | 6 | 7 | 8 | 9 | 10 |

138c • Problem Typing

30 minutes

Problem 1—Business Letter with Table

50-space line   Date on line 18   Modified block   Blocked ¶'s   Mixed punctuation   Carbon copy   Small envelope

• Indent the first column of the table 5 spaces from the left margin. Leave 5 spaces between the columns. Double-space before and after the table.

May 9, 197– / Kinman & Kuhn Clothiers / 2018 Carmel Avenue / Pocatello, Idaho 83217 / Gentlemen: / SUBJECT: Advertising Plans / It is always a pleasure to participate with our customers in a cooperative advertising program. (¶) According to the terms of our agreement, it is necessary for us to receive from you two full tear sheets covering each advertisement. Will you please send us another tear sheet to cover the following advertisements:

Twin Falls News-Dispatch	April 23
Idaho Falls Telegram	April 25
Pocatello Journal	May 1

We look forward to continued cooperation with you in your advertising plans. / Very truly yours, / LENNAN MANUFACTURING COMPANY / Winston W. Nelson / Advertising Director / (xx)

Problem 2—Business Letter with Table

Directions – 1. Type the letter in Problem 1 in block style, with open punctuation, and address it to:

Jack's Men's Wear
1867 Moroa Avenue
Modesto, California   95350

2. Insert the following table in place of the one used in Problem 1:

Sacramento Bee	April 18
Monterey Herald	May 1
San Francisco Chronicle	May 3

• Lesson 139 • *70-space line*

139a • Keyboard Review • Each line at least three times

5 minutes

All letters SS   We made only the best quality kegs for all our expensive frozen juice.
Figure-Symbol   If I add 3,682 and 57, I certainly should not get 4,032 for an answer!   Quick, sharp
Difficult reach   The executive was aware that exemptions were awarded, then taken away.   strokes
Easy   Eight of the new men were so tired they slept right through the night.

| | 1 | 2 | 3 | 4 | 5 | 6 | 7 | 8 | 9 | 10 | 11 | 12 | 13 | 14 |

139b • Speed Builder

10 minutes

Directions – 1. Type a 1-minute writing to determine your goal word.

2. Type a 5-minute writing At the end of each minute the return will be called. Try to reach your goal.

	Words
DS Years ago some unsung hero realized that when a large group of	13
people faced the same kind of risks, only a few really suffered a	26
65 words 1.4 si loss. This gave him a bright idea. If everyone would agree to share	40
the losses of a few, the threat of total disaster would be removed	53
from all. Thus it was that the idea of insurance was born.	65

Position of Wrists

Don't buckle
your wrists   Keep the
                     wrists low

←——— Wrong   Right ——→

9e • Sentence Skill Builder

Directions – Type two 1-minute writings on each sentence.
Figure your gross words a minute (*gwam*).

1   Keith can do the job if I have the tools he needs.

2   I can learn to do the things that need to be done.   Keep the
                                                                 wrists low
3   I can gain a high skill goal for the job if I try.

| 1 | 2 | 3 | 4 | 5 | 6 | 7 | 8 | 9 | 10 |

• Lesson 10

• *Spacing: Double.*
• *Margins: 50-space line.*

10a • Keyboard Review • Type once — then repeat

o   lol lol ol ol old bold sold fold hold cold so sort

b   fbf fbf bf bf bluff be bell belt ball bag bug burn   Eyes on copy

v, y   vf yj vf yj dry try drive guy give hay have strive

Shift   Jake Todd and Sue Bell; Frank Johns and June Trent

                                                                 Quick, sharp
All letters   Keith can buy the stove for you if Grace sells it.   strokes
taught
         Jay can buy it. He can buy it for you. I had it.

| 1 | 2 | 3 | 4 | 5 | 6 | 7 | 8 | 9 | 10 |

10b • Location of X and P

Find **x** on the chart. Find it on your ←— REACH TO X   REACH TO P —→ Find **p** on the chart. Find it on your
typewriter keyboard.   typewriter keyboard.
Place your fingers over   Place your fingers over
the home keys. Touch   the home keys. Touch
xs lightly, lifting the   ;p lightly, keeping your
little finger slightly to   elbow quiet and hold-
give your s finger free-   ing the other fingers in
dom of movement.   typing position.

TYPE x WITH   TYPE p WITH
THE s FINGER   THE ; FINGER

sxs sxs xs xs six six six   • Type twice on same line •   ;p; ;p; p; p; par par par

• Lesson 138 • *70-space line*

All letters	SS	Jasper waited in the quaint city of Bozeman before going to Knoxville.
Figure-Symbol		Type policy numbers without commas: His insurance policy is #9235874.
"s-w" comb.		Shrewd witnesses will wisely swear they saw shadows on the white snow.
Easy		Making a mistake is often the best thing in the world if you admit it.

Reach with your fingers

| 1 | 2 | 3 | 4 | 5 | 6 | 7 | 8 | 9 | 10 | 11 | 12 | 13 | 14 |

138b • Speed Stretcher • Use Speed Stretchers for 5-minute writings, or use each paragraph for 1-minute writings.   *10 minutes*

All letters

			G W A M
			1' 5'

**¶ 1
66 words
1.4 si** **DS** Try this little test. First, type your name in full; then, type   13 3 54
it again. The second time, however, skip every other letter. Which   27 5 56
was easier and faster—the first or the second typing? The first typing   41 8 59
probably was easier and quicker, even though you typed twice as many   55 11 62
letters. Why was this true? What did the test prove?   66 13 64

**¶ 2
68 words
1.4 si** When you typed your full name the first time, you typed it from   13 16 67
habit. Habit, however, did not help you on the second typing. You had   27 19 70
to concentrate on each letter separately as you typed it. As a result,   42 22 73
you typed slowly. Good habits are a valuable aid in typing as well as   56 24 75
in almost everything else you do. They often save you time.   68 27 78

**¶ 3
64 words
1.4 si** There are just two things to remember about building good habits.   13 29 80
First, when you type, type correctly. If you remember that the right   27 32 83
way is the easy way, this rule should not be too hard to follow. Next,   42 35 86
practice zealously! You simply cannot expect to type well if you waste   56 38 89
part of your practice period every day.   64 40 91

**¶ 4
55 words
1.4 si** Have you ever attempted to break a bad habit? Everyone says the   13 42 93
job is not easy. Although it might not seem like it, good habits are   27 45 96
no easier to eliminate than bad ones. Once you learn to type correctly,   42 48 99

**All ¶'s
1.4 si** you are on the way because your good habits will take over for you.   55 51 102

| 1' | 1 | 2 | 3 | 4 | 5 | 6 | 7 | 8 | 9 | 10 | 11 | 12 | 13 | 14 |
| 5' | | | 1 | | | 2 | | | 3 | | | |

10c • Location Drills — X and P

Directions – Type each line once with your teacher. Type the lines again by yourself.

Technique Goal – Reach to the new keys with your fingers. Keep the wrists low.

1   x   sxs sxs sxs sxs xs xs xs xs six six fix fix ox box   Type x with the s finger

2   lax lax flax flax flex flex next next fox fox hoax

3   p   ;p; ;p; ;p; ;p; p; p; p; p; par par part part pert   Type p with the ; finger

4   pack pack pale pale pad pad lap lap trip trip trap

Space-Bar Control

Curve right thumb over space bar ←   → Strike with quick down-and-in motion

10d • Technique Builder — Down-and-in Motion of Right Thumb • Single spacing Each line twice

1   xs p; xs p; xs p; flax flax pelt pelt cap caps six

2   fox tax fox lax six jinx box hex coax hoax vex axe   Strike space bar with quick down-and-in motion

3   top stop lot plot lay play rap strap nap snap snip

4   fix the snap; snap the hex; pay the tax; six steps

5   Pat can fix it. He can fix the pad. Al paid Pat.   Wrists and elbows still

6   Rex paid the six boys for the job they did for Al.

     | 1 | 2 | 3 | 4 | 5 | 6 | 7 | 8 | 9 | 10 |

10e • Paragraph Typing

Directions – Set machine for a 5-space paragraph indention and double spacing. Type twice. Repeat if time permits.

Technique Goal (*Manual*) – Hold the tab bar or key down until the carriage stops.

Words

Tab ———→   You can type at a high rate if you hold your   , 9

hands still as you reach for the keys. Just keep   19

your eyes on this copy. It is the right thing to   29

do as you type. Try it and see. Try it and see.   39

     | 1 | 2 | 3 | 4 | 5 | 6 | 7 | 8 | 9 | 10 |

• Lesson 137 • *70-space line*

137a • Keyboard Review • Each line at least three times   *5 minutes*

All letters   SS   I have been lucky to exceed my first high quota and win a major prize.

Figure-Symbol   By 1967, no fewer than 84 men had cracked the 4-minute mile "barrier"!   Type with

Weak fingers   We saw he was lax and had acquired lazy habits playing weak opponents.   your fingers

Easy   They kept their goals before them during the time they were in charge.

| 1 | 2 | 3 | 4 | 5 | 6 | 7 | 8 | 9 | 10 | 11 | 12 | 13 | 14 |

137b • Paragraph Guided Writings • As directed in 126b, page 201   *10 minutes*

DS   Very few foods are more American than the hot dog. The billions   Words 13

eaten each year prove it. Still, there are two other sandwiches that   27

65 words   1.4 si   rank ahead of the famous weiner and bun. Would you believe that peanut   41

butter and jelly is first and the hamburger second? Because of this,   55

those who sell hot dogs will have to try harder.   65

137c • Problem Typing   *30 minutes*

Problem 1—Business Letter with Postscript

• *Type a postscript a double space below the reference initials. It need not be preceded by the letters P. S.*

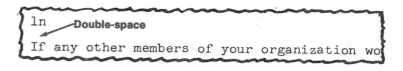

50-space line   Blocked ¶'s   Carbon copy   Modified block

Mixed punctuation   Date on line 18   Small envelope

May 14, 196– / Mrs. Margaret Matheson / 948 Lupin Drive / Miami, Florida   33155 / Dear Mrs. Matheson: / SUBJECT: Your Recent Visit / On behalf of the Association and its Board of Directors, I should like to express our appreciation to you for visiting our office yesterday. In visiting us, you indicated a keen interest in the citrus fruit industry. As you know, this is one of the most important industries to the economy of our area. (¶) It was a pleasure for me personally to show you through our facilities and explain our Association and its operation. I sincerely hope that your visit was a pleasant one. / Very truly yours, / Howard A. Forrest / (xx) / If any other members of your organization would like to make a similar tour in the future, we shall be happy to accommodate them.

Problem 2—Composing a Business Letter

Directions – 1. Compose and type a personal business letter to Valley Citrus Association / 1740 Harvard Avenue / Fresno, California   93732 / Attention Mr. Howard A. Forrest / Gentlemen /

2. Thank Mr. Forrest for permitting you to visit the offices and plant of his company. Tell him that you were impressed with the care taken by the members of his company to make sure that the oranges handled were clean and fresh.

3. Type the letter in modified block style, indented ¶'s, mixed punctuation. Use today's date.

4. Use your own address in the heading.

5. Address a small envelope. Remember to type the attention line below the company name.

• Lesson 11

11a • Keyboard Review

Directions – Type once; then repeat.

Posture Goal – Body centered opposite the **h** key, 6 to 8 inches from front frame of typewriter.

x	sxs sxs xs xs six six lax flax next next flex flex
p	;p; ;p; p; p; par part pal pail plan pain rip trip
b, o	bf ol bf ol bold bolt boil rob robe job born board
"un" reach	sun sun gun gun fun fun run run hunt hunt runt sun

Quick carriage return

All letters taught	Play your part to the hilt; try to reach the goal.
	Have Fred buy the six good books on parks in June.

| 1 | 2 | 3 | 4 | 5 | 6 | 7 | 8 | 9 | 10 |

11b • Location of W and M

Find **w** on the chart. Find it on your typewriter keyboard. Place your fingers over the home keys. Touch **ws** lightly, lifting the little finger slightly to give your **s** finger freedom of movement.

←— REACH TO W   REACH TO M —→

Find **m** on the chart. Find it on your typewriter keyboard. Place your fingers over the home keys. Touch **mj** lightly without twisting your hand or moving the other fingers from their typing position.

TYPE w WITH THE s FINGER

TYPE m WITH THE j FINGER

sws sws ws wish wish wish   • Type twice on same line •   jmj jmj mj mj jam jam jam

11c • Location Drills — W and M

Directions – Type each line once with your teacher. Type the lines again by yourself.

Technique Goal – Keep your fingers deeply curved. Reach with your fingers; keep wrists still.

w	sws sws sws sws ws ws ws ws wish wish win win wind
	wall wall walk walk well well how how way way laws
m	jmj jmj jmj jmj mj mj mj mj jam jam make make made
	mix mix lame lame stem stem come come much much am
	am same game game more more from from sum sum drum

Type w with the s finger

Type m with the j finger

		GWAM 1' 5'

All letters

¶ 1
44 words
1.4 si

DS   A few years back it would have been tough to find someone who knew   13 | 3 | 55

much about automation. This word did not exist in the dictionary. Now   28 | 6 | 58

it blares at us from the daily papers. Some headlines glow. Others   42 | 8 | 60

seem gloomy.   44 | 9 | 61

¶ 2
48 words
1.4 si

One story may shout the good news that some new device promises   57 | 11 | 63

relief for those workers who must put in long hours at boring tasks.   71 | 14 | 66

Another will warn of the tragedy that comes when these automated plants   85 | 17 | 69

force thousands out of their jobs.   92 | 18 | 70

¶ 3
52 words
1.3 si

The electronic marvels in use these days range from simple machines   106 | 21 | 73

that can furnish us with orange pop or an ice cream bar to huge systems   120 | 24 | 76

which run whole factories. Computers have been used to make decisions.   135 | 27 | 79

Some of these machines can play chess with you.   144 | 29 | 81

¶ 4
56 words
1.4 si

As machines take over and production goes up, there should be a   157 | 31 | 83

rise in our standard of living. The workweek will be shorter, so many   171 | 34 | 86

of us will have more free time for rest and recreation. Workers who   185 | 37 | 89

have been displaced will likely now have to be retrained for different   199 | 40 | 92

jobs.   200 | 40 | 92

¶ 5
60 words
1.3 si

What does all this mean to the boys and girls in school today?   213 | 43 | 95

It means that they must realize it is the unskilled worker, the one   226 | 45 | 97

without an adequate education, who is most likely to suffer in the   240 | 48 | 100

world of automation. Never before has the need for good schooling   253 | 51 | 103

All ¶'s
1.4 si

been brought home with such force.   260 | 52 | 104

1' | 1 | 2 | 3 | 4 | 5 | 6 | 7 | 8 | 9 | 10 | 11 | 12 | 13 | 14 |
5' | | | 1 | | | | 2 | | | | 3 | | | |

136d • Creative Typing • Compose a paragraph based on the following
quotation, as directed in 111d, page 184.   *10 minutes*

"There are no elevators in the house of success."

11d • Technique Builder — Quick, Sharp Stroking

Directions – Change to single spacing. Type each line two times.

Technique Goal – Don't rest your fingers heavily on the home keys. Barely touch them with your fingertips. Feel the keys; don't smother them. Make short, direct reaches. Strike the keys; don't push them.

Strike, don't push!

1   ws mj ws mj ws mj who whom who whom mow mower when

2   how show we well wall walk much much mar mark miss   Light touch

3   me mew mad made so some low slow win wind aim fame

4   will win; will take; will make; will move; will be   Quick, sharp

5   who may; who makes; who must; some walk; some show   strokes

6   Meet each new day with a smile if you wish to win.

| 1 | 2 | 3 | 4 | 5 | 6 | 7 | 8 | 9 | 10 |

11e • Sentence Skill Builder.

Directions – Type a 1-minute writing on each sentence. Figure your *gwam* on each sentence.

Technique Goal – Barely touch the keys with your fingertips. Strike the keys quickly; don't push them.

1   There is a right way to type; use it in your work.

2   Strike a key with a short stroke. Do not push it.   Quick, crisp, short strokes

3   I can learn to like to do the things I need to do.

| 1 | 2 | 3 | 4 | 5 | 6 | 7 | 8 | 9 | 10 |

11f • Paragraph Skill Builder

Directions – Five-space paragraph indention; double spacing. Type three 1-minute writings on the paragraph. Figure your *gwam* on the best writing.

• *To figure your gwam on paragraph copy, note the figure at the end of the last complete line typed in the column at the right. To it, add the words in a line partially typed by noting the scale at the bottom. Use the figure nearest the last stroke typed. The total is your gross words a minute (gwam).*

                                          Words

Tab ⟶   We all have minds that can be used. This is   9

    a gift that all of us have. Use that gift to add   19

    to the things that you can do.   25

| 1 | 2 | 3 | 4 | 5 | 6 | 7 | 8 | 9 | 10 |

135c • Problem Typing

Problem 1—Business Letter with Attention Line

- *An attention line is used to direct a letter to a particular person. It is usually typed on the second line below the address, as illustrated at the right. (In addressing the envelope, type the attention line immediately below the company name.)*

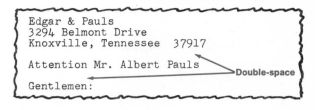

```
Edgar & Pauls
3294 Belmont Drive
Knoxville, Tennessee  37917

Attention Mr. Albert Pauls        Double-space

Gentlemen:
```

| 60-space line | Date on line 18 | Mixed punctuation | Block style | Large envelope |

June 12, 197– / Edgar & Pauls / 3294 Belmont Drive / Knoxville, Tennessee 37917 / Attention Mr. Albert Pauls / Gentlemen: / In order for us to take appropriate action in handling the claim I mentioned on Monday, we must receive a complete accident report from you by June 20. A copy of the accident file is enclosed. (¶) I recommend that you get in touch with the Blackburn family in Knoxville, as well as the driver and passengers in the Blackburn car. Mr. & Mrs. Blackburn now live in or near Louisville, Kentucky. (¶) As we are not certain about injuries, we want you to give this matter priority over other files. With the assistance of your thorough service, we should be able to reach a final decision early in July. / Very truly yours, / G. A. Eckenrod, Claims Department / (xx) Enclosure

Problem 2—Business Letter with Subject Line

- *When a subject line is used in a letter, it may be typed on the second line below the salutation and centered; or it may be typed at the left margin as illustrated.*

```
Mr. Howard Christensen
1244 Elmwood Drive
St. Louis, Missouri  63159

Dear Mr. Christensen          Double-space

SUBJECT:  Lincoln School Specifications
```

| 50-space line | Date on line 18 | Modified block | Blocked paragraphs | Open punctuation | Small envelope |

May 12, 196– / Mr. Howard Christensen / 1244 Elmwood Drive / St. Louis, Missouri 63159 / Dear Mr. Christensen / SUBJECT: Lincoln School Specifications / Plans and specifications for the Lincoln School are now complete. We should appreciate your coming to our office at 3 p.m. on June 12 so that we might go over the details for this job. (¶) After a discussion of the particulars, you may wish to take the plans with you for further study. It will be necessary for us to have your bid not later than August 1. (¶) If it will not be convenient for you to meet on June 12, please let us know. Any day that week will be satisfactory. / Yours very truly / ROYAL CONSTRUCTION COMPANY / H. G. "Tony" Royal, President / (xx)

• Lesson 136 • *70-space line*

136a • Keyboard Review • Each line at least three times

All letters SS	Policemen request extra heavy fur jackets to wear during the blizzard.	
Figure-Symbol	The stocks that sold for $104.37 in 1929 had risen to $568.60 by 1969.	Think as
Long reach	Myra was quite mystified by a myriad of mysterious symbols on my door.	you type
Easy	Both of the girls spent their time working to aid others in the class.	

| 1 | 2 | 3 | 4 | 5 | 6 | 7 | 8 | 9 | 10 | 11 | 12 | 13 | 14 |

136b • Skill Comparison • Type three 1-minute writings each on 107b, page 178 and 134c, page 216. Compare rates.

• Lesson 12

• *Spacing: Double.*
• *Margins: 50-space line.*

12a • Keyboard Review

Directions – Type once; then repeat.

Posture Goal – Elbows near body; wrists held low and steady.

w	sws sws ws ws wish wise win wind wall walk who how
j	jmj jmj mj mj jam jam me met melt mad made arm sum
x, p	xs p; xs p; xs p; par part lax flax lap slaps coax
"pl" comb.	play plays plan plans plate plow place plane plush

Elbows in

Wrists low

All letters taught

We must know that the key to a man is his thought.

Have Jack take the six maps to the school in Lima.

| 1 | 2 | 3 | 4 | 5 | 6 | 7 | 8 | 9 | 10 |

12b • Location of Q and , (comma)

Find q on the chart. Find it on your ←— REACH TO Q   REACH TO , —→ Find the **comma** on the chart. Find it typewriter keyboard. Place your fingers over the home keys. Touch qa lightly without moving the elbow in or out. Hold the elbow steady.

TYPE q WITH THE a FINGER

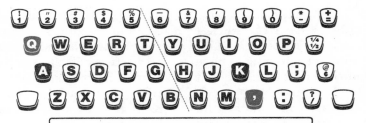

on your typewriter keyboard. Place your fingers over the home keys. Touch ,k lightly, lifting the **j** finger slightly to give you freedom of action.

TYPE , WITH THE k FINGER

aqa aqa qa quit quit quit   • Type twice on same line •   k,k k,k ,k irk, irk, irk,

12c • Location Drills — Q and , (comma)

Directions – Type each line once with your teacher. Type the lines again by yourself.

Spacing Guide – Space once after a comma (,).

q	aqa aqa aqa qa qa quit quiet quite quip quay equip
	pique quilt square squirt queen queer quote quotes
	squid quaint quake quick queue equal quarry squeak

Type q with the a finger

, (comma)	k,k k,k k,k ,k ,k work, rock, broke, trick, truck,
	fork, forks, sock, socks, dock, dike, lock, clock,
	kick, choke, steak, rake, kale, king, chock, soak,

Type , with the k finger

134d • Problem Typing

30 minutes

Problem 1—Business Letter in Modified Block Style

• *An enclosure notation is used when a paper (or papers) is sent with the letter. Type the notation at the left margin a double space below the reference initials. Use the plural, Enclosures, if two or more items will be enclosed.*

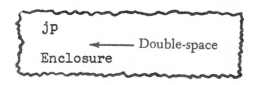

| 60-space line | Date on line 18 | Modified block | Indented ¶'s | Mixed punctuation | Large envelope |

• *In the lessons that follow, the necessary directions for typing the letters will be given as shown above. The line on which the date is to be typed is included.*

October 5, 197– / Mr. Glen Blomgren / 248 Abbey Street / Milwaukee, Wisconsin 53221 / Dear Mr. Blomgren: / Enclosed is the report you asked for regarding the use of passenger cars in our division during the past six months. You should keep in mind that this was not a typical period since our new model was not received until August 1. Another fact to remember is that Mr. Powers was working out of the Madison office during September and was therefore using one of their cars during that time. (¶) Please notice on page 2 that mileage figures as of the last day of each month are shown in Column 4. (¶) If you have any questions after reading the report, please let me know. Very truly yours, Irving Davis / Chief Accountant / (xx) Enclosure

Problem 2—Business Letter in Block Style

| 50-space line | Date on line 18 | Block style | Open punctuation | Current date | Large envelope |

Mr. Raymond L. Puck / 260 Crescent Way / Laramie, Wyoming 82047 / Dear Mr. Puck / Thank you for your comments about BRITE toothpaste. It is indeed most encouraging to have a valued customer confirm our opinion about what we feel is an outstanding product. (¶) You may be interested to learn that we manufacture and distribute many other items that are useful in the modern home. The enclosed brochure contains a complete listing of those available. (¶) We are pleased to enclose also a complimentary gift certificate which we hope you will use. It may be redeemed at all leading stores where BRITE products are sold. / Cordially yours / Kent R. Meyer / Customer Relations / (xx) / Enclosures

Problem 3—Business Letter in Modified Block Style

Directions – Type the letter in Problem 2 in modified block style with indented paragraphs. Use mixed punctuation. Address a large envelope.

• Lesson 135 • *70-space line*

135a • Keyboard Review • Each line at least three times

5 minutes

All letters SS	He quickly explained most of Mr. Beltzig's peculiar views to the jury.	
Figure-Symbol	A $1 bet on a race horse, "Wishing Ring," won $1,213 on June 17, 1912.	Quick
Balanced- and one-hand	if they see, if they look, if they wear, if they jump, if they address	carriage return
Easy	The less of it that one has, the more willing he is to speak his mind.	

| 1 | 2 | 3 | 4 | 5 | 6 | 7 | 8 | 9 | 10 | 11 | 12 | 13 | 14 |

135b • Timed Writings • Type a 1- and a 5-minute writing on 131c, page 210. Circle errors. Compute gwam.

10 minutes

12d • Technique Builder — Eyes on Copy

Directions – Single spacing. Type each line twice; then type 1-minute writings on the last three lines.

Technique Goal – Don't look from the copy to your typewriter and back again. Type right! Keep your eyes on the copy at all times.

1   qa ,k qa ,k qa ,k quit, qualm, quip, quite, squeal

2   quick, quill, queen, quote, plaque, quilt, squinch

3   to quote, to quit, the quick, the queen, the quilt

4   He was quick to quote the man about the red quilt.   Space once after comma

5   Drive right, as the life you save may be your own.

6   As you type, use quick, short, firm, sure strokes.

7   He can gain the high skill he needs for this work.

| 1 | 2 | 3 | 4 | 5 | 6 | 7 | 8 | 9 | 10 |

12e • Paragraph Skill Builder

Directions – Five-space paragraph indention; double spacing. Type the paragraph once for practice; then type three 1-minute writings on it. Figure your *gwam* on the best writing.

	Words
Tab⟶ He said that the men who sling mud must give	9
ground. There is much truth in these words. You	19
will lose more than you gain when you give way to	29
the use of words and thoughts that are too harsh.	39

| 1 | 2 | 3 | 4 | 5 | 6 | 7 | 8 | 9 | 10 |

• Lesson 13

- *Spacing: Double.*
- *Margins: 50-space line.*

13a • Keyboard Review • Type once — then repeat

q   aqa aqa qa qa quit quits quote quotes quart quarts

, (comma)   k,k k,k ,k ,k work, all, fork, fill, dark, squall,   Sit erect

w, m   ws mj ws mj ws mj warm warm mow mow whom whom home

"mu" reach   mud mug mugs must much mull mulls muff muffs mules   Wrists low

All letters taught   Type with a fixed goal in mind; use quick strokes.

A job will give you the chance to test your skill.

| 1 | 2 | 3 | 4 | 5 | 6 | 7 | 8 | 9 | 10 |

Problem 3—Business Letter in Block Style

Directions – Type as shown on page 215. Type today's date on line 18; use a 50-space line. Address a small envelope.

- *The symbol (¶) in the copy below indicates the point at which a new paragraph begins.*

Miss Janice Gordon / 2190 Princeton Street / Portland, Oregon 97233 / Dear Miss Gordon / Thank you for your check. It pays your loan in full. I want to compliment you on the prompt manner in which you handled this account. (¶) Now that we are well acquainted, the First National Bank is the logical place to come whenever you may again be in need of extra cash. We hope, too, that you will consider opening a savings account with us in the near future. An account can be started with as little as one dollar or as much as you desire. (¶) Please stop in soon. We shall be happy to serve you. / Yours very truly / FIRST NATIONAL BANK / Lloyd Johnson, Manager / (xx)

• Lesson 134 • *70-space line*

134a • Keyboard Review • Each line at least three times

5 minutes

All letters	SS	Wes misjudged people even after checking boxes and analyzing requests.
Figure		The Pittsburgh Pirates won their 1902 pennant by a margin of 27 games.
Right-hand		Look in on my nylon mill, John Polk; I'll hook pink poplin on my loom.
Easy		The flies that make the loudest noise are the ones that get hit first.

Quiet wrists and arms

| 1 | 2 | 3 | 4 | 5 | 6 | 7 | 8 | 9 | 10 | 11 | 12 | 13 | 14 |

134b • Number Expression Guides — Amounts of Money

5 minutes

Directions – Type each sentence three times. The first line gives the rule; the remaining lines apply it.

1 SS Amounts of money, either dollars or cents, should be typed in figures.

2 If you want the books, too, the cost of the set is $17.50, not $14.39.

3 The price of these booklets is 23 cents; the cards cost 18 cents each.

4 Use ¢ and @ in typing bills: Ship them 500 ripe melons @ 3½ ¢ a pound.

Reach with your fingers

| 1 | 2 | 3 | 4 | 5 | 6 | 7 | 8 | 9 | 10 | 11 | 12 | 13 | 14 |

134c • Skill Builder from Rough Draft • Type four 1-minute writings.

5 minutes

	Words
DS If you are looking for an new and unusual hobby, you might want to	13
consider keeping raising bees. Bee keeping maybe thought of as an academic	27
66 words **1.4 si** pursuit. It is easy to think hobby. You can even think of bees as people, since they have a madness habit	41
for of storing far more honey than they could ever use. Like humans people, they	55
work hard to gathering wealth for which have no they don't need.	66

13b • Location of Z and ?

Find z on the chart. Find it on your typewriter keyboard. Place your fingers over the home keys. Touch za lightly, keeping the other fingers in typing position.

◄——— REACH TO Z   REACH TO ? ———►

Find ? on the chart. Find it on your typewriter keyboard. Place your fingers over the home keys. Touch ?; lightly several times. Remember to shift to type ?.

TYPE z WITH
THE a FINGER

TYPE ? WITH
THE ; FINGER

aza aza za zone zone zone   • Type twice on same line •   ;?; ;?; ?; Why? Why? Why?

13c • Location Drills — Z and ?

Directions – Type each line once with your teacher. Type the lines again by yourself.

Spacing Guide – Space once after a question mark within a sentence; twice after a question mark at the end of a sentence.

z   aza aza aza za za za zone zones zero zip zeal zinc

zoo zing maze maze gaze graze doze quiz quiz froze

?   ;?; ;?; ;?; ?; ?; ?; Is it? Can they go? Why go?

Can he tell them how? or why? Whom did they take?

Type z with the a finger

Type ? with the ; finger — Note spacing guide above

13d • Technique Builder — Shift-Key Control • Single spacing; each line two times. Type 1-minute writings on the last three lines.

1   za ?; za ?; What zinc? Who froze it? Whose zone?

2   Will they care? When will he come? Are you sure?

3   Can we go? Is this the zone? Was her prize here?

4   Does he prize the things that count in life? How?

5   Do you hit all the keys with quick, sharp strokes?
     | 1 | 2 | 3 | 4 | 5 | 6 | 7 | 8 | 9 | 10 |

Hold shift key down; release it quickly

13e • Paragraph Skill Builder • Double spacing; three 1-minute writings

Tab ———►   We know that the one who learns to type well

can type as he thinks. This is the right goal to

have in your mind. It is one that you can reach.
| 1 | 2 | 3 | 4 | 5 | 6 | 7 | 8 | 9 | 10 |

Words
9

19

29

PARAMOUNT PEN COMPANY

8469 WILSHIRE BOULEVARD   LOS ANGELES, CALIFORNIA 90048   213-272-2449

		Words
18th line space	April 9, 197-	3
	4th line space	
Address	Mr. Paul E. Mooradian	7
	483 East Shields Avenue	12
	St. Louis, Missouri 63136	17
Salutation	Dear Paul	19
Body	You will be happy to know I was able to make the	29
	return trip to Los Angeles without any airline prob-	40
	lems. In spite of the bad weather that was forecast,	50
	every flight was right on schedule. Now I must	60
	settle down immediately to the grind of getting	70
	ready for the summer season.	76
	Thank you so much for the many courtesies extended	86
	me during my week with your sales force. It was	96
	certainly a most valuable experience and one that I	106
	shall not soon forget.	111
	Please convey my appreciation to Mr. Johnson and the	121
	others.	123
	Sincerely yours	126
Company name in closing	PARAMOUNT PEN COMPANY	131
	Dennis Lynch	
Typed name and official title	Dennis Lynch **4th line space**	133
	Sales Manager	136
Reference initials	fp	137

Business letter in block style

Improving Your Typewriting Techniques

General Directions • Lessons 14 – 20

1. Single-space (SS) sentences and drill lines. Double-space between repeated groups of lines.
2. Double-space (DS) paragraph copy. Set a tabulator stop for a 5-space paragraph indention.

Time Schedule: Beginning with this unit, practice time is given for each section of a lesson. If it seems best to vary the schedule, do so with the approval of your instructor.

• Lesson 14

• *Use a 50-space line for all lessons in this unit.*

14a • Keyboard Review • Each line twice   *7 minutes*

z	SS	aza aza za za zeal zone doze quiz maze graze zesty	
?		;?; ;?; ?; ?; Who? Where? How many? Is he here?	Sit erect
"gr" reach		gr gr gray green grill grow grown growth grit gray	
		A quick fox jumped over the high fence at the zoo.	Feet on the floor
All letters		The long bridge over the bay will be closed today.	

| 1 | 2 | 3 | 4 | 5 | 6 | 7 | 8 | 9 | 10 |

14b • Technique Builder — Typing Whole Words • Type each line twice as your teacher dictates.   *5 minutes*

1	SS	to to do do to do to do if if he he if he if he is	
2		it it is is it is it is if it is if he is if it is	Think and type whole words
3		go go to go to go if it is to go if it is to go to	
4		he the the to the if the if it is the if it is the	

14c • Sentence Skill Builder   *10 minutes*

Directions – Type each sentence twice; then type a 1-minute writing on each. Figure your *gwam.*

Technique Goal – Try typing the short, easy words as a whole. Just think the words; type them.

1	SS	He can do the job now all right if he is to do it.	
2		If it is to be done, he and I can do it all right.	
3		If he is to go there to do the work, he can do it.	Type short words as a whole
4		He can type right if he thinks the words he types.	
5		He can do the drill right if he types whole words.	

| 1 | 2 | 3 | 4 | 5 | 6 | 7 | 8 | 9 | 10 |

133b • Speed Stretcher • Use Speed Stretchers for 5-minute writings, or use each paragraph for 1-minute writings.

10 minutes

All letters

| | | G W A M |
| | | 1' 5' |

¶ 1
63 words
1.4 si

DS   Eventually, you will have to face the question about the kind of   13 3 49

career you will follow. You may have been advised already to choose a   27 5 51

career while you are still in school so that you can get ready for it.   42 8 54

Almost all jobs require some special training. Hopefully, you will   55 11 57

realize this fact before it's too late.   63 13 59

¶ 2
64 words
1.4 si

Just dreaming lazily about a career is not sufficient. Examine   13 15 61

yourself carefully. What can you do best? What do you enjoy doing?   27 18 64

Your parents and teachers have urged you to make a careful choice, and   41 21 67

then resolve to be the best in your field. This is wise advice. There   55 24 70

is room in any area if you are good enough.   64 25 71

¶ 3
41 words
1.4 si

You cannot expect to get very far in your career if you're one of   13 28 74

those who know a little about a great many things and not too much about   28 31 77

anything in particular. The world has plenty of people like that.   41 34 80

¶ 4
64 words
1.4 si

Thousands of careers are available to almost anyone who wishes to   13 36 82

enter them. The problem is to discover the one that you can do well   27 39 85

and that you enjoy doing. If you cannot do it well, you'll fail. If   41 42 88

you dislike it, you'll miss one of the thrills life holds for us. You   55 45 91

All ¶'s
1.4 si

certainly must select your career with care.   64 46 92

```
1' | 1 | 2 | 3 | 4 | 5 | 6 | 7 | 8 | 9 | 10 | 11 | 12 | 13 | 14 |
5' |       1       |       2       |       3       |
```

133c • Problem Typing

30 minutes

Problem 1—Business Letter in Block Style

Directions – Type the model letter shown on page 215. Type the date on the 18th line space. (*If necessary, see directions for addressing a small envelope which appear on page 85.*)

• *If a workbook is not available, use a small envelope or paper cut to small envelope size (6½" by 3⅝").*

Problem 2—Business Letter in Block Style

Directions – Type the letter in Problem 1, but address it to Mr. Kenneth C. Chmelka / 2000 South Rustin Street / Omaha, Nebraska 68135. Supply an appropriate salutation. Address a small envelope.

Proofreading Your Work

Making typing errors cannot be avoided even if you try very hard not to make them. As you master reaches to keys and learn to type with good form,

1. Circle the whole word containing an error. Count only one error to a word.

2. A cut-off capital letter is an error.

3. Failure to space between words is an error.

4. A stroke that does not show is an error.

5. The wrong letter or a strikeover is an error.

6. An omitted or an added word is an error.

7. A missed or wrong punctuation mark is an error.

you will make fewer errors. You must learn to find and mark your errors, however. Some common errors are shown below.

(Hole) your (rist) low and stil

(Do) not arch or move them up and

(thekeys). (Youcan) learn to type r

Keep (y ur) eyes on this book

drills. Do (mot) look at the (keys

be able to gain⌃high rate (if) if

you (peck,)

14d • Continuity Practice

15 minutes

Directions – Type the copy below; circle your errors. Repeat. Try to make fewer errors.

Technique Goals – Type without pauses. Return the carriage quickly. Resume typing at once.

- *The syllable intensity (si) is given for the paragraphs below. It is a guide to the difficulty of the material. Copy of average difficulty is said to have a si of 1.4. The material in these paragraphs is thus quite easy.*

			Words in Para.	Total Words
¶1 27 words 1.0 si	DS	Hold your wrists low and still as you type.	9	9
		Do not arch or move them up and down as you strike	19	19
		the keys. You can learn to type right.	27	27
¶2 30 words 1.0 si		Keep your eyes on this book as you type the	9	36
		drills. Do not look at the keys, as you will not	19	46
		be able to gain a high rate if you must peek as	28	55
		you peck.	30	57

| 1 | 2 | 3 | 4 | 5 | 6 | 7 | 8 | 9 | 10 |

14e • Paragraph Skill Builder

8 minutes

Directions – Type two 1-minute writings on each of the two paragraphs in 14d. Figure your *gwam.* Type additional 1-minute writings on the paragraph on which you made your lowest score.

132c • Problem Typing

Problem 1—Business Letter in Modified Block Style

Directions – 1. Type the model letter shown on page 212. Type the date on the 18th line space.

2. Address a small envelope.

- *If necessary, see directions for addressing a small envelope which appear on page 85.*

- *Envelopes are printed on the back of the letterhead paper in the workbook. If a workbook is not available, use a small envelope or paper cut to small envelope size (6½" by 3⅝").*

Problem 2—Business Letter in Modified Block Style

50-space line
Modified block
Indented ¶'s
Mixed punctuation
Small envelope

Directions – Type this letter exactly as shown in the model on page 212.

Words

July 8, 197–   3

Mr. Frank Clemente   6
15 West Eighth Street   11
Tulsa, Oklahoma   74119   15

Dear Mr. Clemente: 19

    I am sure that you and your family will enjoy   29
staying at the Drake Hotel while you are attending   39
our annual conference. Several men made similar   49
arrangements last year, and all seemed well pleased. 59

    The meetings have been scheduled only until noon   69
each day, so members will have the rest of the day   79
free to do as they wish.   85

    If you can stop by the office on Monday morning,   94
we can discuss final plans for the opening session. 105

- *For this letter and for remaining letters in the book, use your own initials as reference initials.*

    Cordially yours,   108

    Nicholas Hein, Chairman   113

• Lesson 133 • *70-space line*

133a • Keyboard Review • Each line at least three times

All letters   SS   The expensive, liquid-fueled rocket jars big windows when it zooms by.

Figure   In 1884, a champion ice skater went 10 miles in 31 minutes 11 seconds.

Eyes on copy as you return the carriage

Left-hand   Sweet tastes were decreased as excess treats were served as a dessert.

Easy   Arguments begin whenever two people try to get in the last word first.

| 1 | 2 | 3 | 4 | 5 | 6 | 7 | 8 | 9 | 10 | 11 | 12 | 13 | 14 |

• Lesson 15 • *50-space line*

15a • **Keyboard Review** • Each line twice

n	SS	jnj jnj nj nj no not note need nest next knew know
t		ftf ftf tf tf to tone tune tack take ton torn this
"tr" reach		tr tr true truth tray stray trip trap train strain
		Jack may quote the expert on bridges in this zone.
All letters		Zoe may see the wall from the cliff above the bay.

Sit erect

Eyes on copy

| 1 | 2 | 3 | 4 | 5 | 6 | 7 | 8 | 9 | 10 |

15b • **Technique Builder — Typing Whole Words** • Each line three times; then type a 1-minute writing on each line.

12 minutes

1	SS	He is to do the job all right if he can do it now.
2		How you type has a lot to do with how well you do.
3		Can he go to the lake to see the work on the dock?
4		He can take a train to the game if the teams play.

Type short
words as
a whole

| 1 | 2 | 3 | 4 | 5 | 6 | 7 | 8 | 9 | 10 |

15c • **Continuity Practice** • Type the copy below; circle the errors. Repeat, trying to make fewer errors.

10 minutes

G W A M
1' 2'

All letters
¶ 1
28 words
1.0 si

DS

Take some; give a lot. Try this thought on | 9 5

for size. Keep it in mind. In the long run, you | 19 10

may find that you will get more than you give. | 28 14

¶ 2
36 words
1.0 si

Be quick to give praise; slow to take it. | 9 19

There is no tax on kind words. Use them to raise | 19 24

the hopes of those who need help. Just have the | 28 28

faith you like to see in your friends. | 36 32

1' | 1 | 2 | 3 | 4 | 5 | 6 | 7 | 8 | 9 | 10 |
2' | 1 | 2 | 3 | 4 | 5 |

15d • **Sustained Skill Building**

16 minutes

Directions – 1. Type two 1-minute writings on each paragraph in 15c. Circle errors. Figure *gwam*.
2. Type two 2-minute writings. Circle errors. Figure *gwam*. Compare rates on short and long writings.

• *In figuring your gwam for the writings on the paragraphs, use the 1-minute column at the right and the 1-minute scale underneath the paragraph to figure your 1-minute rate. Use the 2-minute column and scale to figure your 2-minute rate.*

LESSON 15 • PAGE 27

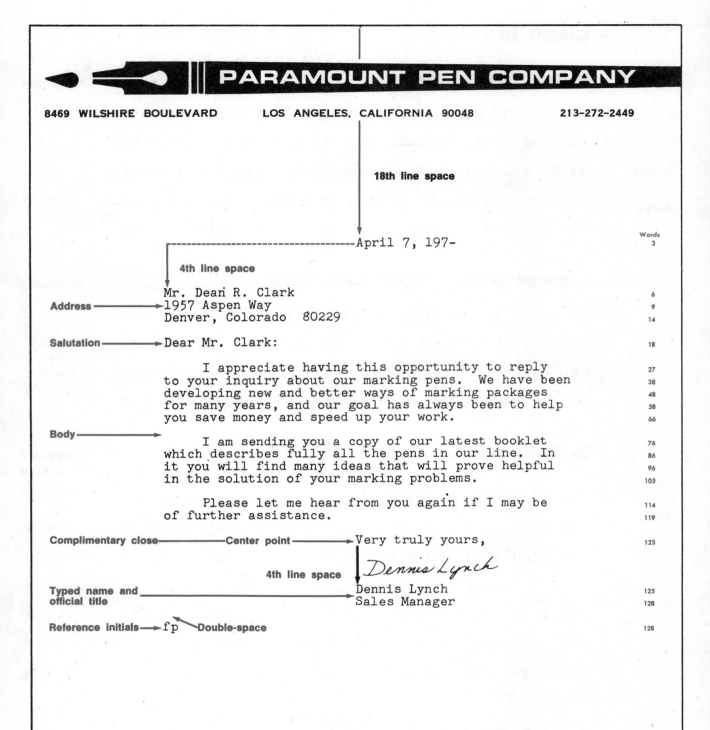

PARAMOUNT PEN COMPANY

8469 WILSHIRE BOULEVARD   LOS ANGELES, CALIFORNIA 90048   213-272-2449

Words

18th line space

--April 7, 197-   3

4th line space

Mr. Dean R. Clark   6
Address ——————→ 1957 Aspen Way   9
Denver, Colorado 80229   14

Salutation ——————→ Dear Mr. Clark: 18

     I appreciate having this opportunity to reply   27
to your inquiry about our marking pens. We have been   38
developing new and better ways of marking packages   48
for many years, and our goal has always been to help   58
you save money and speed up your work.   66

Body ——————→   I am sending you a copy of our latest booklet   76
which describes fully all the pens in our line. In   86
it you will find many ideas that will prove helpful   96
in the solution of your marking problems.   105

     Please let me hear from you again if I may be   114
of further assistance.   119

Complimentary close——————Center point——————→ Very truly yours,   123

4th line space   *Dennis Lynch*

Typed name and   Dennis Lynch   125
official title   Sales Manager   128

Reference initials ——→ fp   Double-space   128

Business letter in modified block style

• Lesson 16 • *50-space line*

16a • Keyboard Review • Each line twice
7 minutes

b	SS	bfb bfb bf bf bid bind bow bowl ban band bit built
p		;p; ;p; p; p; par part up upon pot port pure pearl	Elbows in
"un" reach		un un unit unite united sun sung run rung gun lung
All letters		You can see many bright flowers in this zone then.	Eyes on book
		Six barges are packed with antique jugs and vases.

| 1 | 2 | 3 | 4 | 5 | 6 | 7 | 8 | 9 | 10 |

Adjusting the Ribbon-Control Lever

1. Your typewriter has a ribbon-control lever (No. 22). Find it on your machine.
2. Set the ribbon-control lever to type on the upper portion of the ribbon.
3. Note the position of the ribbon-control lever.
4. At the beginning of a lesson, check the ribbon-control lever to see that it is in this position.

16b • Technique Builder — Typing Whole Words
5 minutes

1	SS	he	he	did	he did	he did	he did it	he did the
2		and	and he	and he	and the	and if he	and if he	Think words
3		for	for	it	it	for it	for it is	for it is the	Space quickly
4		do	go	do go	do go to	and do	and do go	and go

16c • Sentence Guided Writings
15 minutes

Directions – 1. Type each line twice for practice. 2. Type each line for one minute with the call of the guide. Try to complete each line as the guide is called. (Your teacher will tell you how the guide will be called.) 3. Type 1-minute writings on the last sentence without the call of the guide.

			Words in Line	GWAM 20" Guide
1	SS	You can type right if you try.	6	18
2		I can do this drill at a good rate.	7	21
3		Try to type each line as time is called.	8	24
4		I must try to type with quiet hands and arms.	9	27
5		If I type well, I can win the prize of high speed.	10	30

| 1 | 2 | 3 | 4 | 5 | 6 | 7 | 8 | 9 | 10 |

132a • Keyboard Review • Each line at least three times   5 minutes

All letters SS   Howard ate five big pretzels and drank exactly two quarts of my juice.

Figure   All 34 eighth graders did Spelling Lesson 1-B on page 368 for Tuesday.   Type without pauses

Double letters   All room committees agreed that baggage accommodations were very good.

Easy   Talk becomes cheap when there is a bigger supply than there is demand.
              | 1 | 2 | 3 | 4 | 5 | 6 | 7 | 8 | 9 | 10 | 11 | 12 | 13 | 14 |

132b • Paragraph Guided Writings • As directed in 126b, page 201   10 minutes

	Words
DS These rules were written for telephone repairmen many years ago:	13
"Treat others as you like to be treated, including your horse. To	27
65 words understand the horse's side of it, merely remove your coat and hat some	41
1.4 si day, hitch yourself to the same post with your belt, and stand for two	55
hours. In the future, don't forget his blanket."	65

| 1 | 2 | 3 | 4 | 5 | 6 | 7 | 8 | 9 | 10 | 11 | 12 | 13 | 14 |

INFORMATION ABOUT BUSINESS LETTERS

Letter Styles – With slight variations, the modified block style shown on page 212 is used in almost all business letters. Another style that is growing in usage is the block style illustrated on page 215.

Punctuation Styles – Two commonly used punctuation style are open and mixed. In *open* punctuation no punctuation marks are used after the salutation or the complimentary close. In *mixed* punctuation a colon is placed after the salutation and a comma after the complimentary close.

Vertical Placement of Dateline – Vertical placement of the date varies with the length of the letter. However, in the majority of business letters the date is typed on line 18. The address is typed on the 4th line space (3 blank spaces) below the date.

Abbreviations – Excessive abbreviations should be avoided. It is acceptable, however, to abbreviate the state name in an address when using a ZIP Code in order to maintain uniformity of line length. Leave two spaces between state name and ZIP Code.

Reference Initials – The typist should always type his reference initials two line spaces below the typed name of the writer of the letter.

Stationery Size – Most business letters are typed on 8½- by 11-inch stationery that is imprinted with the name and address of the company.

Envelopes – Use small envelopes for one-page letters and large envelopes for two-page letters or when enclosing materials within a letter.

16d • Continuity Practice

10 minutes

Directions – Type the copy below; circle the errors. Repeat, trying to make fewer errors.

Technique Goal – Return the carriage quickly. Resume typing at once.

| | | | G W A M |
| | | | 1' 2' |

All letters

¶ 1
29 words
1.1 si

DS

It will pay you to think and type some of the   9   5

words in this copy as a whole. Just read and type   19 10

them as units. Do not spell them as you type.   29 15

¶ 2
33 words
1.1 si

Use quick, short, sharp strokes. Keep your   9   19

wrists low and firm. Relax, but sit erect. Have   19 24

a clear goal in mind; then work with zeal. You   28 29

can learn to type right.   33 31

1' | 1 | 2 | 3 | 4 | 5 | 6 | 7 | 8 | 9 | 10 |
2' | 1 | 2 | 3 | 4 | 5 |

16e • Sustained Skill Building

8 minutes

Directions – Type a 1-minute, then two 2-minute writings on the paragraphs in 16d. Try to equal your 1-minute rate on the 2-minute writings.

Technique Goals – Type without a sense of hurry. Gain speed by cutting out pauses and waste movements in your arms, elbows, and wrists.

• Lesson 17 • *50-space line*

Hold the Wrists Low and Steady

Curve the fingers, not your wrists. Make the reaches to the keys with your fingers. Hold your wrists low and steady.

17a • Keyboard Review • Each line twice

7 minutes

y   SS   jyj jyj yj yj yet year you your yes yarn yearn eye

q   aqa aqa qa qa quart quire squire square quiet quit

"br" reach   br br br bring broth brain braid bride brake broke

All letters   Burton will pay for the ticket so save it for him.

                 Rex found the quartz in a jagged rock near Mexico.

                 | 1 | 2 | 3 | 4 | 5 | 6 | 7 | 8 | 9 | 10 |

Fingers
deeply
curved

131c • **Speed Ladder Paragraphs** • As directed in 126b, p. 202   *20 minutes*

● All letters are used in these paragraphs

		G W A M
		1' 5'

¶ 1   DS   As you have nearly completed your personal typewriting course,   13 3 55
44 words
1.4 si   it's well to take a brief glance at what you have accomplished. The   26 5 57

fact that you have typed this paragraph proves that some learning must   41 8 60

have taken place.   44 9 61

¶ 2   Your reasons for enrolling in this class likely differed. Some   57 11 63
48 words
1.3 si   wanted to learn to type because they felt it would help them in their   71 14 66

schoolwork. Others had an eye on the future, and they decided typing   85 17 69

might prove useful in getting a job.   92 18 70

¶ 3   Then, too, several students may have signed up because they felt   105 21 73
52 words
1.4 si   that learning to operate a typewriter would be fun. Chances are good   119 24 76

that you were not disappointed. It is fun to take a class in which   133 27 79

you do actually see the results of what you have learned.   144 29 81

¶ 4   No matter what your reasons for taking typing might have been, you   157 31 83
56 words
1.4 si   are sure to have gained enough basic skill to utilize this new tool to a   172 34 86

great extent. The personal-use typist needs to have the same command of   187 37 89

techniques as those students who take the class for vocational use.   200 40 92

¶ 5   It has required long hours of practice for you to reach your pres-   213 43 95
60 words
1.4 si   ent level of ability. If you neglect to maintain your speed, it will   227 45 97

gradually slip away from you. You have developed a skill that can be   241 48 100

of great assistance in the future. Make good use of it in your classes   256 51 103

All ¶'s
1.4 si   and in your daily life.   260 52 104

1' | 1 | 2 | 3 | 4 | 5 | 6 | 7 | 8 | 9 | 10 | 11 | 12 | 13 | 14 |
5' | 1 | 2 | 3 |

131d • **Creative Typing** • Compose a paragraph based on the following quotation, as directed in 111d, page 184.   *10 minutes*

"If it is to be, it is up to me."

17b • Sentence Guided Writings

• As directed in 16c, page 28

15 minutes

Words GWAM
in   20"
Line Guide

1 SS Do the job as well as you can.   6   18

2 *Hard work is the secret of success.*   7   21

3 Plan your work right if you wish to win.   8   24

4 *Plan to make some gain in your work each day.*   9   27

5 Now is the day to do these lines in the right way.   10   30

| | 1 | 2 | 3 | 4 | 5 | 6 | 7 | 8 | 9 | 10 | |

17c • Continuity Practice

10 minutes

Directions – Type the copy below; circle the errors. Repeat; try to make fewer errors.

Technique Goal – Read, think, and type the short words as units, not letter by letter.

GWAM
1' 2'

DS   It is said that our friends are like melons.   9   5

In order to find just one we like, we must try a   19   10

dozen or more. This may be quite true, all right,   29   15

**All letters
60 words
1.1 si**

but do not expect to find your friends in a melon   39   20

patch. You will not find them there. The best   49   25

way to find a close friend is to be a good one   58   29

yourself.   60   30

1' | | 1 | 2 | 3 | 4 | 5 | 6 | 7 | 8 | 9 | 10 | |
2' | | 1 | | 2 | | 3 | | 4 | | 5 | |

17d • Sustained Skill Building

8 minutes

Directions – Type a 1-minute, then two 2-minute writings on the paragraph in 17c. Try to equal your 1-minute rate on the 2-minute writings.

Technique Goals – Gain speed by using quick, sharp strokes. Snap the finger toward the palm of the hand after each stroke.

17e • Centering Paragraph Copy

5 minutes

Directions – Type the paragraph in 17c on a half sheet of paper so that the space above and below the paragraph is even. Try typing the paragraph with no more than two errors.

Solution: a. Count lines in the half sheet.   33

b. Count lines and spaces between the lines in the paragraph.   13

c. Subtract b from a.   20

d. Divide by 2.   10

e. From top edge of paper, space down to the 11th space. Start typing.

Cycle 4 •

Introduction to Business Typewriting

This cycle introduces you to some of the typewriting duties performed in the typical office.

Typing Business Letters – The two basic letter styles introduced in Cycle 2 are presented here as they are commonly used in business correspondence. You will learn how to set up letters of different lengths so that they are placed properly on the page.

Typing Business Forms – In Unit 17 you will type interoffice memorandums and invoices.

Extra-Credit Assignments – Problems are given at the end of the following Lessons for students who finish assignments: 140, 145, and 150.

Improving Your Basic Skills – By this time you have acquired considerable typewriting speed and control. Increases in speed do not come so rapidly now as they did early in the year. The skill-building material provided in this cycle will put the finishing touches on your typewriting skill.

• Unit 16

Typing Business Letters

General Directions • Lessons 131 – 140

Machine Adjustments – Use a 70-space line for drills and timed writings in this unit. Single-space sentences and drill lines. Double-space between groups of repeated lines. Double-space paragraph copy. Much of the problem copy that you will type will be set in lines either longer or shorter than those for which your margins are set. It will be necessary for you to listen for the bell, to use the right margin release, and to divide long words coming at the ends of lines.

Erasing – Your teacher will tell you whether or not you are to erase errors made on problem copy.

Special Forms – Type the problems on the special forms provided in the workbook or on plain paper.

• Lesson 131

131a • Keyboard Review • Each line at least three times   *5 minutes*

All letters SS	Jules got very few dark boxes of any size in the shipment from Quincy.	Begin slowly;
Figure-Symbol	The problem stated that he purchased 15 new transistor radios @ $9.95.	increase
Vowels—e, i	Their niece received a prize when she hiked over here in nine minutes.	speed
Easy	A word that you can use is like a key because it can unlock your mind.	gradually

| 1 | 2 | 3 | 4 | 5 | 6 | 7 | 8 | 9 | 10 | 11 | 12 | 13 | 14 |

131b • Speed Ladder Sentences • Two 1-minute writings on each sentence. Your teacher may call the guide for you.   *10 minutes*

			G W A M 15″ 12″ 10″
1	SS	Decide what level of skill you believe you can acquire.	44 55 66
2		Be determined to attain the level you have set for yourself.	48 60 72
3		During every practice session, keep this goal fixed in your mind.	52 65 78
4		If you heed these suggestions, your typing ability is sure to improve.	56 70 84

| 1 | 2 | 3 | 4 | 5 | 6 | 7 | 8 | 9 | 10 | 11 | 12 | 13 | 14 |

• Lesson 18 • *50-space line*

18a • Keyboard Review

• If time permits after typing each line twice, type 1-minute writings on the last two lines. Figure your gwam. Compare rates.

7 minutes

x   SS   sxs sxs xs xs lax lax mix mix fix fix box axe axle

p   ;p; ;p; p; p; play play plate plate plan plan pray

"wa" comb.   wa wa wade want warn ward was wall watch wand wasp

          Dave flew from Quebec to Danzig in just six hours.

All letters   It will pay him to keep his fingers deeply curved.

| | 1 | 2 | 3 | 4 | 5 | 6 | 7 | 8 | 9 | 10 | |

Quick carriage return

Resume typing at once

18b • Technique Builder — Typing Whole Words • Each line twice

5 minutes

1   SS   he the then an and hand go got to torn he the they

2   end lend land fur for form fir firm me men man may

3   go got to torn do down he held did dig so also rug

4   He may pay the men to fix the torn fur rug for us.

| | 1 | 2 | 3 | 4 | 5 | 6 | 7 | 8 | 9 | 10 | |

Type whole words

18c • Continuity Practice

10 minutes

Directions – Type twice. Repeat if time permits.

Technique Goal – Return the carriage quickly. Start typing at once.

			GWAM	
			1'	3'

All letters
¶ 1   DS
38 words
1.1 si

Jack Dempsey, one of the great boxers of his   9   3   29

day, told a group of young men that there are no   19   6   32

shortcuts in sports. To win, you should play a   28   9   35

clean, hard game. You must be quick and smart.   38   13   39

¶ 2
39 words
1.2 si

The same rule applies to your work in school.   47   16   42

Punch hard; work with zeal. Do not look for any   57   19   45

shortcuts. The things you learn now will help you   67   22   48

solve many of the problems you will face later.   77   26   52

1' | 1 | 2 | 3 | 4 | 5 | 6 | 7 | 8 | 9 | 10 |
3' | 1   2   3   4 |

130d • Problem Measurement

Problem 1—One-Page Report

Directions – 1. Type this one-page report in regular report style.

2. Type the footnote in correct form at the bottom of the page.

• *Directions for typing a one-page report are given in the problem on page 95. Directions for typing footnotes are given on page 150. Refer to these pages if necessary.*

HOW TO USE THE LIBRARY

When you go to the library to study or read for pleasure, you go to a room with something more than just four walls and a number of tables. No other room in your school is quite like it. It is here that you can find the key that opens the door to a whole new world for you. It is here that you can meet the wisest and wittiest men of all time.

Plato will not mind it at all if you want to turn back the pages of time to get his views on philosophy—neither will Mozart if you want to get his help in composing an opera. On the other hand, if you feel like laughing, Bennett Cerf will be glad to oblige with some of the funniest stories ever told.

One excellent reference on library usage reminds you that in most of your courses you will want to seek information beyond that given in your classes. School libraries provide the materials and reference aids that enable you to find this information by yourself. In this way they give you a sense of independence in your search for an education.[1]

Books are arranged according to a system that has been worked out by librarians. Learn enough about the system to help you get the books you want quickly and easily.

---

[1] Beauel M. Santa and Lois Lynn Hardy, How to Use the Library (Palo Alto, California: Pacific Books, 1966), p. 11.

Problem 2—Outline

Directions – 1. Type this brief outline of a speech on a half sheet of paper.

2. Indent, space, capitalize, and punctuate the outline correctly. Place it in the exact vertical center of the page.

• *You may want to refer to 92c, page 157, for assistance in spacing your outline correctly.*

using an encyclopedia

I   introduction
   A   importance of encyclopedia as a reference
   B   rules for library use
II body
   A   how to locate information
      1   look first in the regular alphabetical place
      2   always look for last names of persons
      3   in words of two or more parts, look for the first part
   B   miscellaneous hints
III conclusion

130e • Extra-Credit Typing

Problem 1

Type a note of regret to a friend who has asked you to attend a movie. Look at Problem 2, page 203, for ideas, but type the message in your own words.

Problem 2

Type a postal card announcement for one of the clubs in your school. If necessary, refer to Problem 1, page 203, for help in arranging your material.

18d • Sustained Skill Building

Directions – Type 1-, 2-, and 3-minute writings on the paragraphs in 18c. Circle errors; figure *gwam*. Try to equal your 1-minute rate on the longer writings.

• *Use the 1- and 3-minute columns and scales to figure the 1- and 3-minute rates. For the 2-minute rate, use the 1-minute column and scale to get total words; then divide by 2.*

18e • Centering Paragraph Copy

10 minutes

Directions – Type the paragraphs in 18c on a half sheet of paper so that the space above and below them is even.

• Lesson 19 • *50-space line*

19a • Keyboard Review

7 minutes

z   SS   aza aza za za zone zero size lazy doze dozen prize

c   dcd dcd cd cd cut ice cap cape can cancel cost cow

"pol" comb.   pol pol pole polar polite poll pollen police polka   Wrists and elbows still

All letters   Five quart cans of wax kept my jeep glazed bright.

              As a rule, the men who throw mud must give ground.

`| 1 | 2 | 3 | 4 | 5 | 6 | 7 | 8 | 9 | 10 |`

19b • Technique Builder — One-Hand Words • Each line twice

5 minutes

1   SS   up as in we at my saw hip far him see upon care on   Type letter by letter

2   was ink car pop red inn bag pull read hill wet you

3   wear milk save lion star noon acre pink gave pupil   Wrists low and still

4   A brave pupil gave John See a savage lion at noon.

`| 1 | 2 | 3 | 4 | 5 | 6 | 7 | 8 | 9 | 10 |`

19c • Sentence Guided Writings • As directed in 16c, page 28

15 minutes

		Words in Line	GWAM 20" Guide
1	SS Most of us do far less than we can.	7	21
2	*Can you keep your fingers deeply curved?*	8	24
3	We fail to test the real power that is in us.	9	27
4	*I find that the more I know the more I must learn.*	10	30
5	How much is it? Where do I pay? Can John see it?	10	30

`| 1 | 2 | 3 | 4 | 5 | 6 | 7 | 8 | 9 | 10 |`

129e • Division Sign and Degree Symbol • Each line three times   *5 minutes*

Division sign –
Type the hyphen
over the colon.

Degree symbol – Pull the ratchet-release lever (No. 6) forward. Turn the left cylinder knob toward you slightly; type the small letter *o* without space between the figure
and the symbol; return the ratchet-release lever to its original position.

1   SS   Here are my three problems: $96 \div 8 = 12$. $96 \div 4 = 24$. $248 \div 8 = 31$.

Sit erect

2   He knows that water boils at $212°$; milk, at $215°$; and alcohol at $152°$.

| 1 | 2 | 3 | 4 | 5 | 6 | 7 | 8 | 9 | 10 | 11 | 12 | 13 | 14 |

• Lesson 130 • *70-space line*

130a • Keyboard Review • Each line at least three times   *5 minutes*

All letters   SS   Barry, the quizmaster, expected Francis to give a just answer quickly.

Figure-Symbol   I said the famous Dempsey-Tunney fight was held on September 22, 1927.

Quiet wrists
and arms

4th finger   All the people we saw appeared happy with the apparatus at the bazaar.

Easy   To write a good report, you should learn all you can about your topic.

| 1 | 2 | 3 | 4 | 5 | 6 | 7 | 8 | 9 | 10 | 11 | 12 | 13 | 14 |

130b • Number Expression Guides • Read the explanations. Type each
example sentence three times.   *5 minutes*

Line 1 – Use figures to type dates. When the day
date comes before the month, use a figure
and follow it with *th, st,* or *d*.

Line 2 – Spell a number beginning a sentence even

though figures may be used later in the
sentence.

Line 3 – Use figures with *a.m.* and *p.m.* Use words
with *o'clock*.

1   SS   We moved on May 26, 1970. I started to work on the 15th of September.

2   Fifty men were needed; only 25 applied. Seventy dollars is the price.

3   I will arrive at 9:45 p.m. I can leave at six o'clock in the morning.

| 1 | 2 | 3 | 4 | 5 | 6 | 7 | 8 | 9 | 10 | 11 | 12 | 13 | 14 |

130c • Speed Builder • As directed in 117b, page 192   *5 minutes*

DS   It is true that clothes don't make a man, but they can make a good

impression for him. They may, however, make quite an unfavorable one.

60 words
1.4 si

The instant a clown appears in the circus ring, his clothing evokes

Flowing,
rhythmic
stroking

laughter, even before his actions do. Be sure your clothes make the

best impression for you.

19d • Continuity Practice

Directions – Twice. Repeat if time permits.   Technique Goals – Space quickly. Return carriage without looking from the copy.

	GWAM 1'	3'

¶ 1
47 words
1.1 si

DS   Mark Twain said that nothing needs changing   9 3 35

so much as the habits of others. He was thinking   19 6 38

of the quirks all of us have. We spend most of   28 9 41

our lives getting rid of them. No one knows just   38 13 45

how much time we spend on this crazy game.   47 16 48

¶ 2
48 words
1.1 si

We all know that some habits are good; some   56 19 51

are bad. The bad ones can trap us as much as the   66 22 54

good ones can help. We must feed well the traits   76 25 57

that help. We must also put a sharp axe to those   86 29 61

that can trap us before they grow into habits.   95 32 64

```
1' | 1  | 2  | 3  | 4  | 5  | 6  | 7  | 8  | 9  | 10 |
3' |   1    |    2    |     3    |    4    |
```

19e • Sustained Skill Building

Directions – Type 1-, 2-, and 3-minute writings on the paragraphs in 19d. Try to equal your 1-minute rate on the longer writings.   Technique Goals – Feet on floor; body relaxed but erect. Fingers deeply curved; wrists low and still.

• Lesson 20 • *50-space line*

20a • Keyboard Review • Each line twice

All letters   SS Zoe paid a tax on my quince jelly when it arrived.

You are quite right; they can do this job for Kim.   Quick, crisp, short strokes

Easy   A sharp goal will help you get the skill you want.

Easy   Try to do this work just as well as you can do it.

```
| 1  | 2  | 3  | 4  | 5  | 6  | 7  | 8  | 9  | 10 |
```

20b • Technique Builder — Flowing Rhythm • Each line three times from dictation

1   SS to my | and look | to see | to date | for him | for you   Flowing rhythm

2   with you | and get | if you | it was | and be | did see

129b • Punctuation Guides — Apostrophe • Read the explanation carefully; then type each example sentence twice. *15 minutes*

Line 1 – Use an apostrophe in writing contractions.

Line 2 – *It's* means *it is*. *Its*, the possessive pronoun, does not take an apostrophe.

Line 3 – Use the contraction o'clock (of the clock) in writing time.

Line 4 – Add *'s* to form the possessive of any singular noun.

Line 5 – Add an *'s* to plural nouns that do not end in *s*.

Line 6 – If a plural noun does end in *s*, add only an apostrophe after the *s*.

Line 7 – The apostrophe denotes possession. Do not use it merely to form the plural of a noun.

Line 8 – Use an *'s*, however, to form the plural of figures, letters, signs, and words referred to as words.

Line 9 – Add an apostrophe and *s* to a proper name of one syllable which ends in *s* to show possession.

Line 10 – Add only an apostrophe to a proper name of more than one syllable which ends in *s* to show possession.

1 SS It's here. He's ill today. Don't go yet. I'll go, but I can't stay.

2   The sophomore class will hold its picnic soon; I hope it's a nice day.

3   If they're not here by four o'clock, we'll have to go on without them.

4   every man's rights, my son-in-law's car, their firm's rules, Hal's cap

5   five women, five women's coats; men, men's ties; these firemen's coats

6   six girls, six girls' geography books; two couples, two couples' house

7   There were only three girls in the room. This is the new girl's room.

8   My i's look just like e's; my 3's, like 5's. Take out all the that's.

9   Mr. Jones's land is several miles down the road from the Sims's ranch.

10   Aunt Virginia enjoyed reading the story to Mrs. Roberts' son, William.

Type steadily

| 1 | 2 | 3 | 4 | 5 | 6 | 7 | 8 | 9 | 10 | 11 | 12 | 13 | 14 |

129c • Paragraph Guided Writings • As directed in 126b, page 201 *10 minutes*

DS   It seems that most people just can't resist trying to look into the future. As yet, though, no one has found a surefire method for predicting all aspects of it. Our hunger to learn what lies ahead is not mere curiosity. We need to possess some knowledge of the future in order to plan our actions.

60 words
1.4 si

Blend fast and slow stroking for flowing rhythm

129d • Skill Comparison • Two 1-minute writings on each sentence. Compare rates. *10 minutes*

1.0 si   SS   To know how to do work well and to know that you know is a good thing.

1.2 si   We can learn to work, as there are many ways open to the right person.

1.3 si   Everyone should learn to work well with others on many kinds of tasks.

1.4 si   Men who enjoy their work will likely lead a much more satisfying life.

Flowing rhythm

| 1 | 2 | 3 | 4 | 5 | 6 | 7 | 8 | 9 | 10 | 11 | 12 | 13 | 14 |

20c • Sentence Guided Writings

• As directed in 16c, page 28

• As directed in 16c, page 28

15 minutes

			Words in Line	GWAM 20" Guide
1	SS	*This drill will help you type well.*	7	21
2		We start many jobs that we never finish.	8	24
3		*A clear, sharp goal will help you type right.*	9	27
4		Start a job on time; do not stop until it is done.	10	30
5		*You will gain skill if you do a job the right way.*	10	30

| 1 | 2 | 3 | 4 | 5 | 6 | 7 | 8 | 9 | 10 |

20d • Continuity Practice

10 minutes

Directions – Two times. Repeat if time permits.

Technique Goals – Return the carriage quickly; resume typing at once.

	GWAM	
	1'	3'

DS

	1'	3'
Someone with a quick wit once said that hay	9	3 33
is something we must make between the time we get	19	6 36
out of it and the time we hit it. These, I think,	29	10 40
are his exact words. The jet age, with its stress	39	13 43
on speed, moves the world along at a dizzy pace.	49	16 46
More work must be done than ever. There seems to	59	20 50
be much less time to do it; still we can squeeze	69	23 53
enough hours into a day to get our work done if we	79	26 56
keep in mind that the jet age makes each second	89	30 60
count.	90	30 60

All letters
90 words
1.1 si

| 1' | 1 | 2 | 3 | 4 | 5 | 6 | 7 | 8 | 9 | 10 |
| 3' | | 1 | | 2 | | 3 | | 4 |

20e • Timed Writings

8 minutes

Directions – Type two 3-minute writings on 20d. Circle errors; figure *gwam*. Submit the better writing.

20f • Extra-Credit Typing

Directions – Type the paragraph in 20d on a half sheet of paper so that the space above and below it is even.

128c • Problem Measurement

Problem 1—Personal Business Letter

Full sheet
50-space line
Indented paragraphs
Mixed punctuation

Directions – 1. Type the letter below as a personal business letter in modified block style. Type the address on the 10th line space from the date.

2. Prepare a carbon copy. Address a small envelope. Fold the letter; insert it.

Return address—115 Orange Drive / Pekin, Illinois   61554 / *Current date*

Address—Miss Karen Fleming / Karen's Specialty Shop / 38 Clovis Avenue / Chicago, Illinois   60646

Dear Miss Fleming:

Thank you very much for sending me the special birthday candle I ordered when I was in your shop last Saturday.

I am glad to learn that in the future I shall be able to order these candles by mail. They make such unique birthday gifts.

Enclosed is the list of names I promised to send you. You will find all of these people potential customers, I'm sure.

Sincerely yours,

Lorraine Johnson

Problem 2—Poem

Directions – 1. Type the poem in the exact vertical center on a half sheet of paper.

2. Center the copy horizontally by the second line of the first verse.

Loco-Motive

Down at the station I like to see the trains
Sticking out their chests and coming down the lanes
Dinging and a-hooing, reaching out their light--
How I wish that trains wouldn't cry at night.

Out in the country, rushing through the grass,
Trains seem happy, purring as they pass,
Or across the highway, clatter-banging by--
Why in the night time do the trains cry?

— Augusta Towner Reid

Problem 3—Personal Business Letter

Full sheet
50-space line
Open punctuation

Directions – 1. Type the letter in Problem 1, above, as a personal business letter in block style. Type the address on the 10th line space from the date.

• Lesson 129 • *70-space line*

129a • Keyboard Review • Each line at least three times

5 minutes

All letters SS	A just, quick, but exact mind will help you develop a zest for living.
Figure-Symbol	The * was typed after 265 of the 1,843 students' names listed in 1970.
Shift	Last August, Donald went to Atlanta to see the Braves play the Giants.
Easy	They were to type their last names right below the title of the theme.

Quick, crisp, short strokes

| 1 | 2 | 3 | 4 | 5 | 6 | 7 | 8 | 9 | 10 | 11 | 12 | 13 | 14 |

Learning the Figure and Symbol Keys

General Directions ● Lessons 21 – 30

1. Single-space sentences and drill lines. Double-space between repeated groups of lines.

2. Double-space paragraph copy. Set a tabulator stop for a 5-space paragraph indention.

● *Use a 50-space line for all lessons in this unit.*

● Lesson 21

21a ● Keyboard Review ● Each line twice   *7 minutes*

● *If figure 1 appears on the top row of your machine, strike it with the a finger. If it does not have a special key for the figure 1, use the small letter l to type 1.*

SS   I hope that Godfrey may receive his expert advice.

All letters   His new job in Mexico will require pluck and zeal.

l   I saw 111 deer in 11 weeks. He drove 111.1 miles.

Type 1 with the a finger or use small letter l

Easy   To type well, you must keep your eyes on the book.

Easy   Keep your fingers well curved as you hit the keys.

| 1 | 2 | 3 | 4 | 5 | 6 | 7 | 8 | 9 | 10 |

21b ● Location of 3 and 7   *5 minutes*

● *Reread the plan for learning the location and stroking of new keys given on page 5.*

Find 3 on the chart. Find it on your ←—REACH TO 3   REACH TO 7—→ Find 7 on the chart. Find it on your typewriter keyboard. Place your fingers over the home keys. Touch d3d lightly two or three times. Lift the first finger slightly to make the reach easily and naturally.

typewriter keyboard. Place your fingers over the home keys. Touch j7j lightly two or three times. Make the reach without arching your wrist. Hold the other fingers in typing position.

TYPE 3 WITH
THE d FINGER

TYPE 7 WITH
THE j FINGER

d3d d3d d3d d3d 3d 3d d3d   ● Type twice on same line ●   j7j j7j j7j j7j 7j 7j j7j

• Lesson 128 • *70-space line*

128a • Keyboard Review • Each line at least three times   *5 minutes*

All letters SS   I'm amazed to know the fall gym party and major banquet are exclusive.

Figure-Symbol   The symbol for the ampersand (&), illustrated on page 64, means "and."   *Flowing rhythmic stroking*

Long reach   He joined in the annual hunting fun with the gun snugly under his arm.

Easy   It is not trite but true that we must set goals for ourselves in life.

| 1 | 2 | 3 | 4 | 5 | 6 | 7 | 8 | 9 | 10 | 11 | 12 | 13 | 14 |

128b • Speed Stretcher • Use Speed Stretchers for 5-minute writings, or use each paragraph for 1-minute writings.   *10 minutes*

GWAM
1'   5'

All letters
¶ 1   DS
64 words
1.4 si

The renting business seems to be growing by leaps and bounds these   13 3 48
days. Just about everyone rents something at one time or other. It's   28 6 51
true that you can rent almost anything you need—even an elephant. The   42 8 53
price is a little high, of course, so you may want to consider a lion;   56 11 56
they cost only about one-third as much.   64 13 58

¶ 2
55 words
1.4 si

Renting is often cheaper than buying. In cities where parking   13 15 60
costs a lot, people rent autos so they don't have to pay for space in   27 18 63
a garage. It can be an inexpensive way to impress others. Some women   41 21 66
rent fur coats for special evenings. Some men rent flashy sports cars.   55 24 69

¶ 3
50 words
1.4 si

Storage can be a problem for the buyer. Those who live in small   13 26 71
houses or apartments rent things they don't use very often, such as   27 29 74
tuxedos and power tools. They come out ahead because they don't have   41 32 77
to wonder about where to store them afterwards.   50 34 79

¶ 4
54 words
1.4 si

You'll probably be amazed to discover that it is possible to rent   13 36 81
a new lawn for an outdoor party. The lawn comes in squares of grass.   27 39 84
They are laid like tiles in less than an hour. After the party the   41 42 87

All ¶'s
1.4 si

grass is removed, and the lawn reverts to its original condition.   54 45 90

1' | 1 | 2 | 3 | 4 | 5 | 6 | 7 | 8 | 9 | 10 | 11 | 12 | 13 | 14 |
5' | 1 | 2 | 3 |

21c • Location Drills — 3 and 7

10 minutes

Directions – Each line twice.   **Technique Goal** – Think the figure as you type it.

3   SS   d3d d3d d3d 3d 3d 3d 33 days, 333 hours, 33 and 33   Type 3 with
                                                                      the d finger
          Give us 333 feet.   Take 3,333 gallons.   I have 33.

7   j7j j7j j7j 7j 7j 7j 77 jars, 77 jolts, 77 and 777   Type 7 with
                                                                      the j finger
          Send 77 sets.   Paint 777 frames.   Ship 7,777 pens.

Number
fluency   He sent us 33 feet of wire and 77 pounds of nails.

          Only 37 of the 73 boys were at the game on May 13.

          | 1 | 2 | 3 | 4 | 5 | 6 | 7 | 8 | 9 | 10 |

21d • Technique Builder — Flowing Rhythm • Five times from dictation

6 minutes

1   SS   and date | and look | and grade | and limp | and right

2   to regard | to jump | to show | to fear | to do | to be   Flowing
                                                                       rhythm
3   the date | the rest | the fee | the order | the letter

21e • Continuity Practice

17 minutes

Directions – 1. Type the paragraph.   2. Type the paragraph again. Center it on
When you complete typing it, circle   a half sheet of paper. Circle your errors.
any errors you may have made.   Try to make no more than four errors.

	GWAM
	1' 3'

DS   School trains you to do the things you should   9 3 34

          even though you may think they are a waste of time.   20 7 38

          In growing up, you will find that·it is the little   30 10 41

          things that count.   From small deeds well done, you   40 13 44

All letters   learn how to handle jobs of large size.   You may   50 17 48
93 words
1.1 si   not be quite ready to run your school, but you can   60 20 51

          do a lot of things to help.   Do those things extra   71 24 55

          well.   In time, they may teach you to run a school,   81 27 58

          solve the problems of peace, or fly a spaceship to   91 30 61

          the moon.   93 31 62

      1' | 1 | 2 | 3 | 4 | 5 | 6 | 7 | 8 | 9 | 10 |
      3' | 1 | 2 | 3 | 4 |

• Lesson 127 • *70-space line*

127a • Keyboard Review • Each line at least three times   *5 minutes*

All letters **ss** Benjamin expects to have twelve dozen big prints made from it quickly.

Figure   The 1,256 scouts marched 38 blocks before more than 24,970 spectators.   *Wrists and
elbows still*

Long words   Periodically, specimens of fish never before identified are recovered.

Easy   The man who uses few words does not have to take so many of them back.

| 1 | 2 | 3 | 4 | 5 | 6 | 7 | 8 | 9 | 10 | 11 | 12 | 13 | 14 |

127b • Concentration Practice • Type as many times as you can in the time allowed.   *10 minutes*

Words

ds   Irving Berlin has written over 800 songs, including those for 26   13

stage shows and several movies. A few of the most famous are "God Bless   28

**60 words
1.5 si** America," "There's No Business Like Show Business," "White Christmas,"   42

and "Easter Parade." When he was 74, Mr. Berlin was back on Broadway   56

with "Mr. President."   60

| 1 | 2 | 3 | 4 | 5 | 6 | 7 | 8 | 9 | 10 | 11 | 12 | 13 | 14 |

127c • Problem Measurement   *30 minutes*

Problem 1—Postal Card Announcement

Directions – 1. Use a postal card or paper cut to proper size (5 by 3 inches). Insert the card, short side at the left, in your typewriter.

2. Center each line horizontally. Center the announcement vertically.

3. Address the card to your name and address. No return address.

• *Directions for finding the center of odd-size paper are on page 68.*

EDUCATION COMMITTEE MEETINGS
TO BE AT HIGH SCHOOL
Please watch bulletin for dates and times

For further information, call:

Mrs. Myra Young, Chairman
3982 East Gettysburg Avenue, 225-4850
or
Mrs. Pauline Russell, Cochairman
5167 North Fourth Street, 435-8062

Problem 2—Informal Regret to Invitation

Directions – Type the informal regret below. Use 4-by 5-inch stationery. Arrange the copy attractively.

2948 Palm Way / Dallas, Texas   75206 /
Current date

Dear Paula

You were so thoughtful to ask us to attend the Community Theater performance on Wednesday evening. Unfortunately, Ken has to work late that week and we cannot accept your kind invitation.

Thanks for thinking of us, Paula. I hope we can take a rain check for a future time.
Sincerely,

Problem 3—Postal Card Announcement

Directions – Follow the directions given in Problem 1. Type your own name, address, and telephone number as chairman. Type the same kind of information about a friend you want to designate as your cochairman.

• Lesson 22 • *50-space line*

22a • Keyboard Review • Each line twice
7 minutes

All letters | SS | Axel made a very quick trip to the Azores in July.
He saw a large fleet of boats in the small harbor.

Quiet wrists and arms

3 | d3d d3d 3d 3d 313 desks, 33 sets, 33 and 33 and 13

7 | j7j j7j 7j 7j 717 pints, 77 pens, 77 and 77 and 17

Easy | Hit all the keys with short, quick, sharp strokes.

| 1 | 2 | 3 | 4 | 5 | 6 | 7 | 8 | 9 | 10 |

22b • Location of # and & • Each line twice
6 minutes

is the shift of 3. Before a figure, # stands for number. After a figure, # stands for pounds. There is no space between the sign and the number.

& is the shift of 7. The & (ampersand) is a substitute for the word *and*. When using the ampersand, place a space before and after it.

| SS | d3d d#d d3d d#d #d #d #133, ship #373, #13 and #17
He ordered #173. We sent #731 and #133. Buy 37#.

 # shift of 3

& | j7j j&j j7j j&j &j &j Day & Night, Brown & Johnson
Bell & Day sold 77 sets. Buy 771 from Bell & Day.

& shift of 7

22c • Location of 5 and 9
5 minutes

Find **5** on the chart. Find it on your typewriter keyboard. Place your fingers over the home keys. Touch **f5f** lightly two or three times. Keep your left wrist low as you make the reach. Avoid moving your hand forward.

← REACH TO 5   REACH TO 9 →

Find **9** on the chart. Find it on your typewriter keyboard. Place your fingers over the home keys. Touch **l9l** lightly two or three times. Lift the first and second fingers slightly to make the reach to **9** easily.

TYPE 5 WITH THE f FINGER

TYPE 9 WITH THE l FINGER

f5f f5f f5f f5f 5f 5f f5f   • Type twice on same line •   l9l l9l l9l l9l 9l 9l l9l

22d • Location Drills — 5 and 9
6 minutes

Directions – Each line twice.

Technique Goal – Think the figure as you type it.

5 | SS | f5f f5f f5f 5f 5f 5f 55 files, 551 feet, 55 and 55
Sell 515 sets. Order 5,551 books. Mail 515 pins.

Type 5 with the f finger

9 | l9l l9l l9l 9l 9l 9l 99 lakes, 919 lids, 99 and 99
Buy 19 dozen. Sell 191 sets. Pay for 19 and 991.

Type 9 with the l finger

126d • Speed Ladder Paragraphs

• The following paragraphs are in speed ladder form. They may be used for a variety of drills. Two practice suggestions are described here. Your teacher will tell you which one to use.

20 minutes

Speed Ladder – Type the first paragraph for 1 minute. When you can type it at the rate specified, type the next paragraph. Keep climbing the ladder until you reach the top.

Control Ladder – Type the first paragraph for 1 minute. When you can type it at the rate specified *without error*, type the next one. Move from paragraph to paragraph only when you type at the specified rate without error.

		GWAM 1' 5'
All letters		
¶ 1 DS	While no one needs to be an expert on Emily Post to make his way	13 3 55
44 words	in the world, all of us need to treat others with courtesy. We are	27 5 57
1.3 si	simply using standard ways of showing courtesy when we practice the	40 8 60
	rules of etiquette.	44 9 61
¶ 2	When you are not quite sure of the rules about good conduct in a	57 11 63
48 words	certain situation, just think about the other person's feelings. Act	71 14 66
1.4 si	in a manner that will make him feel comfortable. You cannot go far	85 17 69
	wrong if you heed this bit of advice.	92 18 70
¶ 3	Good manners are but ways of showing consideration for the other	105 21 73
52 words	person. You eat with a fork because no one would want to look at you	119 24 76
1.3 si	if you ate with your fingers. Bad manners simply indicate that you	133 27 79
	care more for the food than for the company at the table.	144 29 81
¶ 4	When you use good manners, you merely put another person's comfort	157 31 83
56 words	ahead of your own. That's the acid test of good manners. Do you make	172 34 86
1.4 si	the people with whom you associate feel at ease? Do they prize your	185 37 89
	friendship? Let these questions guide you in your relations with others.	200 40 92
¶ 5	In any relationship with others the use of good manners seems to	213 43 95
60 words	invoke the Golden Rule. One is as likely to return kindness for kind-	227 45 97
1.4 si	ness as he is to return insult for insult. It is a rogue, indeed, who	241 48 100
	will not respond in kind to the lure of good manners. Practice yours;	255 51 103
All ¶'s 1.4 si	see if you don't agree.	260 52 104

```
1' | 1 | 2 | 3 | 4 | 5 | 6 | 7 | 8 | 9 | 10 | 11 | 12 | 13 | 14 |
5' |          1          |          2          |          3          |
```

22e • Sentence Guided Writings

10 minutes

Directions – Type each sentence for a 1-minute writing with the call of the guide each 20 seconds. Try to complete each sentence as the guide is called.

			Words in Line	GWAM 20" Guide
1	SS	Try to type each line as time is called.	8	24
2		*Type with a keen mind and quick strokes!*	8	24
3		I must try to type with quiet hands and arms.	9	27
4		*Try to raise your rate by one word each line.*	9	27
5		If I type well, I can win the prize of high speed.	10	30
6		*When work takes the place of words, we gain skill.*	10	30

| 1 | 2 | 3 | 4 | 5 | 6 | 7 | 8 | 9 | 10 |

22f • Sustained Skill Building

11 minutes

Directions – Type a 1-, 2-, and two 3-minute writings on the paragraph in 21e, page 36. Compute *gwam*. Try to equal your 1-minute rate on the longer writings.

• For the 2-minute rate, use the 1-minute column and scale to get total words; then divide by 2.

• Lesson 23 • *50-space line*

23a • Keyboard Review • Each line twice

7 minutes

All letters	SS	The quick brown fox can jump over those lazy dogs.	
5, 9		f5f 191 f5f 191 5f 91 55 fans, 99 lads, 191 and 55	
#, &		d3d d#d j7j j&j 13# of #17, Cooke & Eat, #73 files	Eyes on this copy
Easy		Work is fun if you make it fun and do it all well.	

| 1 | 2 | 3 | 4 | 5 | 6 | 7 | 8 | 9 | 10 |

23b • Location of % and (• Each line twice

6 minutes

% is the shift of 5. Do not space between the number and the percent sign.

(is the shift of 9. Do not space between the left parenthesis and the material it encloses.

%	SS	f5f f%f f5f f%f %f %f 15%, 37%, 19%, at 5%, for 3%	% shift of 5
		We got a discount of 5%. He got 15% and I got 7%.	
(		191 1(1 191 1(1 To type (, shift and strike the 9.	(shift of 9
		The (is the left parenthesis. Strike 9; then (9.	

Improving Your Basic Skills — Measurement

General Directions • Lessons 126 – 130

Machine Adjustments – Follow the general directions given in earlier units of this cycle.
Measurement – Measurement of straight-copy and problem typing skills is included in this unit.

The problems are similar to those covered in Cycle 3. Very few directions are given with the problems. Apply what you have learned in earlier lessons to the typing of these problems.

• Lesson 126

• *Use a 70-space line for all lessons in this unit.*

126a • Keyboard Review • Each line at least three times

5 minutes

All letters	SS	Pale, excited men inquired about a few objects hovering in a hazy sky.
Figure-Symbol		Type percentages in figures: They pay 6½% interest on this $875 loan.
3d finger		Millions of colorful followers all over the world tolled solemn bells.
Easy		The world does not owe you a living today; it is your duty to earn it.

Quick, sharp strokes

| 1 | 2 | 3 | 4 | 5 | 6 | 7 | 8 | 9 | 10 | 11 | 12 | 13 | 14 |

126b • Paragraph Guided Writings

10 minutes

Directions – 1. Set goals of 40, 50, and 60 words a minute. Type two 1-minute writings at each rate. Try to type your goal word just as time is called for writings at the various rates.

2. Your teacher may call the quarter or half minutes to guide you.
3. Type additional writings at the 50- and 60-word rates as time permits.

DS

If you are planning to enter one certain trade or profession, it is important to study your fitness for such work. If you find that you are weak in certain traits, you will know where to concentrate your efforts to improve yourself. You may find that you have greater aptitude for some other work.

60 words
1.4 si

Resume typing at once

126c • Technique Builder — Stroking • Two 1-minute writings on each sentence

10 minutes

First finger	SS	That runner had run too far to return to first base after Burt's bunt.
Second finger		Did Dick and Eddie Decker pick up all the kids' kites from their deck?
Third finger		I saw an old notice about Lois Olson's solo in the school talent show.
Fourth finger		I'm puzzled now, Paul; are they to write a paper and/or take the quiz?

Even stroking

| 1 | 2 | 3 | 4 | 5 | 6 | 7 | 8 | 9 | 10 | 11 | 12 | 13 | 14 |

23c • Location of 4 and 8

5 minutes

Find 4 on the chart. Find it on your ⟵REACH TO 4   REACH TO 8⟶ Find 8 on the chart. Find it on your typewriter keyboard. Place your fingers over the home keys. Touch f4f lightly two or three times. Keep your wrist low and quiet. Do not move your hand forward.

TYPE 4 WITH THE f FINGER

f4f f4f f4f f4f 4f 4f f4f   • Type twice on same line •   k8k k8k k8k k8k 8k 8k k8k

typewriter keyboard. Place your fingers over the home keys. Touch k8k lightly two or three times. Keep the other fingers over their keys as you reach to the 8. Keep your wrist low.

TYPE 8 WITH THE k FINGER

23d • Location Drills — 4 and 8 • Each line twice Eyes on copy

6 minutes

4   SS   f4f f4f f4f 4f 4f 4f 44 firs, 414 files, 4414 feet

Pay in 44 days.   Mark 4,414 tags.   Send 14 and 44.

Type 4 with the f finger

8   k8k k8k k8k 8k 8k 8k 88 kits, 18 kites, 8,818 ties

Dig 818 feet.   Walk 18 miles.   Buy 8,188 new sets.

Type 8 with the k finger

23e • Technique Builder — Flowing Rhythm • Each line three times; 1-minute writing on each. Compare gwam.

10 minutes

Word   SS   This is his job, and he is to do it now if he can.

Think words

Letter   Phillip Aster was at ease in Red Cave in Honolulu.

Think letters

Combination   Grace may see the sign at the end of Union Street.

We saw John jump at the lake; he was in rare form.

Flowing rhythm

| 1 | 2 | 3 | 4 | 5 | 6 | 7 | 8 | 9 | 10 |

23f • Paragraph Guided Writings

11 minutes

Directions – 1. Type for one minute. Note the *gwam*. Add four words to your *gwam* for a new goal.

2. Type three more 1-minute writings. Try to reach your new goal on each writing.

3. Type for one minute at your first rate. Your goal this time is to type without error.

		Words
DS	My guide said that man is like a tree. As	9
	long as it is growing toward sunlight, it may fill	19
48 words 1.1 si	its place in the forest. It fights for root space	29
	in the earth and for sun and air among the other	39
	trees. When it gives up the struggle, it dies.	48

| 1 | 2 | 3 | 4 | 5 | 6 | 7 | 8 | 9 | 10 |

124b • Timed Writings

10 minutes

Directions – 1. Type two 1-minute writings on paragraph 1, 101d, page 170. Compute the *gwam* on the better writing.

2. Type a 5-minute writing on all the paragraphs in 101d. Circle errors. Compute *gwam*.

124c • Problem Typing

30 minutes

Problem 1—Sentence Outline

Directions – 1. Type the outline in 57d, Problem 1, page 101, according to the directions given.

2. Remember to use the new center point.

3. Type the page number and identifying title.

Problem 2—Topic Outline

Directions – 1. Type the outline in 92c, Problem 1, page 157, following the directions given.

2. Remember to use the new center point.

3. Type the page number and identifying title.

• Lesson 125 • *70-space line*

125a • Keyboard Review • Each line at least three times

5 minutes

All letters   SS   Jane and William quickly packed the five dozen very big express boxes.

Figure   On April 11, 1965, tornadoes struck the Middle West at least 37 times.

Right-hand weak fingers   Opal paid for the opera tickets. I will oppose the plan to supply it.

Even stroking

Easy   The busy men who keep rowing their boat will not have the time to rock it.

| 1 | 2 | 3 | 4 | 5 | 6 | 7 | 8 | 9 | 10 | 11 | 12 | 13 | 14 |

125b • Timed Writings

10 minutes

Directions – 1. Type two 1-minute writings on paragraph 1, 106d, page 177. Compute the *gwam* on the better writing.

2. Type a 5-minute writing on all the paragraphs in 106d. Circle errors. Compute *gwam*.

125c • Problem Typing

30 minutes

Problem 1—Notice and Agenda of a Meeting

Directions – 1. Type the notice and agenda of a meeting in 102c, Problem 1, page 171, following the directions given with the problem.

2. Remember to use the new center point.

3. Type the page number and identifying title.

Problem 2—Minutes of Meeting

Directions – 1. Type the minutes in 103c, page 173, following the directions given with the problem.

2. Remember to use the new center point.

3. Type the page number and identifying title.

24a • **Keyboard Review** • Each line twice

All letters SS The tax questions puzzled that jury of twelve men.
Judge Sawyer blocked their motion for a new trial.

Sit erect

4, 8 f4f k8k f4f k8k 4f 8k 44 firs, 88 kits, 881 and 44

Quiet wrists and arms

%, (f5f f%f 191 1(1 15%, (is shift of 9, for 8% or 4%

Easy We know that tact fails the instant it is noticed.

| 1 | 2 | 3 | 4 | 5 | 6 | 7 | 8 | 9 | 10 |

24b • **Location of $ and '** • Each line twice

$ is the shift of 4. Do not space between the $ sign and the number which follows it.

' (apostrophe) is the shift of 8. The apostrophe does not have a space before or after it.

• *For drills on the location of the ' on electric typewriters, see p. xiii.*

**$** SS f4f f$f f4f f$f $f $f $44, $48, $74.54, $14 and $4
He sent $94. I spent $437.17. Pay $45. Get $74.

$ shift of 4

' k8k k'k k8k k'k 'k 'k don't, can't, isn't, Frank's
We can't go. It's in Jay's bag. It doesn't work.

' shift of 8

24c • **Sentence Skill Builder — Numbers and Symbols** • Each line three times

1 SS I must have 85 cents to see the game on August 14.

2 The % is the shift of 5. Our interest rate is 5%.

Wrists low and still

3 The # is the shift of 3. We must have Form #7195.

4 The & is the shift of 7. Send Jay & Lark 75 maps.

| 1 | 2 | 3 | 4 | 5 | 6 | 7 | 8 | 9 | 10 |

24d • **Script Skill Builder**

Directions – Type the paragraph twice for practice; then type two 1-minute writings. Figure *gwam*.

Technique Goal – Read the copy carefully. Type without pauses.

Words

DS *It is said that many good things come to him* — 9

34 words
1.1 si
who waits if he knows what he desires. Do not wait — 19

for typing skill to come to you, as you will learn — 30

only if you work for it. — 34

| 1 | 2 | 3 | 4 | 5 | 6 | 7 | 8 | 9 | 10 |

Problem 2—Personal Letter in Semibusiness Form

Directions – 1. Type the letter in 80c, Problem 1, page 136. Follow the directions given for the problem.

2. Paste this letter on an 8½- by 11-inch sheet of paper; place it so that it appears centered when bound at the left margin.

3. Type the page and identifying title.

• Lesson 123 • *70-space line*

123a • Keyboard Review • Each line at least three times

5 minutes

All letters   SS   Wendy bought an exquisite Navajo necklace for me on a trip to Arizona.

Figure-Symbol   This country has 6.5% of the world's people and 5.7% of its land area.

Vowels—o, i   Most older pilots violently opposed revision of admission regulations.

Fingers deeply curved

Easy   The man who loses his head is probably the type who would not miss it.

| 1 | 2 | 3 | 4 | 5 | 6 | 7 | 8 | 9 | 10 | 11 | 12 | 13 | 14 |

123b • Timed Writings

10 minutes

Directions – 1. Type two 1-minute writings on paragraph 1, 96c, page 163. Compute the *gwam* on the better writing.

2. Type a 5-minute writing on all the paragraphs in 96c. Circle errors. Compute *gwam*.

123c • Problem Typing

30 minutes

Problem 1—One-Page Theme

Directions – 1. Type the theme on page 95. Follow the directions given in 53c, page 94.

2. Remember to use the new center point.

3. Type the page number and identifying title.

Problem 2—First Page of Theme with Footnotes

Directions – 1. Type the theme on page 151 in the form illustrated.

2. Remember to use the new center point.

3. Type the page number and identifying title. Center the identifying title a double space below the last footnote.

• Lesson 124 • *70-space line*

124a • Keyboard Review • Each line at least three times

5 minutes

All letters   SS   Banjo players who balked were required to memorize five complex songs.

Figure-Symbol   He could buy $28,750 worth of protection for $14.96 a month at age 32.

Left-hand weak fingers   I passed the science quiz. Zelda got an extra quill for the desk set.

Type without pauses

Easy   It is not right to talk when your mouth is full or your head is empty.

| 1 | 2 | 3 | 4 | 5 | 6 | 7 | 8 | 9 | 10 | 11 | 12 | 13 | 14 |

24e • Continuity Practice

12 minutes

Directions – 1. Type the two paragraphs twice. Circle any errors you may make. 2. Center the first paragraph on a half sheet of paper. Try for no more than two errors.

GWAM
1' 3'

All letters DS
¶ 1
44 words
1.2 si

A good grade is the prize you get when you bet   9 3 34
on yourself. You can collect the prize if you lay   20 7 38
your talents and your will to learn each lesson on   30 10 41
the line. Your efforts must be equal to the prize   40 13 44
if you expect to win.   44 15 46

¶ 2
48 words
1.2 si

Do not forget that the grade is just a symbol.   10 18 49
What counts are the things you learn and the new   19 21 52
skills you acquire. These are the lasting rewards   30 25 56
of learning. A poor grade is the only thing you   39 28 59
can get in this world without working for it.   48 31 62

1' | 1 | 2 | 3 | 4 | 5 | 6 | 7 | 8 | 9 | 10 |
3' | 1 | 2 | 3 | 4 |

• Lesson 25 • *50-space line*

25a • Keyboard Review • Each line twice

7 minutes

SS
All letters

Jack expects to take the very hard quiz in August.
Fran, Mark, and Beth will take the quiz then, too.

Figures
and
Symbols

Please send Moore & Bell a check for $594 at once.
Send 44 or 45 quarts. Pay $54. I may deduct 17%.

Sit erect
with elbows in

Easy

You can judge a man by the books he likes to read.

| 1 | 2 | 3 | 4 | 5 | 6 | 7 | 8 | 9 | 10 |

25b • Technique Builder — Flowing Rhythm

5 minutes

Directions – Each line five times from dictation.   **Technique Goal** – Blend your typing into flowing rhythm.

1   SS   and the set | and the sea | and the ink | and the oil

2   if they bet | if they hop | if they see | if they get   Flowing rhythm

3   for the ear | for the car | for the set | for the inn

Problem 2—Table of Contents

Directions – 1. Type the table of contents below for your style guide.

2. Set your margins for a 60-space line. (Remember that the center point should be 3 spaces to the right of the point normally used.)

3. Allow a 2-inch top margin. Triple-space between the title and the heading for the page numbers. Double-space between items.

TABLE OF CONTENTS

Problem 3—Personal Business Letter in Modified Block Style

Directions – 1. Type the letter in 47d, Problem 1, page 82. Use the directions given for the problem.

2. In setting margins for a 50-space line, remember to use the new center point.

3. Refer to the style guide general directions on page 197 for the placement of the page number and the identifying title.

• Lesson 122 • *70-space line*

122a • Keyboard Review • Each line at least three times   *5 minutes*

All letters	SS	Their own quaint jujitsu expert amazed folks on the block every night.
Figure		The Great Pyramid, 755 feet across by 481 feet high, covered 13 acres.
Shift		Early typewriter inventors included Pratt, Sholes, Glidden, and Soule.
Easy		Profit depends on whether you keep your mind or your feet on the desk.

Instant release

| 1 | 2 | 3 | 4 | 5 | 6 | 7 | 8 | 9 | 10 | 11 | 12 | 13 | 14 |

122b • Timed Writings   *10 minutes*

Directions – 1. Type two 1-minute writings on paragraph 1, 91d, page 156. Compute the *gwam* on the better writing.

2. Type a 5-minute writing on all the paragraphs in 91d. Circle errors. Compute *gwam*.

122c • Problem Typing   *30 minutes*

Problem 1—Personal Business Letter in Block Style

Directions – 1. Type the letter in 83d, Problem 1, page 142. Follow the directions given for the problem.

2. Remember that the center point should be 3 spaces to the right of the point normally used.

3. Type the page number and identifying title.

25c • Location of 2 and 0

5 minutes

Find **2** on the chart. Find it on your ←—REACH TO 2   REACH TO 0—→ Find **0** on the chart. Find it on your keyboard. Place your fingers over the home keys. Touch ;0; lightly two or three times. Keep elbows quiet and hold the other fingers in typing position.

typewriter keyboard. Place your fingers on the home keys. Touch s2s lightly two or three times. Lift the little finger slightly to give you freedom of action.

TYPE 2 WITH
THE s FINGER

TYPE 0 WITH
THE ; FINGER

s2s s2s s2s s2s 2s 2s s2s   • Type twice on same line •   ;0; ;0; ;0; ;0; 0; 0; ;0;

25d • Location Drills — 2 and 0

6 minutes

Directions – Each line twice.   **Technique Goal** – Keep the elbows and wrists motionless.

2   SS   s2s s2s s2s 2s 2s 2s 22 suits, 212 slides, 22 sets

        I am 22.   I walked 212 miles in 22 days, 12 hours.   Type 2 with the s finger

0   ;0; ;0; ;0; 0; 0; 0; 100 pets, 110 pints, 909 tons   Type 0 with the ; finger

        He may have 20, 30, 40, or 50 of these long forms.

25e • Sentence Guided Writings

10 minutes

Directions – Type each sentence for a 1-minute writing with the call of the guide each 20 seconds. Try to complete each sentence as the guide is called.

			Words in Line	GWAM 20" Guide
1	SS	Please send them 5,500 prints.	6	18
2		John paid $20 for it; she paid $22.	7	21
3		You may take either 40, 44, or 48 books.	8	24
4		They sold 99 tickets to the game on April 19.	9	27
5		David's sister is 22 years old; his brother is 27.	10	30

    | 1 | 2 | 3 | 4 | 5 | 6 | 7 | 8 | 9 | 10 |

25f • Sustained Skill Building

12 minutes

Directions – 1. Type two 1-minute writings on ¶ 1, 24e, page 41; then type two 1-minute writings on ¶ 2. Figure your *gwam*.

2. Type two 3-minute writings on both paragraphs. Circle errors. Figure *gwam* on the better writing. Compare your 3-minute rate with your 1-minute rate.

Preparing a Student-Writer's Style Guide

General Directions • Lessons 121 – 125

Machine Adjustments – Follow the general directions given in earlier units of this cycle.

• Lesson 121

• *Use a 70-space line for all lessons in this unit.*

121a • Keyboard Review • Each line at least three times

5 minutes

All letters	SS	Mark will need seven jars of equal size for this next biology project.
Figure-Symbol		Their bill came to $465.80, but it was not due until December 3, 1972.
Adjacent keys		Bob believed their voices were barely audible above the verbal battle.
Easy		People should realize there is nothing much busier than an idle rumor.

Eyes on this copy

| 1 | 2 | 3 | 4 | 5 | 6 | 7 | 8 | 9 | 10 | 11 | 12 | 13 | 14 |

121b • Timed Writings

10 minutes

Directions – 1. Type two 1-minute writings on paragraph 1, 86d, page 147. Compute the *gwam* on the better writing.

2. Type a 5-minute writing on all the paragraphs in 86d. Circle errors. Compute *gwam*.

STUDENT WRITER'S STYLE GUIDE

• *In the problems of this unit, you will prepare a booklet entitled STUDENT WRITER'S STYLE GUIDE. The following general instructions apply to all these problems.*

1. Keep the pages you prepare in this unit until the entire booklet is finished. (The booklet will contain 11 pages in all.)

2. Erase and correct errors.

3. Number the pages as indicated in the table of contents. Type page numbers on the fourth line space from the top, 1 inch from the right edge of the paper.

4. Pages which follow the table of contents will contain the identifying title shown in the table of contents. Except as otherwise directed, center this title in capital letters on the sixth line space from the bottom of the page.

5. The booklet will be stapled at the left side. Thus, for all pages in the booklet, except the title page, the center point is 3 spaces to the right of the point normally used. Use this center point in centering titles and in setting margins when the directions call for setting a certain space line, such as a 50-space line.

121c • Problem Typing

30 minutes

Problem 1—Title Page of Style Guide

Directions – 1. Prepare a title page similar to the one shown on page 154. Type the title, STUDENT WRITER'S STYLE GUIDE, your name, and the current date on the page.

2. If you wish, type a simple border consisting of asterisks (*) about 1½ inches from top, bottom, and side margins.

• Lesson 26 • *50-space line*

26a • Keyboard Review • Each line twice

7 minutes

All letters   SS   The quick brown fox jumped over the lazy old dogs.

2   s2s s2s 2s 2s 22 sacks, 212 stamps, 22 and 2 and 2

0   ;0; ;0; 0; 0; 100 pies, 101 lids, 10 and 20 and 30

Quiet wrists and arms

Easy   Hold the wrists low and still as you hit the keys.

| 1 | 2 | 3 | 4 | 5 | 6 | 7 | 8 | 9 | 10 |

26b • Location of " and) • Each line twice

5 minutes

" is the shift of 2. Type it without a space between it and the word it encloses.

) is the shift of 0. Do not space between the right parenthesis and the material it encloses.

• *For drills on the location of the " on electric typewriters, see p. xiii.*

"   SS   s2s s"s s2s s"s "s "s "ninety" for "ninty," "Gigi"

           Type "forty," not "fourty." Read "Tinker's Itch."

" shift of 2

)   ;0; ;); ;0; ;););); type), type), type) again

           Most of the men (84 to be exact) passed the tests.

) shift of 0

26c • Location of 6 and Hyphen

5 minutes

Find **6** on the chart. Find it on your typewriter keyboard. Place your fingers over the home keys. Touch **j6j** lightly two or three times. Make the reach without arching your wrist. Hold other fingers in typing position.

← REACH TO 6   REACH TO – →

Find – (hyphen) on the chart. Find it on your typewriter keyboard. Place your fingers over the home keys. Touch **;–;** lightly two or three times without moving the other fingers from their typing position.

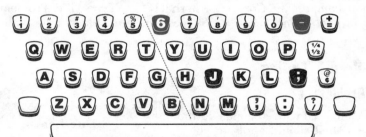

TYPE 6 WITH THE j FINGER

TYPE – WITH THE ; FINGER

j6j j6j j6j j6j 6j 6j j6j   • Type twice on same line •   ;–; ;–; ;–; ;–; –; –; ;–;

26d • Location Drills — 6 and Hyphen • Each line twice

6 minutes

6   SS   j6j j6j j6j 6j 6j 6j 66 jolts, 6166 jets, 16 and 6

           I weigh 66 pounds. Send 161 now. Collect 16,616.

Type 6 with the j finger

– (hyphen)   ;–; ;–; ;–; –; –; –; re-tread, clear-cut, send-off

           My son-in-law had a clear-cut view of that parade.

Type – with the ; finger

• **Lesson 120** • *70-space line*

120a • **Keyboard Review** • Each line at least three times

5 minutes

All letters SS We looked up at a majestic flag flying in the quiet breeze over Texas.

Figure Track and field events attracted 427,171 persons at the 1932 Olympics.

Long reach Millions of tiny ornaments have been made annually by the old artists.

Easy I know that kindness is the chain by which all men are bound together.

| 1 | 2 | 3 | 4 | 5 | 6 | 7 | 8 | 9 | 10 | 11 | 12 | 13 | 14 |

Type with your fingers

120b • **Timed Writings**

15 minutes

Directions – Type two 5-minute writings on 116c, page 191. Compute your *gwam*. Submit the better of the two writings.

120c • **Problem Typing**

25 minutes

Problem—Letter of Application

Directions – 1. Compose and type a letter of application similar to the one in 117c, Problem 1, page 192. Don't copy your letter. Write one that fits you.
2. Assume that you saw an advertisement in your local paper for a salesclerk, boy or girl, for the summer months.

• *Type your letter as you compose it. Correct it; then, retype it in final form.*

3. Type the letter in modified block style, blocked paragraphs, open punctuation. Arrange it neatly on a full sheet.
4. Address your letter to Mr. John V. Brown, Manager, Brown Variety Store, 175 Main Street, *your* city, state, and ZIP Code. Use May 15, 197– as the date.

Alternate Suggestion – Type 117c, Problems 1 and 2, pages 192-93, in block style with open punctuation.

120d • **Extra-Credit Typing**

Problem 1

Directions – Prepare a personal data sheet similar to the one in 118c, page 194. It should apply to you.

Problem 2

Directions – Type the problem you did not type for 120c, above.

Problem 3

Directions – Prepare an article for the school newspaper based on the ideas expressed in 116c, page 191. Write the article in your own words. Give it a title. Prepare it in the form prescribed in the General Directions on page 187.

Problem 4

Directions – Write a letter of thanks for an interview. Assume that you had an interview as a result of the application letter you wrote to Mr. Brown in 120c, above. Use May 25, 197– as the date. Modified block style; blocked paragraphs; open punctuation.

Problem 5

Directions – If you do not have a workbook, obtain an application blank from your school placement bureau. Fill it in on the typewriter with employment and personal information that pertains to you.

26e • Sentence Guided Writings

12 minutes

Directions – 1. Type each sentence for a 1-minute writing with the call of the guide each 20 seconds. Try to complete each sentence as the guide is called.

2. Type the last two sentences for additional 1-minute writings, as time permits, without the call of the guide.

			Words in Line	GWAM 20" Guide
1	SS	Type with your fingers well curved.	7	21
2		I read 25 pages for today's lesson.	7	21
3		Try to strike the keys in the right way.	8	24
4		I set a new record (157 miles per hour).	8	24
5		To type right, hold the wrists low and quiet.	9	27
6		He will need 44 tons of sand for the highway.	9	27
7		Human life and turnips remain cheap and plentiful.	10	30
8		Highway 366 doesn't run through the scenic valley.	10	30

| 1 | 2 | 3 | 4 | 5 | 6 | 7 | 8 | 9 | 10 |

26f • Paragraph Guided Writings • As directed in 23f, page 39

10 minutes

DS

48 words
1.1 si

	Words
If you cannot find the time to do a job right	9
the first time, how in the world do you expect to	19
find the time to do it over? There is a lot of	29
sense in these few words. Think about them. Save	39
time; do a job right the first time you do it.	48

| 1 | 2 | 3 | 4 | 5 | 6 | 7 | 8 | 9 | 10 |

• Lesson 27 • 50-space line

27a • Keyboard Review • Each line twice

7 minutes

SS   Jim's trip takes in Cadiz, Taxco, Quito, and Bonn.

All letters

We have tickets for the Olympic games this summer.

6   j6j j6j 6j 6j 66 jars, 616 jumps, 66 and 616 and 6   Type steadily

– (hyphen)   ;-; ;-; -; -; son-in-law, 33-foot pole, 2-pint jar

Easy   Keep your mind on your work as you type this copy.

| 1 | 2 | 3 | 4 | 5 | 6 | 7 | 8 | 9 | 10 |

119b • Minus and Plus Signs • Each line three times

5 minutes

Minus sign – Strike the hyphen; space before and after it.

Plus sign – If you do not have a plus key on your typewriter, strike the hyphen over the diagonal; space before and after it.

1   SS   They are sure that she got the balance as follows: $160 — $50 = $110.

2   Frank got the answer to this problem as follows: 238 + 41 + 27 = 306.

Type with your fingers

| 1 | 2 | 3 | 4 | 5 | 6 | 7 | 8 | 9 | 10 | 11 | 12 | 13 | 14 |

119c • Control Builder • Type four 1-minute writings at your control rate.

5 minutes

DS

A real friend is one who stands near when he is needed. Friends satisfy different needs, but you appreciate them most when they are there to share the important events of your life. When your friends have important news, make your friendship mean something special by sharing their joys or sorrows.

60 words
1.4 si

Type steadily

119d • Problem Typing

30 minutes

Problem 1—Permit to Work

• *The Fair Labor Standards Act of 1938 requires minors to obtain work permits. These may be obtained, as a rule, from school offices. A permit provides proof of age. You will type such a permit in this problem.*

Directions – 1. Type the work permit at the right on a 5- by 3-inch card or paper cut to that size.

2. Arrange the data as illustrated. Single and double spacing are used for the first four lines of copy; 1½ line spacing is used beginning with the name line.

• *For typewriters which do not have vertical half-spacing, 1½ line spacing is obtained as follows: (1) using the variable line spacer, roll the cylinder back until the alignment scale is at the top of a lower case letter such as m (do not use lower case letters, such as l, which extend higher than m), (2) double-space.*

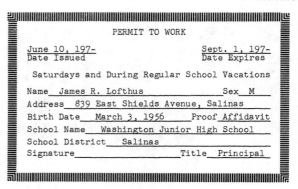

Problem 2—Affidavit of Age of Minor

• *A certificate of birth or baptism, an insurance policy, a Bible record, a passport, or the combination of a school record and affidavit may be used as proof of the age of a minor applying for work. This problem illustrates an affidavit.*

Directions – 1. Type the affidavit of age at the right on a 5- by 3-inch card or paper cut to that size.

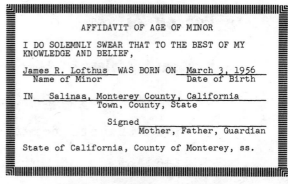

Affidavit of age of minor

2. Arrange the data as illustrated using single and double spacing.

BACKSPACING

- *The backspace key assists you in positioning the carriage. In 27b you will learn how the backspace key assists you in underlining words.*

Manual Machines – The backspace key on manual machines is located at the extreme left of the fourth row. Depress the key with the little finger as you keep the **f** finger in its proper position and the **d** and **s** fingers on or near their home row positions.

Alternate Suggestion – If your little finger is weak, operate the backspace key with one of the other fingers. To use a finger other than your little finger, move your entire hand to the fourth row and return it to the home keys after backspacing.

- *On some portable and electric machines the backspace key is at the extreme right of the fourth row of keys. In this case use the little finger of the right hand for controlling the backspace key.*

27b • Location of Underline and * • Each line twice   6 minutes

The underline is the shift of **6**.
The asterisk is the shift of **–**.

- *For drills on the location of the underline and the asterisk on electric typewriters, see p. xiii.*

- *In underlining words type the material to be underlined, then backspace to the first letter of the word (or move the carriage by hand) and strike the underline. If several words are to be underlined, use the shift lock. Use an unbroken line or break the line between words, whichever you prefer. Both practices are correct.*

_ (underline)   SS   j6j j_j j6j j_j _j _j <u>only</u>, <u>at once</u>, <u>now</u>, <u>Newsweek</u>

I buy the <u>Reader's Digest</u> and <u>Fortune</u> every month.   _ shift of 6

*   ;-; ;*; ;-; ;*; *; *; The * is the shift of the -.   * shift of –

Use * for some footnotes. He quoted Bing Crosby.*

27c • Technique Builder — Stroking • Two 1-minute writings on each line   15 minutes

1   SS   Our words are to our minds what keys are to doors.

2   *Time is on the side of the man who plans his work.*

3   He must think the words as he types to gain speed.   Quick, sharp strokes

4   *Give her time, and she will do the work all right.*

5   Use your head and your hands to learn how to type.

| 1 | 2 | 3 | 4 | 5 | 6 | 7 | 8 | 9 | 10 |

27d • Paragraph Guided Writings • Paragraphs are on next page   17 minutes

Directions – 1. Type a 1-minute writing on ¶ 1. Note the *gwam*. Add four words to your *gwam* for a new goal. Type two more writings, trying to reach your new goal.
2. Repeat Step 1 for ¶ 2.

3. Center the two paragraphs on a half sheet. Try to make no more than two errors per paragraph.

- *Your teacher may call the half-minute guide on the 1-minute writings to aid you in checking your rate.*

118c • Problem Typing

30 minutes

Problem—Personal Data Sheet

Directions – Use a 60-space line. Allow a 2-inch top margin. See the illustration at the right below.

• *Frequently an applicant for a position will include a personal data sheet with his letter of application. Such a data sheet is given in this problem.*

PERSONAL DATA SHEET
Nancy Sunada
3726 Bullard Avenue
Rochester, Minnesota 55901

Personal Information

Age: 16
Height: 5 feet 3 inches
Weight: 110 pounds
Health: Excellent
Telephone: 825-7316

Education

High School: West Hills High School, Rochester (completing the tenth grade)
Major: Combined academic-business course
Office subjects: Typewriting, with speed of 50 words a minute
Activities: Girls League and Glee Club

Work Experience

Salesclerk in F. W. Woolworth Company last summer
Addressed envelopes for United Crusade this year

References (by permission)

Mr. Lawson Bartell, Manager, F. W. Woolworth Co., 23 Van Ness Ave., Rochester
Mr. William Nuttman, typing teacher, West Hills High School, Rochester
Mrs. Marilyn Johnson, Chairman, United Crusade, 481 Chestnut Street, Rochester

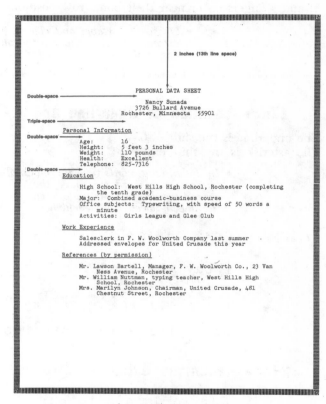

Personal data sheet

• Lesson 119 • *70-space line*

119a • Keyboard Review • Each line at least three times

5 minutes

All letters	SS	The quickness and dexterity of this juggler amazed the viewing public.
Figure		Grange, retired in 1935, carried the ball 32,820 yards in 4,000 tries.
4th finger		Paul and Polly were appalled at the opposite views of the politicians.
Easy		If you get some bumps, it is a sign you are traveling out of your rut.

Wrists low and still

| 1 | 2 | 3 | 4 | 5 | 6 | 7 | 8 | 9 | 10 | 11 | 12 | 13 | 14 |

¶ 1
38 words
1.2 si

DS Mistakes may be a sign of progress. They are   9 3 31

made when we try out new or better ways of doing   19 6 34

a job. The men who succeed do not make the same   29 10 38

mistake twice; they try to make some new ones.   38 13 41

¶ 2
47 words
1.1 si

The world is full of willing people; some are   47 16 44

willing to work; the rest are willing to let them.   58 19 47

You must know that there is no such thing in this   68 23 51

world as something for nothing. We must all be   77 26 54

willing to work for the things we want.   85 28 56

1' | 1 | 2 | 3 | 4 | 5 | 6 | 7 | 8 | 9 | 10 |
3' | 1 | 2 | 3 | 4 |

• Lesson 28 • *50-space line*

28a • Keyboard Review • Each line twice   *7 minutes*

All letters SS Jack Van Glower may buy six dozen quarts of punch.

Think letters

, _   They said that the movie is based on The Sly Fox.

One-hand   As agreed, Fred Barts gave John Lyon a rare award.

Think words

Balanced-hand   The men may work for the big bus firm if they can.

Flowing rhythm

Combination   As they agreed, the men may work for a rare award.

| 1 | 2 | 3 | 4 | 5 | 6 | 7 | 8 | 9 | 10 |

28b • Location of ¢ and ½   *5 minutes*

Find ¢ on your typewriter keyboard. ←REACH TO ¢   REACH TO ½→ Find ½ on your chart. Find it on your
Touch ;¢; lightly two typewriter keyboard.
or three times. There is Place your fingers over
no space between the the home keys. Touch
number and the ¢ sign. ;½; lightly two or three
• *For drills on the lo-* times. There is no space
cation of ¢ on electric between the figure and
typewriters, see p. the fraction.
xiii.

TYPE ¢ WITH
THE ; FINGER

TYPE ½ WITH
THE ; FINGER

;¢; ;¢; ;¢; ;¢; ¢; ¢; ;¢;   • Type twice on same line •   ;½; ;½; ;½; ;½; ½; ½; ;½;

Problem 2—Letter of Thanks for Interview

| Modified block style | 50-space line | 9 spaces between date and address | Return address and inside address as in Problem 1 | Date: May 28, 197— |

Dear Mr. Hull: / Thank you for the interview you gave me on Monday. I believe I can handle the job in your office. (¶) Many of the tasks you described sound similar to those I was assigned in the counseling office at North High. I think my work experience there was very worthwhile. (¶) I can start working on June 6. My home telephone number is 224-1389. / Sincerely, Tim Young

• Lesson 118 • *70-space line*

118a • Keyboard Review • Each line at least three times
5 minutes

All letters SS Dave was quite upset after hearing crazy music from the old jukeboxes.

Figure The population of Phoenix expanded very rapidly between 1950 and 1960.

Double letters A need for referring all necessary letters for approval was discussed.

Space quickly

Easy The thing that matters is not where one is now, but where he is going.

| 1 | 2 | 3 | 4 | 5 | 6 | 7 | 8 | 9 | 10 | 11 | 12 | 13 | 14 |

118b • Speed Stretcher • As directed in 103b, page 172
10 minutes

| | | | G | W | A | M |
| | | | 1' | | 5' | |

All letters
¶ 1
41 words
1.4 si

DS An old saying has it that one man's meat is another man's poison. `13 3 44`
What this really means, of course, is that what's good for one man is `27 5 46`
not necessarily good for another. Is this saying worth remembering? `41 8 49`

¶ 2
50 words
1.4 si

It is worth remembering when you look at the customs of countries `13 11 52`
other than your own. Sometimes you may be tempted to laugh at foreign `27 14 55`
ways. If so, be careful before you pass judgment. You should realize `42 17 58`
their customs exist for very good reasons. `50 18 59`

¶ 3
63 words
1.4 si

These reasons are almost as varied as the customs themselves. As `13 21 62`
a rule, though, customs spring up in one of three ways. They may be `27 24 65`
the solution to a practical problem, or the result of certain events `41 26 67`
such as floods, wars, or new trade routes. They frequently result from `55 29 70`
people's attitudes towards life itself. `63 31 72`

¶ 4
49 words
1.4 si

The American idea of putting in a day's work for a day's pay stems `13 33 74`
in part from our view of competition. Elsewhere in the world people do `28 36 77`

All ¶'s
1.4 si

not look at competition in the same way. Are their attitudes wrong—or `42 39 80`
are they just different from ours? `49 41 82`

| 1' | 1 | 2 | 3 | 4 | 5 | 6 | 7 | 8 | 9 | 10 | 11 | 12 | 13 | 14 |
| 5' | | 1 | | | 2 | | | 3 | |

28c • Location Drills — ¢ and ½ • Each line twice

¢   SS   ;¢; ;¢; 2 for 22¢, 3 for 33¢, 4 for 44¢, 5 for 55¢

We paid 75¢.   The cost was 95¢.   I took 5 for 55¢.

Type ¢ with the ; finger

½   ;½; ;½; 11½ feet, 22½ rods, 15½ meters, 44½ quarts

Send her 82½ yards.   Buy 85½ feet.   Take 14½ feet.

Type ½ with the ; finger

28d • Continuity Practice — Numbers and Symbols • Twice

10 minutes

                                                  Words

DS   Things and people holding records make news.   9

Did you know that Mickey Mantle's 565-foot home run   20

is the longest?   Joe Nuxhall, at 15 years 10 months   30

Figure and symbol review   11 days, was the youngest major league player of   40

all time.   The people living in Connecticut lead   50

all others in incomes ($4,231 per person).   The   59

average for the country is $3,412.   66

    | 1 | 2 | 3 | 4 | 5 | 6 | 7 | 8 | 9 | 10 |

28e • Paragraph Guided Writings • As directed in 27d, page 45

17 minutes

		GWAM 1'	3'

All letters
¶ 1
42 words
1.2 si   DS   Here is one of those pithy quotations that is   9   3   33

worth keeping in mind.   "A man who pulls his own   19   6   36

weight seldom has any left to throw around."   This   29   10   40

is as true in school or on the playing field as it   39   13   43

is on the job.   42   14   44

¶ 2
49 words
1.2 si   Look around, and you will find that a busy man   52   17   47

just does not get into trouble.   He lacks the time   62   21   51

to find it.   The lazy man is always the one who   71   24   54

seems to have an axe to grind.   The first rule of   81   27   57

teamwork, therefore, is to pull your own weight.   91   30   60

1' | 1 | 2 | 3 | 4 | 5 | 6 | 7 | 8 | 9 | 10 |
3' | 1 | 2 | 3 | 4 |

• Lesson 117 • *70-space line*

117a • Keyboard Review • Each line at least three times

All letters	SS	Vickie Morgan did an excellent job of sewing the skirt zipper quickly.
Figure		More than 6,000 people left between June 25, 1897, and March 24, 1923.
Balanced- and one-hand		for you, for trade, for him, for war, for your, for fear, for millions
Easy		You need a keener mind to use good advice than a man needs to give it.

Elbows in

| 1 | 2 | 3 | 4 | 5 | 6 | 7 | 8 | 9 | 10 | 11 | 12 | 13 | 14

117b • Speed Builder • Type 1- and 5-minute writings. The return will be called at the end of each minute.
10 minutes

DS

Not all great ideas have sprung from the minds of those who were — Words 13

searching for answers to certain problems. In fact, a lot of our big — 27

60 words 1.4 si

ideas have come about because someone was sharp enough to build upon — 41

an accident. Ice cream, for example, was the result of some custard — 55

that was frozen by mistake. — 60

PAPERS USED IN APPLYING FOR A JOB

In the lessons of this unit, you will type a number of letters and reports commonly used in applying for a job. Study the examples of letters included in the unit. Follow carefully the directions given with each problem.

117c • Problem Typing
30 minutes

Problem 1—Application Letter

Directions – 1. Type the letter in personal business style, similar to the model illustrated on page 140.

2. Use a 50-space line; leave 6 spaces between the date and the address.

Return Address—3872 Millbrook Avenue / Indianapolis, Indiana 46227 / May 20, 197–

Address—Mr. Frank E. Hull / 478 Fulton Street / Indianapolis, Indiana 46202

Dear Mr. Hull: / I wish to apply for the job of office boy that you have advertised in today's Indianapolis News. (¶) I am sixteen years old and am finishing the tenth grade at North High School. I hope to get a summer job where I can gain some business experience and also save money for my college education. (¶) During the past school year I worked one hour a day in the counseling office at North High. Mr. Ralph Barnes, the head counselor, will be glad to write a letter of recommendation for me. He has given me permission to use his name as a reference. (¶) I can come in any day after school for an interview. My telephone number is 224-1389. Sincerely yours, Tim Young

• Lesson 29 • *50-space line*

29a • Keyboard Review • Each line twice
7 minutes

All letters SS How can Jack Flipsby take a driving quiz next May?

¢, ½ ;¢; ;½; Pay 45¢ for 73½ quarts. Give 83¢ for 62½.
Think letters

One-hand We saw Dave jump in a pool. John saw him at noon.
Think words

Balanced-hand He may sign the forms if Pam can pay for the land.
Flowing rhythm

Combination John saw him sign the forms. Rex may make a pool.

| 1 | 2 | 3 | 4 | 5 | 6 | 7 | 8 | 9 | 10 |

29b • Location of @ and ¼ • Each line twice
6 minutes

@ (symbol for *at*) is the shift of ¢. There is a space before and after the symbol.

¼ is the shift of ½. There is no space between the figure and the fraction.

• *For drills on the location of the @ on electric typewriters, see p. xiii.*

@ SS ;@; ;@; ;@; sell 425 @ 7, buy 66 @ 23, take 22 @ 4
@ shift of ¢

The @ is the shift of ¢. Buy 7 sacks @ 5¢ a sack.

¼ ;¼; ;¼; ;¼; 14¼ yards, 13¼ hours, take 11¼ and 22¼
¼ shift of ½

Sell 475 shares @ 93¼. The discount rate is 12¼%.

29c • Location of / and : • Each line twice
6 minutes

/ (diagonal) is the lower case of ?. Do not space before or after the diagonal.

: is the shift of ;. Space twice after a colon when it is used as a mark of punctuation.

• *The diagonal is used in typing fractions for which there is no special keyboard symbol, as 3/8. Note in Line 1 below how a whole number and a fraction that is not on the keyboard are spaced.*

/ SS ;/; ;/; ;/; 2/3, 2/5, 3 2/3 and 7 1/8, 1/5 and 1/5
/ lower case of ?

Be uniform in typing fractions; thus, 1/2 and 3/8.

: Please send these items: books, stamps, and pens.
: shift of ;

I quote Frost: "Good fences make good neighbors."

29d • Technique Builder — Flowing Rhythm • Five times from dictation
5 minutes

1 SS to do the | to do the work | and did it | and did the

2 if it is | if it is the | if the duty is | if they do
Think words

3 and it | and it is | and it is the | and they did the
Type rapidly

		GWAM 1' 5'

All letters

¶ 1   DS
44 words
1.3 si

Somebody once remarked that when a person is well he has a hundred   13   3   55

wishes; but if he is sick, he has only one. Since good health is a rich   28   6   58

blessing, everyone should do all he can to keep his body in excellent   42   8   60

condition.   44   9   61

¶ 2
48 words
1.3 si

No matter how marvelous the new inventions we come up with these   57   11   63

days, not one of them can compare in complexity with the human body.   71   14   66

This wondrous machine that each of us has to use is not often treated   85   17   69

with the care and respect it needs.   92   18   70

¶ 3
52 words
1.3 si

It is amazing how much punishment our bodies take and still bounce   105   21   73

back for more. When one stops to consider the poor health habits of   119   24   76

some people, one knows this to be true. They treat their bodies with   133   27   79

less respect than they do their mechanical inventions.   144   29   81

¶ 4
56 words
1.3 si

The body needs the right kind of foods, lots of fresh air, and an   157   31   83

adequate amount of rest if it is to work properly. Food provides the   171   34   86

fuel to keep this complex machine running. Fresh air is required to burn   186   37   89

the food. Rest and sleep furnish the time for recovery from exertion.   200   40   92

¶ 5
60 words
1.4 si

These three elements are essential in any program which is planned   213   43   95

for proper care of the human body. When good health practices are fol-   228   46   98

lowed from an early age, they just become habits. The sooner in life   242   48   100

they are formed, the better. These habits will pay off for you in a   255   51   103

All ¶'s
1.3 si

richer and longer life.   260   52   104

```
1' | 1 | 2 | 3 | 4 | 5 | 6 | 7 | 8 | 9 | 10 | 11 | 12 | 13 | 14 |
5' |       1       |        2        |        3        |
```

H. V. Prochnow said, "Parrots don't know what they
are talking about and that makes them almost human."

29e • Skill Comparison

11 minutes

Directions – Type two 1-minute writings on each sentence. Compare *gwam* on the four lines.

Technique Goals – Type without pauses. Space quickly between words. Keep wrists quiet.

Easy · SS · Some things have to be believed to be seen at all.

One-hand · Dexter Lyon saw Milo pull a beaver in a red crate.

Figure · We sold all the land on August 15 at $273 an acre.

Space quickly

Script · *A pound of pluck is worth more than a ton of luck.*

| 1 | 2 | 3 | 4 | 5 | 6 | 7 | 8 | 9 | 10 |

29f • Timed Writings

10 minutes

Directions – Type two 3-minute writings on 28e, page 47. Circle errors. Compute *gwam*. Submit the better writing.

• Lesson 30 • *50-space line*

30a • Keyboard Review • Each line twice

7 minutes

SS · We expect Jeff Quick to take the pole vault prize.

All letters · The two boys saw the young zebra near the big dam.

Wrists low and still

"my" reach · my my army stormy myself mystic myth roomy mystery

"br" reach · br br brush bring break brave broil broad broke br

Reach with your fingers

Easy · They will be judged by the things they do and say.

| 1 | 2 | 3 | 4 | 5 | 6 | 7 | 8 | 9 | 10 |

30b • Exclamation Point and Dash • Each line twice

6 minutes

Exclamation Point – Type the apostrophe; backspace and type the period. Do not space between the word and the exclamation point.

Dash – Type two hyphens. Do not space before or after the dash.

* *On some machines the exclamation point is the shift of Figure 1 on the top row of keys, and the a finger is used to strike the exclamation point. For drills on the location of the ! on electric typewriters, see p. xiii.*

! · SS · Attention! This is our final offer! Act at once!

Apostrophe, backspace, and period

Think what this will mean to you! Call him today!

-- · Return the card now--today--if you can go with us.

Two hyphens

He said that justice--not the majority--must rule.

Problem 2—Article with Justified Right Margin • As directed in Prob. 1, p. 189

SKI CLUB MEMBERS HEAD FOR SLOPES

Badger Pass will be the destination of at least 30 enthusiastic Tioga skiers on Saturday, February 5. The bus will leave from the school at 7:15 a.m.

Betty Steinmetz, club president, has announced that any additional students who want to make the trip must sign up before January 20.

Beginners are welcome. Lessons on a dry ski slope are available each evening during the week at Metry's Sporting Goods on the corner of Ashlan and Blackstone Avenues. Anyone who does not have equipment may rent it from the store for $5.

Mr. Stevenson, club sponsor, says the bus will be back by 8:00 p.m. Saturday evening. Travel permits are required.

115d • Extra-Credit Typing

Problem 1

Directions – Type 99c, page 167, in a form suitable for a school newspaper. Justify the right margin. Provide a suitable title.

Problem 2

Directions – Type a horizontal bar graph, similar to the one on page 179, of your own speed growth in typing class.

• Unit 13
Applying for a Job

General Directions • Lessons 116 – 120

Machine Adjustments – Use the same machine adjustments used in Unit 12.

• Lesson 116

• *Use a 70-space line for all lessons in this unit.*

116a • Keyboard Review • Each line at least three times

5 minutes

All letters SS We expect the judge to question the tax levy before modernizing parks.

Figure On June 30, 1899, Charles C. Murphy bicycled a mile in 57 4/5 seconds.

Eyes and mind on copy as you type

Right hand Paula, please play the part in the play. The play will open in April.

Easy Build faith in yourself, but be sure you can back up words with ideas.

| 1 | 2 | 3 | 4 | 5 | 6 | 7 | 8 | 9 | 10 | 11 | 12 | 13 | 14 |

116b • Sentence Skill Builder • Two 1-minute writings on each sentence

10 minutes

1 SS Be yourself as it is the one thing you can do better than anyone else.

2 Make your job an important one; it is very likely to return the favor.

Type without pauses

3 The man who has both feet on the ground, however, can't fall very far.

4 Many of us fail because we spend our day doing yesterday's work today.

| 1 | 2 | 3 | 4 | 5 | 6 | 7 | 8 | 9 | 10 | 11 | 12 | 13 | 14 |

30c • **Key-Location Practice** • Each line three times

12 minutes

1   ss   They will buy copies of Poppo for $5.74, less 10%.

2   Send 15½ pounds to O'Day; 8¼ pounds to May & Loop.

3   Return 3 1/3 pints @ 19¢ a pint. Buy Form #178-2.

4   The largest garage (Chicago) will hold 2,359 cars.

5   He quoted Emerson: "The first wealth is health."*

6   Get ready! Go! May they--Sue and John--go there?

7   The ¢ and @ are on the same key: Price 195 @ 64¢.

   | 1 | 2 | 3 | 4 | 5 | 6 | 7 | 8 | 9 | 10 |

All figures and symbols taught

30d • **Timed Writings**

10 minutes

Directions – Type two 3-minute writings on this paragraph. Circle errors. Compute *gwam*. Submit the better writing.

G W A M

1'   3'

DS   Morley said that there is one rule for being   9   3 33

a good talker; learn to listen. It is a good   18   6 36

quotation to keep in mind. To talk well, give   28   9 39

others a chance to express their views. Learn   37 12 42

All letters what they know. Try their views on for size.   46 15 45
89 words
1.1 si   Talk only when you have something worth saying.   56 19 49

Just keep in mind that the star of the show is the 66 22 52

one who sings one song too few, not one too many.   77 26 56

Use the same trick to become the star of your   86 29 59

class in school.   89 30 60

   1' | 1 | 2 | 3 | 4 | 5 | 6 | 7 | 8 | 9 | 10 |
   3' | 1 | 2 | 3 | 4 |

30e • **Continuity Practice from Script**

10 minutes

Directions – Type as many copies as time permits.   **Technique Goals** – Eyes on copy; type without pauses.

Words

DS   The important thing to keep in mind in learning   10

35 words to type is good form. There is a right way to strike   20
1.1 si   the keys and handle the machine. Type right; then   31

watch your skill grow.   35

• Lesson 115 • *70-space line*

115a • Keyboard Review • Each line at least three times   *5 minutes*

All letters SS   Joe believed that my trip from Arizona to New York was quite exciting.

Figure   Pike's Peak, at 14,110 feet, ranks 55th among all U.S. mountain peaks.   Eyes on copy
                                                                                          as you return
Direct reach   My Uncle Myron brought my brother and aunt to Briton for the symphony. the carriage

Easy   Your mind is like a good knife; it must be used often to remain sharp.

| 1 | 2 | 3 | 4 | 5 | 6 | 7 | 8 | 9 | 10 | 11 | 12 | 13 | 14 |

115b • Timed Writings   *15 minutes*

Directions – Type two 5-minute writings on 111c, page 184. Compute your *gwam*. Submit the better of the two writings.

JUSTIFYING THE RIGHT MARGIN

School newspapers prepared on a duplicating machine are sometimes typed so that all the lines, except the last one in a paragraph, are even at the right margin. This practice is known as justifying the right margin. The copy then has the appearance of a printed page.

To get an even right margin, extra spaces are added between words to fill out short lines. The copy is first typed as illustrated below. It is then retyped with the extra spaces.

First, type a line of asterisks to indicate the maximum length line: 30 spaces, pica; 36 spaces, elite.

Second, type the article. Add asterisks to the short lines to make them even with the line of asterisks at the top.

Third, retype the article. Add an extra space between words for each asterisk in that line. Try to avoid putting extra spaces in one line under extra spaces in the line above it.

115c • Problem Typing   *25 minutes*

Problem 1—Article with Justified Right Margin

Directions – 1. Type the short article at the right on one of your 4¼- by 11-inch pieces of paper. Type the first draft with the asterisks for the short lines; then the final draft with the justified lines.   *First draft*

2. Follow the same directions you have been using in preparing copy for the school newspaper in Lessons 113 and 114, but justify the right margin.   *Justified draft*

3. Use this title for the article: WHAT'S YOUR TITLE?

```
*******************************************

    No matter what kind of job you***
have these days, you can be sure****
someone will give it a title that***
sounds important.  A janitor is an**
engineer of sanitation; an usher is*
an audience guide; and a dog catcher
is a supervisor of missing canines.


    No matter  what  kind  of  job  you
have   these  days,  you can  be  sure
someone  will  give it  a  title  that
sounds  important.  A  janitor  is  an
engineer  of  sanitation;  an  usher is
an  audience  guide;  and a  dog catcher
is a  supervisor  of  missing  canines.
```

Learning to Use the Special Parts of Your Typewriter

General Directions • Lessons 31 – 35

Line length – Beginning with this lesson, set margin stops for a 60-space line. Make this adjustment at the start of each lesson.

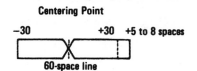

Centering Point

−30   +30   +5 to 8 spaces

60-space line

Spacing – Single-space lines of words and sentences; double-space between repeated groups of lines. Double-space paragraph copy.

• Lesson 31

31a • Keyboard Review • Each line twice

5 minutes

All letters   SS   Jerry Diamond packed the quartz in twelve large, firm boxes.

Figures   The average depth of the Atlantic Ocean is thus 12,800 feet.   Sit erect

Easy   They should read and type many short, easy words as a whole.

| 1 | 2 | 3 | 4 | 5 | 6 | 7 | 8 | 9 | 10 | 11 | 12 |

31b • Spacing After Punctuation Marks — Review

15 minutes

Directions – Each line twice. Read the explanation for a line before you type it.

EXPLANATIONS

Lines 1, 2, and 3 – Space twice after end-of-sentence punctuation.
Line 4 – Do not space after a period within an abbreviation. Space once after a period that ends an abbreviation; twice if that period ends a sentence.
Line 5 – Space once after a comma.

Line 6 – Space twice after a colon. Exception: Do not space before or after a colon in stating time.
Line 7 – Type the dash with two hyphens, without spacing before or after.
Line 8 – Do not space before or after the hyphen in a hyphenated word.

SENTENCES

1   SS   John heard the bell. It rang at night. Al did not hear it.

2   Will they go? Can he drive? Where does he live? Who's it?

3   Dash to the nearest exit! Hurry! Beware! This is madness!

4   I saw him at 11 a.m. They will leave on the 10 p.m. flight.   Eyes and mind on copy as you type

5   She bought statues, jewelry, and other gifts in Rome, Italy.

6   I used these figures: 39, 58, and 20. He left at 4:16 p.m.

7   Ridicule is thus the first—and the last—argument of fools.

8   The well-known skin diver could not find his life preserver.

| 1 | 2 | 3 | 4 | 5 | 6 | 7 | 8 | 9 | 10 | 11 | 12 |

114a • Keyboard Review • Each line at least three times   *5 minutes*

All letters	SS	Excited crowds enjoy big trapeze events and frequently clap them back.
Figure		A plane speed record of 266.59 miles an hour was set November 4, 1923.
Adjacent keys		Right after their retirement, other writers returned to the territory.
Easy		The right mind set will help you make the typewriter do its work well.

Flowing rhythm

| 1 | 2 | 3 | 4 | 5 | 6 | 7 | 8 | 9 | 10 | 11 | 12 | 13 | 14 |

114b • Sentence Skill Builder from Rough Draft • Two 1-minute writings on each sentence   *10 minutes*

1 SS we now that we can see in others some of of our own traits—good or bad.

2 The quickest way to gain your own goals is to help others another gain theirs his.

3 He has the that rare gift of choosing words that to give life to his thoughts.

4 most people can All of us must listen about four times as fast as a person will talk talks.

Think as you type

114c • Problem Typing   *30 minutes*

• *You will continue typing items for the school newspaper in this lesson. Follow the directions given under 113c, page 187.*

Problem 1—Items of Special Interest

Directions – In an article entitled JOHN DOE SAYS—, include the following items. Use an appropriate subheading for each item. Use your name for "John Doe."

75c	Concentration Practice	page 129
86e	Continuity Practice from Script	page 147
92b	Paragraph Skill Builder	page 157

Problem 2—Feature Story

Directions – 1. Compose and type a feature story on one of the following topics. The references following each topic are to similar articles in this textbook. You may get ideas from these articles, but do not copy them. Compose your own story.

2. Type your final copy in the same form that you used in typing the other items for the school newspaper.

3. Type your name as the author. Give your story an appropriate title.

Actions Speak Louder than Words	61e	Paragraph Guided Writings	page 108
Time Marches On	74e	Paragraph Guided Writings	page 128
Is College for Me?	78b	Speed Stretcher	page 133

31c • Speed Ladder Paragraphs

15 minutes

Directions – 1-minute writings. When you can complete the first paragraph in one minute, type the second; then the third, fourth, and fifth. Your teacher may call the half-minutes to guide you.

- The rate increases 5 words a minute with each succeeding paragraph

			Words in ¶	GWAM 3'
¶ 1 20 words 1.2 si	DS	It is common knowledge that a man's mind is the key to	11	4
		his actions. Just think right to type right.	20	7
¶ 2 25 words 1.2 si		Use your mind and save your fingers. Let this be your	11	10
		motto in your typing class. It will pay you to think before	23	14
		you type.	25	15
¶ 3 30 words 1.2 si		Every man must live with himself. He must thus see	10	18
		that he has good company. He should develop in himself the	22	22
		traits he likes to see in his friends.	30	25
¶ 4 35 words 1.2 si		It is often said that temper is such a good thing that	11	29
		we should do our best never to lose it. We are at our very	23	33
		best when we are pleasant. We fail when we lose our temper.	35	37
¶ 5 40 words 1.1 si		Nobody can keep his eyes on the ball and a clock at the	11	40
		same time. If he tries this trick, he will surely strike	23	44
		out. He must measure each day by the work he finishes, not	35	48
All ¶'s 1.2 si		by the hands on the clock.	40	50

```
1' | 1 | 2 | 3 | 4 | 5 | 6 | 7 | 8 | 9 | 10 | 11 | 12 |
3' |    1    |    2    |    3    |    4    |
```

PREPARING NEWSPAPER COPY

Many schools, clubs, fraternities, sororities, and other organizations prepare and issue newspapers and newsletters of the type you will prepare in the next three lessons. Items of interest are composed and typed in accordance with set rules and given to an editor. The editor checks the items and arranges the copy on plan sheets. The copy is typed from the plan sheets on master sheets for spirit duplication or on stencils for mimeographing. The paper is duplicated, stapled, and distributed.

- *In the next three lessons you will prepare copy for the editor. This copy is for a two-column newspaper duplicated on 8½- by 11-inch paper.*

113c • Problem Typing

30 minutes

1. Cut several sheets of 8½- by 11-inch paper in half lengthwise. Each piece should be 4¼ by 11 inches.

2. Type each article or item on a separate piece of paper.

3. Type main headings in all capitals, centered. Type subheadings, if used, in capital and lower case, with triple spacing before and double spacing after.

4. Set margins for a 3-inch line—30 spaces, pica; 36 spaces, elite. (When justifying the right margin, the maximum line length is 30 or 36.)

5. Single-space the final copy; double-space between paragraphs. Indent paragraphs 3 spaces.

6. You need not center the copy vertically. Start typing each article about one inch from the top.

- *Directions for centering lines on odd-size paper are on page 68.*

Problem 1—Feature Article

Directions – 1. Type 106d, page 177, as a feature story for the school newspaper. Use the following heading: THE PERFECT GIFT.

2. In typing your copy, follow the general directions given above.

3. Your copy should look like the copy in the partial illustration at the right.

```
         THE PERFECT GIFT

     The next time you are faced with
the problem of what to buy the person
who has everything, why not consider
getting him a mule?  While the idea
may sound odd at first, you must real-
ize the many advantages of such a
gift.

     Here are just a couple of them.
First of all, a mule requires much
less upkeep than a nifty sports car
```

Problem 2—Special Items

Directions – 1. The second sentence in many Keyboard Reviews in Cycle 3 is a factual statement of general interest. Select six or more of these sentences for an article. Use the following heading: FACTS OF LIFE.

2. Use your own name as the author.

3. Your copy should look like the copy in the partial illustration at the right.

```
         FACTS OF LIFE

            Your name

     On January 24, 1966, nearly
263 million tons of snow fell on the
U.S.

     Ted Williams, who hit .406 in
1941, was the last player to reach
.400.
```

Articles typed on 4¼- by 11-inch paper

Problem 3—Short Item

Directions – Type the paragraph in 82b, page 139, as an item for the paper. Provide a suitable title for it. Use your own name as the author.

31d • Technique Builder — Flowing Rhythm

10 minutes

Directions – Each line three times from dictation.   Technique Goal – Blend stroking into flowing rhythm.

1   SS   if he gets | if he sees | if he reads | if he cares | if he were

2   he did see | he did look | he did get | he did pull | he did set

3   if they join | if they trade | if they jump | to my | if it only

4   he may set | he may oil | he may rest | he may ink | he may wear

Think words

• Lesson 32 • *60-space line*

32a • Keyboard Review • Type each line twice

5 minutes

All letters   SS   Nick gave them Paula's exquisite old jewelry for the bazaar.

Figure-Symbol   John and Bob's bill is for $48. They worked there 15 hours.

Easy   A man who empties his purse into his head will lose neither.
| 1 | 2 | 3 | 4 | 5 | 6 | 7 | 8 | 9 | 10 | 11 | 12 |

Eyes on
this copy

32b • Spacing of Symbols and Figures — Review

10 minutes

Directions – Each line twice. Read the explanation
for a line before you type it.

EXPLANATIONS

Line 1 – Do not space between the dollar sign and
the following figure.
Line 2 – Do not space between a figure and the
percent sign.

Line 3 – Do not space before or after the apostrophe.
Line 4 – Space before and after the ampersand.
Line 5 – Do not space between the quotation marks
and the words they enclose.

SENTENCES

1   SS   We got his check for $95 in today's mail. He still owes $6.

2   These bonds pay interest at the rate of 5%. Vince wants 6%.

3   Honesty pays, but it doesn't pay enough to suit some people.

4   Bob ordered the spring for his watch from Washington & Sons.

5   Ford said, "Money is like an arm or leg—use it or lose it."
| 1 | 2 | 3 | 4 | 5 | 6 | 7 | 8 | 9 | 10 | 11 | 12 |

Think as
you type

Problem 2—Bulletin Board Notice

————PHYSICAL FITNESS PERFORMANCE AWARDS————

Grand Slammer Award   *   Seventh Grade Winner: SANDY SIPOLETT

                      *

DEAN WHITLOW   *   Eighth Grade Winner: LOWELL REYNOLDS

————PHYSICAL FITNESS PERFORMANCE AWARDS————

• Lesson 113 • *70-space line*

113a • Keyboard Review • Each line at least three times   *5 minutes*

All letters SS The judge was quick to penalize the six boys for moving the green car.

Figure-Symbol The United States grows 17.5% of the world's wheat, 41% of its cotton.   Quick, crisp

Shift William A. Burt, Mount Vernon, Michigan, patented his machine in 1829.   short strokes

Easy The best mirror is an old friend; weigh well his kind words of advice.

| 1 | 2 | 3 | 4 | 5 | 6 | 7 | 8 | 9 | 10 | 11 | 12 | 13 | 14 |

113b • Speed Stretcher • As directed in 103b, page 172   *10 minutes*

GWAM 1' 5'

All letters ¶ 1 DS 54 words 1.3 si We envy people who can quote passages from the works of the great writers of the world or remember important facts. Winston Churchill could recall bits of poems to drive home some of the points he made in his talks. He was world famous as an orator. How did he do it? (13 3 42 / 27 5 44 / 41 8 47 / 54 11 50)

¶ 2 71 words 1.3 si The answer is that men who can recall a fact, a few lines of poetry, or an important event memorized these things in the first place. That's the way it must be with you, too. Anyone can memorize what he wants to remember if he is only willing to take the time to do it. In addition, some rules have been worked out that, if followed, are quite helpful. (14 14 53 / 28 16 55 / 43 19 58 / 57 22 61 / 71 25 64)

¶ 3 71 words 1.3 si Repeat what you want to memorize. Get its full meaning. These are the basic rules passed on by mental experts. Memory tricks may be helpful too. Some men learn a foreign language by writing foreign words on one side of a card and the words they stand for in English on the other. (14 28 67 / 28 31 70 / 42 33 72 / 57 36 75)

All ¶'s 1.3 si During their free moments, they just shuffle the cards and study them. (71 39 78)

32c • Timed Writings

10 minutes

Directions – Type two 3-minute writings on 31c, page 52. Compute *gwam*. Submit the better of the two writings.

32d • Tabulator Control • Each sentence three times; single spacing

15 minutes

Directions – 1. Clear the tabulator rack as directed on page vii.
2. Type the first sentence at the left margin.
3. Set a tab stop for the second sentence five spaces from the left margin. Set a tab stop for the third sentence ten spaces from the left margin. Set stops for the fourth and fifth sentences as indicated.

Technique Goal – Depress the tab bar (right index finger) or tab key (right little finger). Hold down the bar or key until the carriage stops. Move quickly back to home position.

Strokes in Line

		Words
60 ──────→ Please keep your eyes on the book as you throw the carriage.		12
5		
55 ──────→ Return, indent, and start the new line without pausing.		11
10		
50 ──────→ They can learn to use the tab bar or key by touch.		10
15		
45 ──────→ Just complete each line without slowing down.		9
20		
40 ──────→ Move your hand to home position quickly.		8

32e • Technique Builder — Repeated Letters

5 minutes

Directions – Each line twice.

Technique Goal – Strike repeated letters with the same force used on the other letters.

1 SS three happy agree room bill week inn message sleep mood well

2 issue guess look good less smooth apply proof speed too free

3 will allow apply feel fall soon floor offer matter add dress

4 full assign buzz funny little rubber spill muzzle poor bluff

Even stroking

• Lesson 33 • *60-space line*

33a • Keyboard Review • Each line twice

5 minutes

All letters SS The expert jumper dazzled Bill Wycoff with his quick diving.

Figure Mt. Whitney ranks among the highest of peaks at 14,495 feet.

Easy Every man shows what he is by what he does with what he has.

| 1 | 2 | 3 | 4 | 5 | 6 | 7 | 8 | 9 | 10 | 11 | 12 |

Fingers deeply curved

• Lesson 112 • *70-space line*

112a • Keyboard Review • Each line at least three times

All letters   SS   All avid track fans were penalized by the exacting major requirements.

Figure   The 985A jet can cruise at 620 miles per hour for the 7,143-mile trip.

Even stroking

"eve" comb.   Have you ever realized that everyone eventually attends every evening?

Easy   Many who neglect to learn in their youth lose the past and the future.

| 1 | 2 | 3 | 4 | 5 | 6 | 7 | 8 | 9 | 10 | 11 | 12 | 13 | 14 |

112b • Punctuation Guides — Quotation Marks

10 minutes

Directions – Read the explanation carefully; then type each example sentence twice.

Line 1 – Place quotation marks around the exact words of a speaker.

Line 2 – When the quotation is broken to identify the speaker, put quotation marks around each part.

Line 3 – If the second part of the quotation is a new sentence, use a capital letter.

Line 4 – Use no quotation marks with an indirect quotation.

Line 5 – Use quotation marks around the titles of articles, songs, poems, themes, short stories, and the like.

Line 6 – Always place the period or comma inside the quotation mark.

1   SS   Professor Cole said, "Only 29 percent of the earth's surface is land."

2   "The deepest mine in the world," they continued, "is 9,811 feet deep."

3   "We are going to Hawaii," she replied softly. "Here are our tickets."

Quick, firm reach to the shift key

4   David said he thinks that the Grand Coulee is the world's biggest dam.

5   Gayle Sobolik wrote the report entitled, "Automation Isn't Automatic."

6   "Sweden," the first speaker insisted, "has the highest literacy rate."

| 1 | 2 | 3 | 4 | 5 | 6 | 7 | 8 | 9 | 10 | 11 | 12 | 13 | 14 |

112c • Problem Typing

30 minutes

Problem 1—Bulletin Board Notice

Directions – Type the bulletin board notice at the right on a half sheet of paper. Arrange your copy attractively.

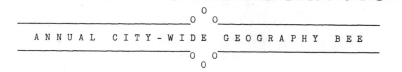

```
                              o   o
                  _____o       o_____
             ANNUAL  CITY-WIDE   GEOGRAPHY  BEE
                  _____o    o_____
                              o


                    Notice to All Contestants

             BUS LEAVES FOR IRWIN JUNIOR HIGH SCHOOL

        Faculty Parking Lot              Wednesday, May 18

                       8:30 a.m.
```

Bulletin board notice

33b • Typing Outside the Right and Left Margins

5 minutes

Right Margin – To type outside the right margin after the carriage is locked, depress the margin-release key (No. 25).

Left Margin – To type outside the left margin, depress the margin release key; then backspace to the desired point.

- *Depress the margin-release key with the ; finger. On some electric typewriters the margin-release key is depressed with the a finger.*

Directions – 1. Using a 60-space line, type the first line. When the carriage locks, depress the margin-release key and complete the line. Repeat.

2. Now, depress the margin-release key, move the carriage five spaces into the left margin, and type the second line. Repeat.

In right margin | Your typewriter has some useful gadgets. Learn to use them well.

In left margin | Your typewriter has some useful gadgets. Learn to use them well.

33c • Dividing Words; Left Margin Release

17 minutes

Directions – 1. Full sheet; 60-space line; single spacing with double spacing between items.

2. Start typing on the 21st line space from the top of the paper.

3. After you type the first line, reset the left margin stop so the carriage stops under the **Y** in *You.* To type the figures 2, 3, 4, etc., move the carriage outside the left margin by depressing the margin-release key and backspacing.

2 spaces

Reset left margin stop →

1. You will divide words at the ends of lines to keep the right margin as even as possible. You can divide words only between syllables, as your-self and foot-ball.

— Double-space

2. When in doubt, use a dictionary to help solve word-division problems. The following guides tell you when not to divide words even though some of them may contain more than one syllable.

3. Naturally, you should not divide words of only one syllable, such as thought, friend, or trained.

4. Do not separate a syllable of one letter at the beginning of a word, such as idea, across, or elect.

5. Do not divide a word of five or fewer letters, such as also, duty, or going.

6. Do not separate a syllable of one or two letters at the end of a word, such as ready, greatly, or greater.

7. Do not separate a syllable that does not contain a vowel from the rest of the word, such as didn't or wouldn't.

8. Avoid, if possible, dividing words at the ends of more than two consecutive lines.

111c • Speed Ladder Paragraphs • As directed in 101d, page 170

20 minutes

		GWAM
		1' 5'

All letters

¶ 1 DS
44 words
1.3 si

When you have formed the habit of politeness, you shouldn't feel   13 3 55
self-conscious about formal courtesies. There are dozens of times when   27 5 57
the poised boys and girls act with ease while some just quaver or feel   42 8 60
embarrassed.   44 9 61

¶ 2
48 words
1.3 si

Lack of poise is caused by lack of knowledge. If you don't know   57 11 63
what to do, you fidget, stammer, and redden. You advertise to others   71 14 66
how bothered you are. Anyone who knows his way about is relaxed. He   85 17 69
neither appears nor acts flustered.   92 18 70

¶ 3
52 words
1.3 si

Most young people like to attend the movies. They often stop   104 21 73
in at a restaurant for a bite to eat on their way home. Here are a   118 24 76
few bits of information you might find helpful. See how many of them   132 26 78
you are aware of and how many you usually put into practice.   144 29 81

¶ 4
56 words
1.4 si

In many restaurants there will be a hostess or a headwaiter on   157 31 83
duty to show you to a table. If not, the boy is responsible for mak-   170 34 86
ing the selection. He should hold the chair to help seat his girl.   184 37 89
She decides what she would prefer from the menu, and he then places   198 40 92
the orders.   200 40 92

¶ 5
60 words
1.4 si

There are several basic rules to remember when finding seats at a   213 43 95
movie. If the usher is present, he normally leads the way, followed by   228 46 98
the girl and then by her escort. If there is no usher, the boy goes   241 48 100
ahead. After locating seats, he steps back for the girl to seat herself   256 51 103

All ¶'s
1.3 si

before he sits down.   260 52 104

```
1' |  1  |  2  |  3  |  4  |  5  |  6  |  7  |  8  |  9  |  10  |  11  |  12  |  13  |  14  |
5' |        1        |        2        |        3        |
```

111d • Creative Typing • Type a paragraph, telling in your own words what the following quotation means to you.

10 minutes

"The best place," Banks said, "to find a helping hand is at the end of your arm."

33d • Listening for the Bell; Right Margin Release

Directions – Type the paragraph with a 50-space line; then with a 60-space line. Let the bell guide you in returning the carriage. If the carriage locks before you complete a word, depress the margin-release key and complete the word. Divide words if necessary, but keep in mind the rules in 33c.

• *Remember to set the right margin 5 to 8 spaces beyond the desired line ending. Doing this will give your copy better horizontal balance.*

Words

46 words
1.2 si

DS

Keep the right margin as straight as you can. — 9
The bell will tell you when you are near the end — 19
of a line. When it rings, finish the word; return — 29
the carriage. Divide long words to keep them from — 40
running into the margin too far. — 46

33e • Continuity Practice

Directions – After typing the paragraph once, circle any errors you may have made. Type correctly three times the word in which you made an error along with the word preceding and the word following the error. See how many times you can type the paragraph without any errors in the time allowed.

Words

46 words
1.2 si

DS

We must all go through life fighting for the things in — 11
which we believe. We must have faith in ourselves and in — 23
our ideas. If we fight the good fight, our days will be — 34
filled with great moments; our lives will be worth living. — 46

| 1 | 2 | 3 | 4 | 5 | 6 | 7 | 8 | 9 | 10 | 11 | 12 |

• Lesson 34 • *60-space line*

34a • Keyboard Review • Each line twice

All letters   SS   The quizmasters expected Biff to give a just answer quickly.

Figure   Type these numbers with your eyes on the copy: 236 347 590.

Quiet wrists
and arms

Easy   If we do not stand for something, we will fall for anything.

| 1 | 2 | 3 | 4 | 5 | 6 | 7 | 8 | 9 | 10 | 11 | 12 |

34b • Typing in All Capital Letters • Type twice

• *To capitalize a whole word, several words, or an entire line, depress the shift lock (No. 29) and type. To release the shift lock, depress either the right or the left shift key.*

Please read the WEEKLY BULLETIN to ALL first period classes.

110c • Problem Typing

Problem—Luncheon Program and Menu

Directions – Follow the directions given in 109d, page 181. Space and arrange the copy attractively on both pages of the fold-over sheet.

Cover Page

LUNCHEON MEETING

JUNIOR ACHIEVEMENT ASSOCIATION

```
        * *
      *     *
    *         *
  *    JA    *
    *         *
      *     *
        * *
```

Crystal Dining Room

Ramada Inn

May 17, 197—

Inside Page

Presiding	Steve McDonald, President
Introductions	Dennis Clark, Vice-President
Keynote Address	Robert A. Flam, Chairman
	Industry-Education Council

Partners in Progress

Awards	R. F. Pietrowski, Manager
	Garabedian Enterprises

LUNCHEON MENU

Tossed Green Salad Green Bean Casserole
Veal Cordon Bleu Rolls, Butter, and Jelly
Baked Potato   Bavarian Cream Pie
Coffee, Tea, Milk

• Lesson 111 • *70-space line*

111a • Keyboard Review • Each line at least three times

All letters	SS	Mr. Brown just received six dozen packages of quilts from the factory.
Figure		A total of 2,819,246 immigrants entered the country between 1955-1964.
Adjacent keys		Robert tried to remove their tires as we drew near on the return trip.
Easy		A fine typist has no problem keeping his eyes on the copy as he types.

Wrists low and still

| 1 | 2 | 3 | 4 | 5 | 6 | 7 | 8 | 9 | 10 | 11 | 12 | 13 | 14 |

111b • Skill Comparison • Type two 1-minute writings on each sentence. Compare gwam.

Easy	SS	Do not rest your fingers on the keys if you wish to reach a high rate.
Figure-Symbol		India leads in cattle. She has 155 million head, or 19% of the total.
Rough draft		the poeple who work hard always seem to get the most fun out off the life.
Shift		Madge saw June and Mildred Avery at the Georgia State Fair in Atlanta.

Type steadily

| 1 | 2 | 3 | 4 | 5 | 6 | 7 | 8 | 9 | 10 | 11 | 12 | 13 | 14 |

34c • Listening for the Bell

Directions – Type the paragraph with a 50-space line; then with a 60-space line. Let the bell guide you in returning the carriage. Use the margin-release key or divide words at ends of lines as needed.

DS

46 words
1.2 si

	Words
Before you take a timed writing, get ready for	9
it. Be sure to have enough clean paper in your ma-	19
chine. Have the margin stops set for the right	29
length of line. Place your copy so it is easy to	39
read. Clear your desk for action.	46

34d • Speed Ladder Paragraphs; Cleaning Your Typewriter

15 minutes

Directions – Type 1-minute writings on the following paragraphs. When you can complete the first paragraph in one minute, type the second; then the third, fourth, and fifth. Your teacher may call the half-minutes to guide you.

			Words in ¶	GWAM 3'
¶ 1 20 words 1.2 si	DS	This is a lesson on keeping your machine in top shape.	11	4
		A cloth, a stiff brush, and oil are needed.	20	7
¶ 2 25 words 1.2 si		Your typewriter must be ready to use at all times. The	11	10
		three steps that follow will help you take good care of your	23	14
		machine.	25	15
¶ 3 30 words 1.2 si		First, wipe the dust from all parts of your machine	10	18
		after each use. If you do not do this, the keys may be	22	22
		sticky, and the carriage will move slowly.	30	25
¶ 4 35 words 1.2 si		Next, using a stiff brush, remove the ink and dirt from	11	29
		the face of the keys. This simple step consumes only a few	23	33
		seconds; yet it will make your copy clean and easy to read.	35	37
¶ 5 40 words 1.2 si		Lastly, with a cloth, clean the grooved bars on which	11	40
		the carriage moves. Apply a little oil on the bars about	22	44
		once a week. If you take good care of your machine, it will	35	48
All ¶'s 1.2 si		help you produce good work.	40	50

1' | 1 | 2 | 3 | 4 | 5 | 6 | 7 | 8 | 9 | 10 | 11 | 12 |
3' | 1 | 2 | 3 | 4 |

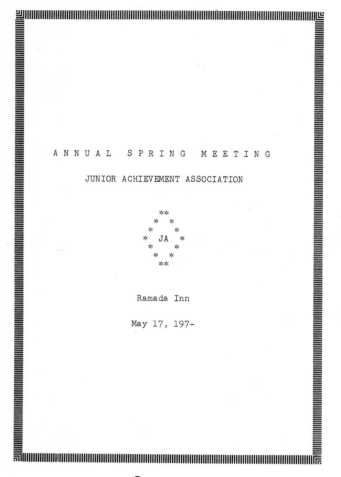

ANNUAL SPRING MEETING

JUNIOR ACHIEVEMENT ASSOCIATION

```
        **
      *    *
    *        *
   *    JA    *
    *        *
      *    *
        **
```

Ramada Inn

May 17, 197-

Cover page

PROGRAM ← Triple-space

9:00	Registration	Lobby, Ramada Inn
	Refreshments	Roundup Room
10:00	General Session	Grand Ballroom
	Greetings	Steve McDonald President
	Welcome	Joseph Brucia, President Marshall Wiley & Company
	Response	Dennis Clark Vice President
	Address	"Looking Ahead to 1980" John Hagen, President Drummond Corporation
11:30	Introduction of Delegates	Ronald Hays Chapter 38
	Special Awards	Steve McDonald President
12:30	Luncheon	Crystal Dining Room

Inside page

One-fold program

• Lesson 110 • *70-space line*

110a • Keyboard Review • Each line at least three times ⟶ 5 minutes

All letters	SS	Karl expected them to realize the use of jargon was very questionable.
Figure		Going 90 miles per hour, a skier jumped 281 feet on February 26, 1933.
Long reach		This is an unpopular policy. He hunted quail near the munitions dump.
Easy		If you like to do a thing, you do it as well as it is in you to do it.

Sit erect

| 1 | 2 | 3 | 4 | 5 | 6 | 7 | 8 | 9 | 10 | 11 | 12 | 13 | 14 |

110b • Timed Writings ⟶ 15 minutes

Directions – Type two 5-minute writings on 106d, page 177. Compute your *gwam*. Submit the better of the two writings.

34e • Tabulator Control

13 minutes

Directions – 1. Clear the tabulator rack as directed on page vii.
2. Check to see that margin stops are set for a 60-space line.
3. Type the first column at the left margin.

4. Set the tab stop for the second column 26 spaces from the left margin. Set the stop for the third column 26 spaces from the second.

5. Type the list of words pertaining to athletics once. Type across the page. Repeat if time permits.

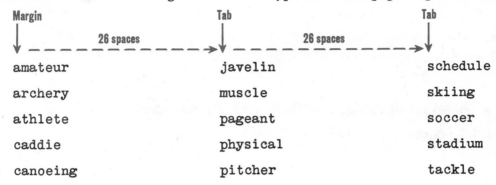

Margin	Tab	Tab
amateur	javelin	schedule
archery	muscle	skiing
athlete	pageant	soccer
caddie	physical	stadium
canoeing	pitcher	tackle

• Lesson 35 • *60-space line*

35a • Keyboard Review • Each line twice

5 minutes

All letters   SS   Max delivered the wrong size pack to Jeff quite by accident.

Figure   Men worked 70 hours a week in 1850—today they work only 40.   Sit erect

Easy   Always type with your fingers well curved and over the keys.

| 1 | 2 | 3 | 4 | 5 | 6 | 7 | 8 | 9 | 10 | 11 | 12 |

35b • Ratchet-Release Lever

5 minutes

Degree Symbol – To type the degree symbol in the first line below, pull the ratchet-release lever (No. 6) forward. Turn the left cylinder knob toward you slightly; type the small letter **o** without space between the figure and the symbol; return the ratchet-release lever to its original position.

Chemistry Symbol – For the second line, type the capital letters, leaving space for the exponents. Backspace to the position for the first exponent; operate the ratchet-release lever and turn the right cylinder knob away from you slightly; type the exponents. Return the lever to its original position.

• *The ratchet-release lever automatically returns the cylinder to the line of writing. The variable line spacer (No. 3), which is used in typing on ruled lines, will not automatically return the cylinder to the line of writing. It should not be used in typing degree symbols, exponents, or footnote reference figures.*

Directions – Each line twice.

1   SS   Bill knows that water freezes at 32° F. and boils at 212° F.

2   The formula for water: H_2O; for sulphuric acid it is H_2SO_4.

109a • Keyboard Review • Each line at least three times

All letters	SS	Mark will require five dozen big boxes for the apricots early in July.
Figure-Symbol		New subscriptions cost $4.87 for 39 weeks and only $6.10 for 52 weeks.
"exa" comb.		I wasn't exactly exalted, but exasperated, at the exaggerated example.
Easy		Find the easy way to do a job; and, as a rule, you find the right way.

Fingers deeply curved

| 1 | 2 | 3 | 4 | 5 | 6 | 7 | 8 | 9 | 10 | 11 | 12 | 13 | 14 |

109b • Punctuation Guides — Dash and Parentheses

5 minutes

Directions – Read the explanation carefully; then type each example sentence twice.

Line 1 – Use a dash to show a sudden break in thought.

Line 2 – Use a dash before the name of an author when it follows a direct quotation.

Line 3 – Use parentheses to enclose an explanation.

• *A dash is made by typing two hyphens without space before or after.*

1	SS	Time may be what all of us want most—but what we often use the worst.
2		"We have nothing to fear but fear itself."—Franklin Delano Roosevelt.
3		He should start typing on the 13th line space (2 inches) from the top.

Reach with your fingers

| 1 | 2 | 3 | 4 | 5 | 6 | 7 | 8 | 9 | 10 | 11 | 12 | 13 | 14 |

109c • Paragraph Skill Builder from Rough Draft • Type four 1-minute writings.

5 minutes

Words

DS ¶ Being able to type well for one minute is one thing; being able — 13

54 words
1.3 si

to type well on a longer writings it's quite another. Your must, of course, — 27

learn to be a steady learner and worker. In a way, this is writing is a — 41

text of your staying power. how will are you meeting the this test? — 54

109d • Problem Typing

30 minutes

Problem—Program of Meeting

Directions – 1. Fold an 8½- by 11-inch sheet of paper to a fold-over program of 5½ by 8½ inches.

2. Insert the folded sheet with the fold at the left.

3. Arrange the copy for the cover page, shown on page 182, in an attractive form.

4. Before typing the inside page, reverse the fold, and reinsert the folded sheet with the fold at the left.

5. Arrange the copy for the inside page as illustrated on page 182. The copy is to be centered vertically with ½-inch side margins.

• *To align items at the right margin, set the carriage at the margin, backspace for the letters and spaces in the item, type.*

• *For directions on how to center lines on paper of odd size, refer to page 68, if necessary.*

35c • Spacing of Symbols and Figures — Review

10 minutes

Directions – Each line twice. Read the explanation for a line before you type it.

Line 1 – Do not space between a figure and ½ or ¼.
Line 2 – Before a figure, # stands for number; after it, for pounds. Do not space between the symbol and a figure.

Line 3 – Space between a whole number and a "made" fraction. Be uniform in typing fractions.
Line 4 – Do not space between the parentheses and the words they enclose.

1   SS   The bank discount rate on these 4¼% bonds is 6½%, is it not?

2   Your Order #7196 is dated May 14. You ordered 61# of nails.

Think as you type

3   I will need 4 1/2 pints of paint and 3 1/8 pints of lacquer.

4   The largest theater (completed 1949) will seat 6,500 people.

| 1 | 2 | 3 | 4 | 5 | 6 | 7 | 8 | 9 | 10 | 11 | 12 |

35d • Timed Writings

10 minutes

Directions – Type two 3-minute writings on 34d, page 57. Compute *gwam*. Submit the better of the two writings.

35e • Continuity Practice from Script

15 minutes

Directions – 1. Type the paragraphs as many times as you can at an easy, sure rate. Your goal: to see how many paragraphs you can type without error.

2. After each typing of the two paragraphs, proofread your copy. Circle any errors you may have made.

			Words in ¶	Total Words
¶ 1 60 words 1.2 si	DS	A miracle, it has been said, is an event described	10	10
		by those to whom it was told by a man or men who did	21	21
		not see it. Miracles do take place, we know, and some-	32	32
		times they occur just when we least expect them. In	42	42
		fact, a miracle takes place when we see value for the	53	53
		first time in the things we learn.	60	60
¶ 2 60 words 1.2 si		The key to riding a bicycle is motion. As long	10	70
		as the wheels turn, we remain upright. When they stop,	21	81
		we fall to the ground. Learning works the same way.	32	92
		We learn as long as we meet new ideas—as long as we	42	102
		keep looking for some new answers to our old prob-	52	112
Both ¶'s 1.2 si		lems. We stop when we close our minds.	60	120

Problem—School Organization Budget

Directions – Standard 2-inch top margin. Space the report vertically as shown below. Leave 10 spaces between the columns.

- *Leaders are made by alternating a period and a space. They are aligned vertically as shown.*

- *Place the $ before the first amount and the total, typed so the $ will be 1 space to the left of the longest amount in the column.*
- *Double lines are made by using the ratchet release to move the carriage forward slightly prior to typing the second line.*

ASSOCIATED STUDENT BODY BUDGET

1971-1972

Triple-space ➡

Anticipated Income

⬅ **Double-space**

Security Bank, Interest.	$ 40.00
Student Body Card Sales.	1,500.00
Vending Machines.	350.00
Total	$1,890.00

⬅ **Triple-space**

Anticipated Expenditures

Activities	$ 625.00
Awards	140.00
Yearbook	250.00
Newspaper.	400.00
Student Body Cards	50.00
Equipment and Supplies	125.00
Total	$1,590.00

Triple-space ➡

Total Budgeted Income.	$1,890.00
Total Budgeted Expense	1,590.00
Total Budgeted Balance	$ 300.00

Budget

Cycle 2 ●

Basic Personal Typewriting Operations

You are now ready to start using the typewriter to prepare some of your school and personal papers. This is a quick preview of some of the kinds of problems you will type in Cycle 2.

Notices, Personal Notes, and Letters – You will type announcements, personal notes, and personal business letters in acceptable form. These papers will be typical of those typed by students.

Themes, Outlines, and Tables – These papers are an important part of school work. The guides that you will be given are those generally used in typing themes, outlines, and tables.

Composing Personal Papers – One of your goals in this course is to be able to compose personal and school papers on the typewriter. The composing drills, spelling aids, and capitalization guides included in this cycle will help you to achieve this goal.

Extra-Credit Assignments – Problems are given at the end of each unit for students who finish assignments ahead of schedule. Type these problems as time permits. Extra credit will be given for them.

Building Basic Skill – The higher your skill becomes on the typewriter, the easier it will be for you to use it for your written work. The ideal is to be able to type so well that you can forget the typewriter and concentrate on the papers you are preparing. That is why you will continue to work on speed and control in Cycle 2.

How You Can Help – Much of what you get out of the lessons in Cycle 2 will depend upon you. Here are some points to keep in mind as you prepare your lessons:

1. Have the desire to improve. Nobody learns much unless he really wants to learn.

2. Have a clear goal in mind for each practice. You can't learn if you don't know what you should be learning. Keep this goal in mind as you type the drills and problems.

3. Learn to plan your work. Part of this job requires you to read and hear directions correctly. You will get some practice in working with directions every day. Make the most of this practice.

● Unit 5

Centering Short Reports and Announcements

General Directions ● Lessons 36 – 40

Machine Adjustments – For the lessons in this unit, use a 60-space line. Single-space lines of words and sentences; double-space between repeated groups of lines. Double-space paragraph copy.

Erasing Errors – Erasing instructions are given in Lesson 39 of this unit. Your teacher will tell you whether or not you are to erase and correct errors on problems in Lessons 39 and 40.

● Lesson 36

36a ● Keyboard Review ● Each line three times   *5 minutes*

All letters	SS	Jack, Bob, and Wayne played five quiz games with Rex Thomas.
Figure-Symbol		Today, Joan had a check for $595 and Nancy had one for $862.
Easy		Anyone who is wrapped in himself makes a very small package.

Quick, sharp strokes

| 1 | 2 | 3 | 4 | 5 | 6 | 7 | 8 | 9 | 10 | 11 | 12 |

Problem 2—Horizontal Bar Graph

FIRST-SEMESTER TYPING SPEED GROWTH FOR KRISTIE ROYAL

Directions – Center the graph on a half sheet; space as directed in Problem 1.

September	xxx
October	xxxxxx
November	xxxxxxxxxxxxxx
December	xxxxxxxxxxxxxxxxxxxxxxxx
January	xxxxxxxxxxxxxxxxxxxxxxxxxxx
GWAM	10 20 30

• Lesson 108 • *70-space line*

108a • Keyboard Review • Each line at least three times   *5 minutes*

All letters	SS	The project was quickly moved by citizens anxious to avoid any fights.	
Figure		The 1964 Civil Rights Act filibuster lasted 75 days, March 26-June 10.	Instant key release
Long words		The correspondent should study the environment and location of a firm.	
Easy		There is no man too busy to take the time to tell just how busy he is.	

| 1 | 2 | 3 | 4 | 5 | 6 | 7 | 8 | 9 | 10 | 11 | 12 | 13 | 14 |

108b • Speed Stretcher • As directed in 103b, page 172   *10 minutes*

			GWAM 1' 5'

All letters
¶ 1
56 words
1.3 si

DS Although they spend many years in school, most students do not know `14 3 39` how to study. Even worse, they don't know what to study. As you read `28 6 42` a lesson, therefore, search for the needle in the haystack—find the `42 8 44` main idea. Look at the headings; study the visual aids in the textbook. `56 11 47`

¶ 2
55 words
1.3 si

When you finish a lesson, try summarizing it in a few words. This `13 14 50` is the real test of learning—putting in your own words the meat of a `27 17 53` lesson. Many students often discover that they learn better if they `41 19 55` recite to themselves. They list the chief points in their own words. `55 22 58`

¶ 3
69 words
1.3 si

It will pay you to overlearn anything you need to learn well. `13 25 61` Reading a lesson through quickly only once is like getting a fish on `26 27 63` your hook and not bothering to land it. Most of us forget about half `40 30 66` of anything we learn the first hour or so after learning it. We need to `55 33 69`

All ¶'s
1.3 si

go over the major points any number of times to fix them in our minds. `69 36 72`

| 1' | 1 | 2 | 3 | 4 | 5 | 6 | 7 | 8 | 9 | 10 | 11 | 12 | 13 | 14 |
| 5' | | | 1 | | | 2 | | | 3 | | |

36b • Technique Builder — Stroking • Each line three times | *10 minutes*

Upper row	SS	Will he try to keep up the treatment as so many others have?
Double letters		The school cannot accept the small books that Dee possesses.
Figure-Symbol		Type amounts as follows: $740 (not $740.00), but $1,935.64.
Difficult reaches		It is doubtful if he will be able to collect any place mats.
Bottom row		We know that the girl held the big soap box when she met us.
Fourth finger		We were asked to apply a quick answer to that quaint puzzle.

| 1 | 2 | 3 | 4 | 5 | 6 | 7 | 8 | 9 | 10 | 11 | 12 |

Fingers deeply curved

Quiet wrists and arms

36c • Spelling and Proofreading Aid • Each line three times | *5 minutes*

• *Accurate spelling is basic to accurate typing and proofreading.*
Teach your fingers to spell the following words correctly.

1	SS	occur yield tempt using coming belief forty kept judge niece
2		believing lose oblige ceiling ninety career typing rare argue
3		since reveal listen knives recent misuse aisle excel possess

Even stroking

36d • Paragraph Guided Writings | *15 minutes*

Directions – 1. Type a 1-minute writing on the first paragraph. Note your *gwam*. Add four words to your *gwam* for a new goal.
2. Type two more 1-minute writings on the paragraph. Try to reach your goal.

3. Now type a 1-minute writing on the paragraph at your first rate. Your goal this time is to type without error.
4. Repeat Steps 1, 2, and 3 for the second and third paragraphs.

			GWAM 1'	3'	
¶ 1 30 words 1.2 si	DS	You have heard it said that if you save your pennies,	11	4	36
		your dollars will take care of themselves. You will find that	23	8	40
		this is true in typewriting, too.	30	10	42
¶ 2 32 words 1.2 si		Watch the little things in typing, and speed will take	41	14	46
		care of itself. Note the position of your fingers. Be sure	53	18	50
		that they are curved and close to your keys.	62	21	53
¶ 3 34 words 1.2 si		Keep your eyes on the copy. Do not waste time glancing	73	24	56
		from the copy to the paper in your machine. When you come	85	28	60
		to the end of a line, just return the carriage quickly.	96	32	64

All ¶'s
1.2 si

| 1' | 1 | 2 | 3 | 4 | 5 | 6 | 7 | 8 | 9 | 10 | 11 | 12 |
| 3' | | 1 | | 2 | | 3 | | | 4 | | |

• Lesson 107 • *70-space line*

107a • Keyboard Review • Each line at least three times

5 minutes

All letters SS Rex must have delivered the wrong size pack to Jeff quite by accident.
Figure-Symbol Ancient card packs had 78 cards—56 ordinary, 21 "tarots" and a "fou."
Shift Steven, Janet, Scott, and Ted all liked Mrs. Severson's English class.
Easy Any man is rich according to what he is, not according to what he has.

| 1 | 2 | 3 | 4 | 5 | 6 | 7 | 8 | 9 | 10 | 11 | 12 | 13 | 14 |

Quick carriage return

107b • Paragraph Skill Builder from Script • Type four 1-minute writings.

5 minutes

Words

DS

So often the little things in life will turn out to be the most — 13
important. The art of printing was suggested by a man who cut letters — 27
60 words
1.3 si
in the bark of a tree. An accident with a red-hot skillet led to the — 41
making of vulcanized rubber. It seems that a thing can't be too small — 55
to demand our attention. — 60

107c • Building Skill on Figures and Symbols • Each line three times

5 minutes

1 SS I read "The Magic Label" by Jack Hankins. It's a very timely article.
2 This bank pays 5¼% interest on savings accounts. Pam received $12.96.
3 Check #529 (dated October 14) will cover this 25¢ charge, will it not?

| 1 | 2 | 3 | 4 | 5 | 6 | 7 | 8 | 9 | 10 | 11 | 12 | 13 | 14 |

Fix key locations in mind

107d • Problem Typing

30 minutes

Problem 1—Horizontal Bar Graph

Directions – 1. Center the graph on a half sheet. **2.** To determine the left margin stop, center the carriage and backspace once for each 2 spaces in the longest name, the space between the names and the bars, and the longest bar. Set a tab stop where the bars begin.

3. Each x represents one word a minute. Place an apostrophe under the first x in each group of ten as shown. Center the GWAM figures under the apostrophe by depressing the backspace key half way.

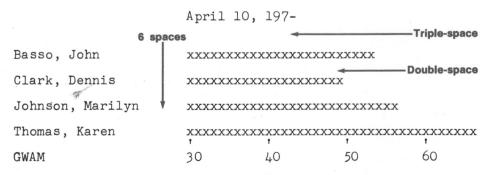

TOP TYPEWRITING SPEEDS OF 1ST PERIOD CLASS

April 10, 197-

6 spaces ← **Triple-space**

Basso, John   XXXXXXXXXXXXXXXXXXXXXXXX
Clark, Dennis   XXXXXXXXXXXXXXXXXX   ← **Double-space**
Johnson, Marilyn   XXXXXXXXXXXXXXXXXXXXXXXXXX
Thomas, Karen   XXXXXXXXXXXXXXXXXXXXXXXXXXXXXXXXXXX
GWAM   30   40   50   60

Bar graph

36e • Composing at the Typewriter

10 minutes

Directions – 1. Type an answer to each question. Use complete sentences.   2. If time permits, retype any sentences in which you made typing errors.

• *An answer is given for the first question as an illustration.*

Questions:

1. What is your favorite sport?
2. What is your favorite subject?
3. Is your typewriter equipped with pica or elite type?
4. What is the name of the astronaut who first walked in space?
5. Name the city in which you were born.
6. Who invented the electric light?

Sample Answer:

```
     1.   My favorite sport is ice hockey.
```

• Lesson 37 • *60-space line*

37a • Keyboard Review • Each line three times

5 minutes

All letters   SS   How can Bud mix five quarts of gray paint for Jack and Liza?

Figure-Symbol   His route home (246 157th Street) avoids Highways 33 and 89.

Easy   Everything is funny as long as it happens to another person.

| 1 | 2 | 3 | 4 | 5 | 6 | 7 | 8 | 9 | 10 | 11 | 12 |

Quiet wrists and arms

37b • Typing from Dictation and Spelling Checkup

5 minutes

Directions – Your teacher will dictate the words in 36c, page 61. Type the words from dictation. Check your work for correct spelling. Retype the words in which you made an error.

37c • Timed Writings

10 minutes

Directions – Type two 3-minute writings on 36d, page 61. Compute *gwam*. Submit the better of the two writings.

VERTICAL CENTERING STEPS

• *Centering material so that it will have uniform top and bottom margins is called vertical centering.*

Step 1 – Count the lines in the copy to be centered. If your copy is to be double spaced, remember to count the spaces between the lines. There is only one line space following each line of copy when material is double spaced.

Step 2 – Subtract the total lines from the lines available on the paper you are using. (There are 33 lines on a half sheet, 66 on a full sheet.)

Step 3 – Divide the number of lines that remain by 2. The answer gives you the number of lines in the top and bottom margins. If the result contains a fraction, disregard it.

Step 4 – Insert your paper so that the top edge is exactly even with the aligning scale (No. 33). Bring the paper up the proper number of line spaces. Start typing on the next line space.

																GWAM 1' 5

All letters
¶ 1   DS   The next time you are faced with the problem of what to buy the   13 3 55
44 words
1.3 si   person who has everything, why not consider getting him a mule? While   27 5 57

the idea may sound odd at first, you must realize the many advantages   41 8 60

of such a gift.   44 9 61

¶ 2   Here are just a couple of them. First of all, a mule requires   57 11 63
48 words
1.3 si   much less upkeep than a nifty sports car and has fewer moving parts   70 14 66

than a wristwatch. To be perfectly frank, I must admit that sometimes   84 17 69

a mule has absolutely no moving parts.   92 18 70

¶ 3   Mules are smart, stubborn, and not the least bit choosy when it   105 21 73
52 words
1.4 si   comes to eating. They will eat whatever is in sight, including wooden   119 24 76

fences. Mule lovers claim their favorite animals have good sense since   133 27 79

they won't do anything that will end up hurting them.   144 29 81

¶ 4   Mules, which often live to be about thirty years old, work until   157 31 83
56 words
1.4 si   the day they die. They are used in national parks, in the movies, in   171 34 86

fishing camps, and on tobacco farms. Armies have used mules to carry   185 37 89

ammunition. West Point football games would never be the same without   199 40 92

one.   200 40 92

¶ 5   Surely you are interested by now. Therefore, it is only fair to   213 43 95
60 words
1.3 si   warn you of one minor problem. A mule's stubborn streak can sometimes   227 45 97

be troublesome. If his ears go down, you had better watch out. You   241 48 100

can always take comfort in the fact, however, that a mule won't kick   255 51 103

All ¶'s
1.3 si   you unless you deserve it.   260 52 104

1' | 1 | 2 | 3 | 4 | 5 | 6 | 7 | 8 | 9 | 10 | 11 | 12 | 13 | 14 |
5' | 1 | 2 | 3 |

106e • **Continuity Practice** • Type the last paragraph of 106d without timing. Type it as many times as you can in the time that remains.   *5 minutes*

37d • Problem Typing

Problem 1—Report on Half Sheet

Half sheet
60-space line
Double spacing

Directions – Center the short report below. Your teacher will tell you where you are to type your name and the problem numbers for the problems you type.

		Words
7		
8	**Start on**	
9	**Line 9** A half sheet of paper contains 33 lines; a full sheet	11
10		
11	has 66 lines. It does not make any difference what kind of	23
12		
13	typewriter you are using. All are the same on this point.	35
14		
15	To center copy vertically, up and down, count the lines in	46
16		
17	the copy. Subtract this total from 33 if you are using a	58
18		
19	half sheet or 66 if you are using a full sheet. Divide the	70
20		
21	difference by 2 to get top and bottom margins for exact cen-	82
22		
23	tering. If the result contains a fraction, just disregard	94
24		
25	it. Type the copy. You will find that it is neatly placed.	106
26		
27	*Lines in half sheet 33*	
28	*Lines and line spaces in copy 17*	
29	*Line spaces in top and bottom margins . . 16*	
30	*Divide by 2. Top margin . . . . 8 °*	
31	*Bottom margin . . . . 8 °*	
32	*° Start typing on the 9th line space from the top.*	
33		

Report centered on half sheet of paper

Problem 2—Report on Full Sheet

Full sheet
60-space line
Double spacing

Directions – Type the short report in Problem 1 again. This time type it on a full sheet. Center it neatly.

• Lesson 38 • *60-space line*

38a • Keyboard Review • Each line three times

All letters   DS   Jack gave Buddy six lemons to squeeze for the Wyman's party.

Figure-Symbol   Tickets for this game are 85¢ each. Don paid $1.70 for two.   **Feet on the floor**

Easy   It is great to show promise; it is tragic not to fulfill it.

| 1 | 2 | 3 | 4 | 5 | 6 | 7 | 8 | 9 | 10 | 11 | 12 |

Problem 3—Typing Postal Card from Script

Directions – 1. Type another postal card containing the message given in Problem 1, page 175.

2. Address the card to Mr. Chris Van Elswyk, 2947 Herndon Avenue, Ellensburg, WA 98926.

• Lesson 106 • *70-space line*

106a • Keyboard Review • Each line at least three times   *5 minutes*

All letters	SS	Hazards of exploring by the dark cave will justify acquiring more aid.
Figure		A full sheet of typing paper is 8½ by 11 inches and contains 66 lines.
Vowels—u, i		They required us to build a building suitable for a public sanitarium.
Easy		The biggest mistake we can make is to believe that we cannot make one.

Fix key locations in mind

| 1 | 2 | 3 | 4 | 5 | 6 | 7 | 8 | 9 | 10 | 11 | 12 | 13 | 14 |

106b • Punctuation Guides — Colon   *5 minutes*

Directions – Read the explanation carefully; then type each example sentence twice.

Line 1 – Use a colon to introduce a list of items or expressions.

Line 2 – Use a colon to separate the hours and minutes when they are expressed in figures.

Line 3 – Use a colon to introduce a question or long quotation.

1   SS   They will ship these items: uniforms, shoes, gloves, bats, and balls.

2   Brian left from Seattle at 7:15 p.m.; he arrived in Butte at 9:20 p.m.

Feet on the floor

3   The question before us is this: Can we complete the projects in time?

| 1 | 2 | 3 | 4 | 5 | 6 | 7 | 8 | 9 | 10 | 11 | 12 | 13 | 14 |

106c • Sentence Control Builder   *10 minutes*

Directions – Type two 1-minute writings on each sentence. Try typing each without error.

1   SS   A person cannot lead anyone else any farther than he has gone himself.

2   The one who thinks too much of himself probably isn't thinking enough.

Space quickly

3   If one could get half his wishes, he would likely double his troubles.

4   You have the right to risk those things if no one else will be harmed.

| 1 | 2 | 3 | 4 | 5 | 6 | 7 | 8 | 9 | 10 | 11 | 12 | 13 | 14 |

38b • Paragraph Guided Writings • As directed in 36d, page 61

As directed in 36d, page 61

15 minutes

• All letters are used in these paragraphs

GWAM
1' 3'

¶ 1 32 words 1.2 si	DS	Do relax your shoulders as you type. Do not sit in a	11 4 38
		tight, cramped position. It will make you tense and tired,	23 8 42
		and you will make more errors than you should.	32 11 45
¶ 2 34 words 1.2 si		Do sit erect; have your feet flat on the floor, with	43 14 48
		one foot just ahead of the other. Don't slump in your seat	55 18 52
		or wrap your feet around the chair legs in a lazy manner.	66 22 56
¶ 3 36 words 1.2 si		Do set the margin stops, and listen for the bell to tell	77 26 60
		you when the lines end. Do not look up for line endings.	89 30 64
		Looking up breaks your rhythm and is a frequent cause of	101 34 68
All ¶'s 1.2 si		errors.	102 34 68

1' | 1 | 2 | 3 | 4 | 5 | 6 | 7 | 8 | 9 | 10 | 11 | 12 |
3' | 1 | 2 | 3 | 4 |

HORIZONTAL CENTERING STEPS

• *Centering headings and paragraph material so that there will be equal left and right margins is called horizontal centering.*

Step 1 – Check the placement of the paper guide. Turn to page vi, and read the directions for adjusting the paper guide.
Step 2 – Move the carriage to the center point.

Step 3 – Backspace once for each 2 spaces in the line to be centered. If there is one letter left, do not backspace for it. Begin to type at the point where the backspacing is completed.

38c • Problem Typing

25 minutes

Practice Problem—Centering Lines Horizontally

Directions – Using practice paper, center each line horizontally as explained above.

FINAL GAME OF THE SEASON

See the Blue and Gold Warriors in Action!

Saturday, November 10, 2 p.m.

Surprise Stunts at Half Time

• Lesson 105 • *70-space line*

105a • Keyboard Review • Each line at least three times

All letters	SS	Janice and David must take that final geography quiz before next week.
Figure-Symbol		John sent Check #6932 (dated February 15) for $78.40 to Long & Strong.
Double letters		All smaller book committees will still meet three weeks in succession.
Easy		If he has a problem when he types, he can check the slant of his hand.

Think as you type

| 1 | 2 | 3 | 4 | 5 | 6 | 7 | 8 | 9 | 10 | 11 | 12 | 13 | 14 |

105b • Timed Writings • Type two 5-minute writings on 101d, page 170. Compute your gwam. Submit the better of the two.

15 *minutes*

105c • Problem Typing • *Illustrations of the proper form for typing postal cards may be found on page 78.*

25 *minutes*

Problem 1—Postal Card from Script

Directions – 1. Type the following message on a postal card or on paper cut to proper size (5½ by 3¼ inches). Use modified block style.

2. Insert the card, short side at the left. Determine the horizontal center; set margin stops for a 48-space line.

3. Address the card to Miss Joy Palmquist, 129 Chestnut Drive, Ellensburg, WA 98926.

4. Type the following return address in the upper left corner of the address side of the postal card: Miss Mary Lou Clark, 15 Poe Street, Seattle, WA 98101.

July 1, 197-/ Dear Service Club Member / Doug Calhoun and I are making arrangements for our club's participation in Orientation Day in the fall. We need the help of as many of our returning members as we can get. (¶) Will you please write me if you can serve as a new student guide during Orientation Day, September 5. I will be visiting at my cousin's home for a few weeks, so please address your card to me at her address. / Mary Lou Clark / Secretary

Problem 2—Composing Postal Card Message

Directions – 1. Assume the message in Problem 1 had been mailed to you. Compose an answer to Mary Lou's request and type it in proper form on a postal card.

2. Explain that you can work as a guide during the morning of September 5 but that you have to work in the testing office in the afternoon.

Problem 1—Centered Announcement

**Half sheet
Double-space**

Directions – Using clean paper, center the practice problem, page 64, vertically. Center each line horizontally. In double-spaced copy, one line space appears between the lines.

Problem 2—Centered Announcement

**Half sheet
Triple-space**

Directions – Center the following problem vertically. Center each line horizontally. In triple-spaced copy, two line spaces appear between the typed lines.

CAMERA CLUB MEETING

Tuesday, November 13, 2:30 p.m.

Room 242

Prizes for Outstanding Photographs

Refreshments

• Lesson 39 • *60-space line*

39a • Keyboard Review • Each line three times   *5 minutes*

All letters SS Foxes move quickly around now, but the lazy dog just sleeps.

Figure-Symbol Joe said, "Don's birthday party is set for May 26 at 8 p.m." Instant release

Easy Frank asked him for his views on the future of atomic power.
| 1 | 2 | 3 | 4 | 5 | 6 | 7 | 8 | 9 | 10 | 11 | 12 |

39b • Speed Ladder Sentences   *10 minutes*

Directions – Type 1-minute writings on each sentence. Try typing each four times in the minute.

Your teacher will call the return of the carriage each 15 seconds to guide you.

• The rate increases 5 words a minute with each succeeding line

GWAM
15"
Guide

1   SS   To type right, sit erect.   20

2   Type the lines with the guides.   25

3   Try typing with the call of the guide.   30

4   The aim is to type this line with the guide. 35

5   Few of us know what a big job a little job can be. 40
| 1 | 2 | 3 | 4 | 5 | 6 | 7 | 8 | 9 | 10 |

• Lesson 104 • *70-space line*

104a • Keyboard Review • Each line at least three times

5 minutes

All letters SS We've organized a mixed quartet to play for joint meetings back there.

Figure-Symbol Johnson, our 36th President, received 61.1% of the votes cast in 1964.

Quick, sharp strokes

4th finger Pat saw that Pal was not able to adapt the apparatus to this aquacade.

Easy A plan will help you do the things you should when you should do them.

| 1 | 2 | 3 | 4 | 5 | 6 | 7 | 8 | 9 | 10 | 11 | 12 | 13 | 14 |

104b • Concentration Practice • Type twice for control—more if time permits. Think the letters and figures as you type.

10 minutes

Words

DS

73 words
1.4 si

On May 20, 1927, a 25-year-old airmail pilot, Captain Charles A.   13
Lindbergh, flew his single-engine plane, The Spirit of St. Louis, from   32
New York to Paris, completing the first nonstop flight, in 33 hours,   46
29 minutes, 30 seconds. On May 26, 1961, Air Force Major W. R. Payne,   60
piloting a B-58, cut the time to 3 hours, 19 minutes, 45 seconds.   73

| 1 | 2 | 3 | 4 | 5 | 6 | 7 | 8 | 9 | 10 | 11 | 12 | 13 | 14 |

104c • Problem Typing • Directions for centering lines on odd-size paper are on page 68.

30 minutes

Problem 1—Typed Admission Tickets

Directions – 1. Type three tickets of the kind illustrated below. Use 5- by 3-inch cards or paper cut to that size. Arrange the copy neatly on the card.

2. Note that some of the lines are centered; some are typed at the left and right margins.

3. Number the cards in sequence, beginning with No. 150.

Problem 2—Typed Membership Cards

Directions – 1. Type three membership cards, using the copy below. Use 5- by 3-inch cards or paper cut to that size. Arrange the copy neatly on the card.

2. Number the cards in sequence, beginning with No. 75.

3. Membership is to June 1 of the next year. Type in the correct year date.

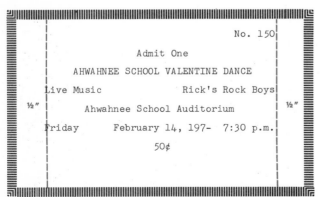

Admission ticket

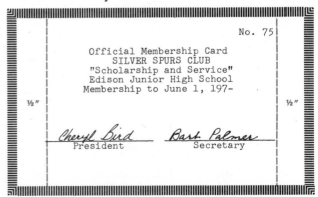

Membership card

DS

There are two kinds of clever people in this world, and both are priceless. One kind thinks of a bright remark in time to say it. The other kind thinks of it in time not to say it. True wit is thus a matter of very careful timing.

47 words
1.2 si

Words
11
23
35
47

ERASING

The errors that you make in themes, personal notes, and other papers you wish to use should be corrected. Therefore, you must learn how to erase typing errors. These instructions are given in Problem 1, below. Read them carefully.

• *Your teacher will tell you whether you are to erase and correct errors made in typing the problems that follow.*

39d • **Problem Typing**   *25 minutes*

Full sheet
60-space line
Double spacing

Problem 1—Short Report

Directions – Center the report vertically on a full sheet. Center the heading horizontally.

ERASING ERRORS

Words
3

Triple-space —————————————————————→

First, move the carriage to one side or the other in order to keep the eraser dust from falling into the typewriter.

Second, roll the paper up two or three spaces to make the erasure. If the correction is to be made near the bottom of the paper, turn the cylinder backward to keep the paper from slipping.

Third, hold the paper firmly against the cylinder with your fingertips. Make the erasure. Blow or brush away the eraser dust.

Fourth, return the paper to typing position. Make the correction.

14
25
27
38
49
61
65
76
88
91
102
104

103c • Problem Typing

30 minutes

Problem—Minutes of Meeting

Directions – Type a copy of the minutes that follow in the form illustrated at the right below. A 1½-inch left margin and a 1-inch right margin is used since minutes are usually placed in a binder.

- *The center point will be 3 spaces to the right of the point normally used. Keep this point in mind in centering headings.*

AHWAHNEE SCHOOL SERVICE CLUB

Minutes of Meeting

Date: September 24, 197—
Time: 12:10 p.m.
Place: Room 119, Ahwahnee School
Present: About 35 students in addition to the advisers, Mr. Holmes and Miss Code

1. Dennis Kerns, President, presided. He introduced the officers and our two advisers.

2. The president outlined the goals of the club and the requirement for membership. Dues are 50¢ per member.

3. Mr. Holmes explained that the principal would like the Service Club to sponsor after-school movies once a month. The cost to students will range from 25¢ to 50¢ depending upon the rental cost of the film.

4. Miss Code asked for volunteers to help paint trash cans after school on September 26.

5. Sue Anderson reported that the Halloween Sock Hop would be held Friday evening, October 31.

6. The president asked members to list their free periods when they would be available to act as guides.

7. A decision was made to hold meetings on the first Wednesday of each month at 12:10 p.m.

8. The president appointed two committees:

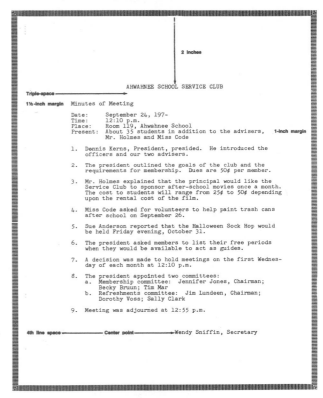

Minutes of meeting

a. Membership committee: Jennifer Jones, Chairman; Becky Bruun; Tim Mar.
b. Refreshments committee: Jim Lundeen, Chairman; Dorothy Voss; Sally Clark.

9. Meeting was adjourned at 12:55 p.m.

Wendy Sniffin, Secretary

Problem 2—Short Report from Rough Draft

Half sheet
60-space line
Double spacing

Directions – Center the report vertically. Center the heading. Make the corrections as you type. If necessary, refer to the proofreaders' marks above.

- *When rough draft copy must be centered, you can count the lines in the draft and add or deduct lines from the total, depending upon the kind of corrections made; or you can type it, with corrections made, on practice paper first. The lines can then be counted, and the second typing can be centered as directed. Your teacher will tell you which practice you are to follow for this problem.*

READING OPENS NEW DOORS

Triple Space ⁋ Have you ever given any thought to the high place that reading holds in your life? It is the key that opens the door to the whole world of ideas and fantasy to you. It puts you in touch with the wise and the witty. More than that, it breaks through the walls of time and space, giving you the chance to become part of any event anywhere in the world, past or present. As some writer once said, "Since men learned to read, no night has been wholly black."

Words
5
16
27
40
52
64
77
88
97

• Lesson 40 • *60-space line*

40a • Keyboard Review • Each line three times   *5 minutes*

All letters   SS   Gary Wells put five dozen quarts of jam in the box for Jack.

Figure-Symbol   Form #58 shows that those 1,970 models weighed 2,540 pounds.   Quick, crisp,
short strokes

Easy   His record will be clear as soon as he pays this large bill.
                    | 1 | 2 | 3 | 4 | 5 | 6 | 7 | 8 | 9 | 10 | 11 | 12 |

Problem 2—Notice and Agenda of a Meeting

Directions – Follow the directions given in Problem 1.

AHWAHNEE SCHOOL "A" CLUB

Regular Meeting, October 15, 197—

Room 126   3:30 p.m.

AGENDA

1. Approval of September 12 minutes

2. Report by Treasurer, Roger Combs

3. Discussion of new business
   a. Need to raise money for club activities
   b. Volunteers to work at October 25 PTA meeting

• Lesson 103 • *70-space line*

103a • Keyboard Review • Each line at least three times   *5 minutes*

All letters	SS	Zealous guardsmen keep daily watch over boxes of their queen's jewels.	
Figure-Symbol		The first electric vacuum cleaner (made about 1905) weighed 92 pounds.	Flowing rhythm
Home keys		According to accepted procedures, no doctor could indicate deductions.	
Easy		He must train himself to think just as he must train himself to write.	

| 1 | 2 | 3 | 4 | 5 | 6 | 7 | 8 | 9 | 10 | 11 | 12 | 13 | 14 |

103b • Speed Stretcher • Use Speed Stretchers for 5-minute writings, or use each paragraph for 1-minute writings.   *10 minutes*

			G W A M 1' 5'

All letters

¶ 1
DS
68 words
1.3 si

What can the student who desires to improve his study habits do — 13 3 38
about the problem? All teachers can give you many hints on this point. — 27 5 40
This paper deals with only one. Get tough with yourself. Do what Teddy — 42 8 43
Roosevelt did in building his willpower. Go out of your way to face a — 56 11 46
few hardships. You should be able to win in spite of them. — 68 14 49

¶ 2
56 words
1.3 si

Do not be afraid to tackle problems which are difficult. In his — 13 16 51
youth, Jack Dempsey often boxed with men who were better than he was. — 27 19 54
He got knocked out many times, but he knew that this was the only way he — 42 22 57
could ever improve. He did improve and became famous the world around. — 56 25 60

¶ 3
51 words
1.3 si

Do not turn away from subjects that are dull or difficult for you. — 14 28 63
Try very hard to conquer them, for once you train your mind to work with- — 28 30 65
out flinching, you will be amazed to learn how easily you can handle — 42 33 68

All ¶'s
1.3 si

the subjects in which you have some interest. — 51 35 70

| 1' | 1 | 2 | 3 | 4 | 5 | 6 | 7 | 8 | 9 | 10 | 11 | 12 | 13 | 14 |
| 5' | | | 1 | | | 2 | | | 3 | | | |

40b • Timed Writings

Directions – Type two 3-minute writings on 38b, page 64. Compute *gwam*. Submit the better of the two writings.

FINDING THE HORIZONTAL CENTER POINT OF ODD-SIZE PAPER OR CARDS

- *In order to center headings on paper or cards of different sizes, you must learn how to find the center point of these papers or cards.*

Step 1 – Insert paper or card into the machine.
Step 2 – Add the numbers on the cylinder scale at the left and right edges of the paper or card.

Step 3 – Divide the sum obtained in Step 2 by 2. The resulting figure gives you the center point of the paper or card.

40c • Problem Typing

Problem 1—Practice Problem

Directions – 1. Insert a half sheet of practice paper (5½″ by 8½″) with the long edge at the left.

2. From the top edge, space down to the 15th line space. Set your machine for triple spacing.

3. Determine the center of the half sheet. Set a tab stop at this point.

4. Center horizontally each line of the problem over the center point of the half sheet.

- *There are six vertical line spaces to an inch. An 8½″ sheet therefore contains 51 vertical line spaces: 8½ x 6 = 51.*

15th line space ——————————————→ THE COMPUTER CLUB
Triple-space ——————————————→

Announces

a Free Demonstration

of the

Universal Language System

Thursday, March 10, 2:30 p.m.

Room 382

****

Problem 2—Announcement on Odd-Size Paper

Directions – Using clean paper, type the practice problem again as directed.

LESSON 40 • PAGE 68

• Lesson 102 • *70-space line*

102a • Keyboard Review • Each line at least three times

All letters SS   His explosive magazine articles were rejected only by a quirk of fate.

Figure   A crowd of 49,936 witnessed the 1966 All-Star game in 100-degree heat.   *Eyes on copy as you return the carriage*

Long reach   I brought the pink linoleum and lumber with me. I broke the monument.

Easy   Turn your book so that it is at the right angle for you when you type.

| 1 | 2 | 3 | 4 | 5 | 6 | 7 | 8 | 9 | 10 | 11 | 12 | 13 | 14 |

102b • Control Ladder Paragraphs
10 minutes

Directions – Type 1-minute writings on the paragraphs in 101d, page 170. When you can type a paragraph without error, move to the next one. Type with control.

102c • Problem Typing
30 minutes

Problem 1—Notice and Agenda of a Meeting

Full sheet
50-space line
2-inch top margin

Directions – 1. Type the notice and agenda of a meeting from the copy below. Follow the form used in the illustration.

2. Items in the third line are to be typed at the left and right margins of the 50-space line.

AHWAHNEE SCHOOL SERVICE CLUB

Notice of the First Meeting

September 24, 197—   12:10 p.m.

Room 119

AGENDA

1. Introduction of officers and advisers
2. Discussion of Service Club organization
   a. Aims
   b. Membership requirements
3. Discussion of major projects for the year
   a. Sponsoring of monthly movies
   b. Club's role in the "Beautify Your School" campaign
   c. Halloween Sock Hop
   d. Guide service for school visitors
4. Decision on meeting dates and time
5. Appointment of program committee
6. Appointment of refreshments committee
7. Adjournment by 12:55 p.m.

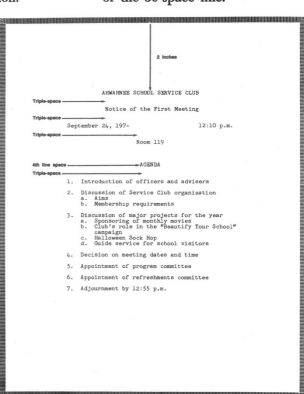

Notice and agenda of meeting

Problem 3—Announcement on Odd-Size Paper

Directions – 1. Insert a half sheet of paper with the long edge at the left.

2. Center each line horizontally. Center the problem vertically, triple-spaced.

- *You must know the number of line spaces in the sheet of paper.*

GLEE CLUB CANDY SALE

at Main Entrance

Friday, October 20

Bring Your Nickels and Dimes

Delicious Candy

Send Glee Club to the District Contest

Problem 4—Announcement on Odd-Size Paper • As directed in Problem 3

- *Do not type the diagonal lines. They indicate carriage-return points.*

JOIN THE EXPLORERS' CLUB / Meetings on Fridays, 2 to 3 p.m. /

Dues Only 50 Cents a Semester / Tours, Exhibits, Demonstrations /

First Meeting, Friday, September 28 / Movie: "Undersea Secrets"

40d • Extra-Credit Typing

Problem—Report from Rough Draft

Full sheet
60-space line
Double spacing

Directions – Provide a heading for the report. Center it on a full sheet. Make the corrections as you type.

	Words
Coin collecting is a *hobby* that some times pays off. A 1914D	12
Lincoln head penny, for exampel, may bring its ~~its~~ owners $30	24
if it is in *good* ~~top~~ condition. Rarest of all our coins is a	35
$5 goldpiece, dated 1822. only three are known to be in exis-	48
tence. It is *so* rare, it is priceless.	56
¶ Any one can become a coin collector. Many *rare* coins ~~are~~ *can* be pur-	69
chased for less than $5. There is always *a* ~~the~~ chance that you	81
will find a collector's *item* ~~coin~~ in your small *change* ~~coins~~.	91

101d • Speed Ladder Paragraphs

20 minutes

Directions – Type as many 1-minute writings as time permits. When you can type the first paragraph at the rate specified, type the next one.

Alternate Procedure – If time remains, start from the beginning. Move from one paragraph to the next only when you have typed without error.

		GWAM 1' 5'

All letters
¶ 1 DS
40 words
1.4 si

Can you imagine wearing a size 38 shoe or buying a man's shirt   13 3 51

that has a size 39 collar? Such items aren't for giants but are for   26 5 53

normal people who use the metric system of weights and measurements.   40 8 56

¶ 2
44 words
1.3 si

In the days before most of the world went metric, chaos reigned.   53 11 59

In fact, if you had crossed Europe a century or two ago, you would have   68 14 62

found that a different system was used in almost every country, town,   82 16 64

or province.   84 17 65

¶ 3
48 words
1.3 si

Systems used throughout the world at one time or other have been   97 19 67

quite varied. Often, common objects such as kernels of grain were used   111 22 70

as weights. According to legend, a yard was the distance from the tip   126 25 73

of a person's thumb to his nose.   132 26 74

¶ 4
52 words
1.3 si

By the close of the middle ages, such odd ways of measuring were   145 29 77

a hindrance to trade. There was a boom in trade because of the finding   159 32 80

of new lands and new routes for travel. At the same time scientists   173 35 83

began to want to measure things with greater accuracy.   184 37 85

¶ 5
56 words
1.3 si

The metric system is not hard to grasp once you have learned a   197 39 87

few basic prefixes. At the end of the last century, people in many   210 42 90

countries the world over were using meters and grams. Some say that   224 45 93

it will be only a matter of time before you will have to be thinking   238 48 96

All ¶'s
1.3 si

metric too.   240 48 96

1' | 1 | 2 | 3 | 4 | 5 | 6 | 7 | 8 | 9 | 10 | 11 | 12 | 13 | 14 |
5' | 1 | 2 | 3 |

101e • Continuity Practice

5 minutes

Directions – Type the last paragraph of 101d as many times as you can without timing.

Technique Goals – Work for continuous stroking, with eyes on copy, and quiet wrists and arms.

Typing Personal Notes and Letters

General Directions • Lessons 41 – 50

Except as otherwise directed, use a 60-space line. Single-space lines of words and sentences, but double-space between repeated groups of lines. Double-space paragraph copy.

• *Your teacher will tell you whether or not to erase and correct errors on problem typing.*

• Lesson 41

41a • Keyboard Review • Each line three times   5 minutes

All letters	SS	David Grable will quickly explain what John made for prizes.
Figure-Symbol		This company's men received a total of $1,596 on October 27.
Easy		Most smart men make mistakes; dull ones keep repeating them.

| 1 | 2 | 3 | 4 | 5 | 6 | 7 | 8 | 9 | 10 | 11 | 12 |

Feet on the floor

41b • Technique Builder — Flowing Rhythm • Each line three times from dictation   10 minutes

1	SS	for him	if the cases	they were	and the date	for the text
2		and the set	to do my	for the only	to see	and read	to be
3		to save	and look	for you	and see	if you	they saw	to my
4		and they join	and she sees	he did trade	go after	for him

Flowing, rhythmic stroking

41c • Sentence Skill Builder from Script   5 minutes

Directions – Type a 1-minute writing on each sentence. Compute *gwam*.

Words

1	SS	The man who has both feet on the ground can't fall very far.	12
2		If one does not say anything, he will not have to repeat it.	12
3		It is harder to hide ignorance than it is to gain knowledge.	12
4		We would rather be ruined by praise than saved by criticism.	12

41d • Spelling and Proofreading Aid • Each line three times   5 minutes

1	SS	recommended Wednesday scheme family gorgeous prior immediate
2		youth volume unnecessary separate receive occurrence leisure
3		accept visible faculty economical remittance wholly February

Type letter by letter

Typing for Club and Community Activities

General Directions • Lessons 101 – 115

Machine Adjustments – Follow the general directions given in earlier units of this cycle.

• Lesson 101

• *Use a 70-space line for all lessons in this unit.*

101a • Keyboard Review • Each line at least three times

5 minutes

All letters	SS	The next evening Jack quickly scanned the horizon from Briarwood Peak.
Figure-Symbol		The price has been reduced from $45,750 to $38,500, effective April 8.
Weak fingers		Patti and/or Paul will acquaint us with techniques of raising azaleas.
Easy		Men can do fine work when they know they are working in the right way.

Wrists and elbows still

| 1 | 2 | 3 | 4 | 5 | 6 | 7 | 8 | 9 | 10 | 11 | 12 | 13 | 14 |

101b • Times and Equal Signs • Each line three times

5 minutes

Times sign – Use a small letter *x* with a space before and after it.

Equal sign – If your typewriter does not have an equal key, type two hyphens, one below the other. In typing the second hyphen, turn the left cylinder knob away from you, or depress the left shift key slightly.

1   SS   Here is the way I figured the discount on this sale: $150 x .06 = $9.

2   Your clerk said that he figured the tax as follows: $650 x .04 = $26.

Feet on the floor

101c • Punctuation Guides — Semicolon

10 minutes

Directions – Read the explanation carefully; then type each example sentence twice.

Lines 1 and 2 – Use a semicolon between the clauses of a compound sentence when no conjunction is used.

Line 3 – If a conjunction is used to join the clauses, use a comma between them.

Lines 4 and 5 – Use a semicolon between the clauses of a compound sentence that are joined by such words as *also, however, therefore,* and *consequently.*

Line 6 – Use a semicolon between a series of phrases or clauses that are dependent upon a main clause.

1   SS   Del Mortimer arrives in Chicago today; he will be in Detroit tomorrow.

2   The boy's softball team won easily; they will play again next Tuesday.

3   Dave plans to be in Memphis today, but he will go to Atlanta tomorrow.

4   This is the current plan; however, it is subject to Harold's approval.

5   Fred and John plan to go; consequently, they will need the automobile.

6   We saw Dick Bell, Ogden; Henry Abels, Reno; and Ed Christensen, Provo.

Think as you type

| 1 | 2 | 3 | 4 | 5 | 6 | 7 | 8 | 9 | 10 | 11 | 12 | 13 | 14 |

41e • Paragraph Guided Writings • As directed in 36d, page 61   *15 minutes*

• All letters are used in these paragraphs

GWAM
1' 3'

¶ 1
34 words
1.2 si

DS   One of the skills you should acquire is the ability to   11   4 40

examine your work with a keen, sharp eye. Oh, you can be   23   8 44

proud of your work, but you can never be content with it.   34 11 47

¶ 2
36 words
1.2 si

If you are satisfied with the quality of work you are   45 15 51

doing at present, your standards may be low; or you may be in   57 19 55

a rut. Set a high goal for yourself; then strive to achieve   69 23 59

it.   70 23 59

¶ 3
38 words
1.3 si

It has been said that the feeling of having done a job   81 27 63

well is a just reward, but knowing that one has done it per-   93 31 67

fectly may spell his doom. It is vital that he maintain   104 35 71

All ¶'s
1.2 si

the zest to excel.   108 36 72

1' | 1 | 2 | 3 | 4 | 5 | 6 | 7 | 8 | 9 | 10 | 11 | 12 |
3' | 1 | 2 | 3 | 4 |

41f • Composing at the Typewriter   *5 minutes*

Directions – Type answers to as many of these questions
as time permits. Use complete sentences.

1. How many vertical line spaces are there on a full sheet of paper?

2. How many vertical line spaces are there on a half sheet of paper?

3. How many vertical line spaces are there on a sheet of paper 6 inches in length?

4. Why should you move the carriage to one side or the other before erasing an error?

• Lesson 42 • *60-space line*

42a • Keyboard Review • Each line three times   *5 minutes*

All letters   SS   Pat Duff will quiz Jack Givens about the extra money he got.

Figure-Symbol   In 1968, the life insurance coverage per family was $18,400.   Sit erect

Easy   Life is a school where we learn what big fools we have been.

| 1 | 2 | 3 | 4 | 5 | 6 | 7 | 8 | 9 | 10 | 11 | 12 |

100a • Keyboard Review • Each line at least three times   *5 minutes*

All letters	SS	Very few sixth graders in the math class ever joked about pop quizzes.
Figure		Arabic numbers like 1, 2, and 3 are sometimes typed (1), (2), and (3).
Adjacent keys		Captain Sam said he was astonished to see several sailors fast asleep.
Easy		If they spend their time working in the right way, they can type more.

Reach with
your fingers

| 1 | 2 | 3 | 4 | 5 | 6 | 7 | 8 | 9 | 10 | 11 | 12 | 13 | 14 |

100b • Timed Writings • Type a 1- and a 5-minute writing on 96c, page 163. Circle errors. Compute gwam.   *10 minutes*

100c • Problem Typing   *30 minutes*

Problem 1—Title Page for Formal Library Report

Directions – 1. Type the title page; use the data given at the right. It is a title page for the report that you have just typed.

2. Follow the directions given on the illustration on page 154, or use any attractive arrangement that is acceptable to your teacher.

WRITING A FORMAL LIBRARY
REPORT

By

Your name
Typewriting II

Current date

Problem 2—Bibliography for Formal Library Report

Directions – 1. Type the bibliography for your formal report on a separate sheet of paper. List the references given below.

2. Assemble your report as follows: title page, body of the report, bibliography. Bind the report at the left.

• *See page 155 for an illustration of a bibliography.*

BIBLIOGRAPHY

Conlin, David A., and George R. Herman. Modern Grammar and Composition. New York: American Book Company, 1965.

Giles, Carl H. The Student Journalist and Feature Writing. Richards Rosen Press, Inc., 1969.

James, T. F. "Hemingway at Work," Cosmopolitan (New York: Hearst Corporation), CXLIII (August, 1957), 54.

Lodge, Helen C., and Gerald L. Trett, New Ways in English. Englewood Cliffs: Prentice-Hall, Inc., 1968.

Post, Homer A. and Harold R. Snodgrass. News in Print. Boston: Allyn and Bacon, Inc., 1967.

Reddick, DeWitt C. Journalism and the School Paper, Fifth Edition. Boston: D. C. Heath and Company, 1963.

Sigband, Norman B. Effective Report Writing. New York: Harper & Brothers, 1960.

100d • Extra-Credit Typing

Problem 1

Directions – Type a short report based on the outline in 92c Problem 1, page 157. Type it in regular report form.

Problem 2

Directions – Type a short report based on the outline in 92c, Problem 2, page 158. Type it in regular report form.

Problem 3

Directions – Type the option you did not type in 96e, page 164. Follow the directions given.

42b • Typing from Dictation and Spelling Checkup

5 minutes

Directions – Your teacher will dictate the words in 41d, page 70. Type the words from dictation. Check for correct spelling. Retype any words in which you made an error.

42c • Timed Writings

10 minutes

Directions – Type two 3-minute writings on 41e, page 71. Circle errors. Compute *gwam*. Submit the better writing.

42d • Problem Typing

25 minutes

Problem 1—Personal Note in Block Style

Half sheet
50-space line
Open punctuation

Directions – Type a copy of the personal note that follows. Type the date on the 7th line space from the top of the paper. (*The date is always typed on the 7th line space in all half-page personal notes.*) Type the salutation on the 5th line space from the date.

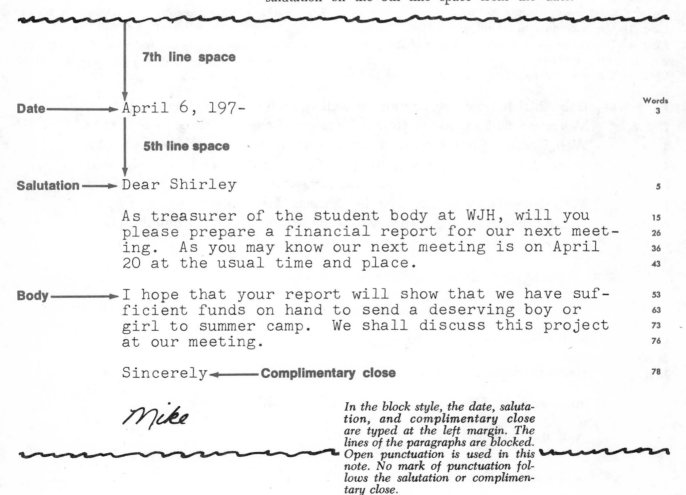

7th line space

Date ─────► April 6, 197-

Words
3

5th line space

Salutation ─────► Dear Shirley

5

As treasurer of the student body at WJH, will you please prepare a financial report for our next meeting. As you may know our next meeting is on April 20 at the usual time and place.

15
26
36
43

Body ─────► I hope that your report will show that we have sufficient funds on hand to send a deserving boy or girl to summer camp. We shall discuss this project at our meeting.

53
63
73
76

Sincerely ◄─────── **Complimentary close**

78

Mike

In the block style, the date, salutation, and complimentary close are typed at the left margin. The lines of the paragraphs are blocked. Open punctuation is used in this note. No mark of punctuation follows the salutation or complimentary close.

Personal note in block style

• Lesson 99 • *70-space line*

99a • Keyboard Review • Each line at least three times

5 minutes

All letters SS   They were required to save the jigsaw puzzles in the black box for me.
Figure   Mt. Everest, India, at 29,018 feet, is the highest point on the earth.   Quiet wrists
Shift   Edmund Hillary and Tenzing Norkey scaled Mt. Everest in the Himalayas.   and arms
Easy   The big men are those who are willing to tell you if they know little.

| 1 | 2 | 3 | 4 | 5 | 6 | 7 | 8 | 9 | 10 | 11 | 12 | 13 | 14 |

99b • Punctuation Guides — Comma

10 minutes

Directions – Read the explanation carefully; then type each example sentence twice.

Line 1 – Use commas to set off parenthetic expressions that break the flow of a sentence.

Line 2 – If the parenthetic expression begins or ends a sentence, use one comma.

Line 3 – Use a comma to set off *yes, no, well, now.*

Line 4 – Use commas to set off the name of the person addressed.

Line 5 – Use commas to set off appositives that give additional information about the same person or object and that can be omitted without changing the meaning of the sentence.

Line 6 – Do not use a comma to separate two nouns, one of which identifies the other.

Line 7 – Use commas to separate the date from the year and the name of a city from the name of the state.

1   SS   Bob Aldrich, however, cannot hit well enough to make the regular team.
2   Moreover, Mike plans to stop at Yosemite Lodge for three or four days.
3   Well, Tommy Anderson saved the game for us by hitting those home runs.
4   Scott, did you really see us there? The first day, Ted, is Wednesday.   Wrists low
5   Mr. Jack Coffey, our new math teacher, wrote a book on wise investing.   and still
6   My husband's sister Sue lives in Chicago. His brother Jim is in Rome.
7   He said the drumming record was set on May 2, 1956, in Columbus, Ohio.

| 1 | 2 | 3 | 4 | 5 | 6 | 7 | 8 | 9 | 10 | 11 | 12 | 13 | 14 |

99c • Paragraph Skill Builder • Type four 1-minute writings.

5 minutes

DS   It has been estimated that a person spends somewhat more than half of his day listening. Listening means more than just hearing sounds. Hearing requires only two ears; but if you listen, you must use your mind as well. Don't merely hear a speaker with your ears turned on and your mind turned off.

60 words
1.3 si

Resume
typing
at once

99d • Problem Typing

25 minutes

Directions – Continue typing the manuscript of the formal library report started in Lesson 97. Keep the margins and spacing uniform throughout the manuscript.

Problem 2—Personal Note in Block Style

Half sheet
60-space line
Open punctuation

Directions – Type the personal note below. Type today's date in the proper place. Type the salutation on the 5th line space from the date.

• *Three words are counted for today's date, although the date used may have more or fewer than 15 strokes.*

	Words
Today's date	3

5th line space

Dear John — 5

	Words
I must write a short paper for my English class on one of	17
our national parks. Since I have never been to any of our	28
parks, this is quite an order. I would like to write a good	41
paper.	42
I recall your telling me that you camped in Yosemite last	54
summer. Do you have any booklets on Yosemite that you could	66
lend me? I shall be sure to return them to you.	76
Sincerely	78

Sign your name

• Lesson 43 • *60-space line*

43a • Keyboard Review • Each line three times
5 minutes

All letters   SS   The quiz kept Jim and Dick Law busy for six very long hours.

Figure-Symbol   He said, "Our club will send Field & King a check for $350."

Quick, sharp strokes

Easy   The greatest of all faults is to believe that you have none.

| 1 | 2 | 3 | 4 | 5 | 6 | 7 | 8 | 9 | 10 | 11 | 12 |

43b • Sentence Skill Builder from Script
10 minutes

Directions – Type two 1-minute writings on each sentence. First writing: push for speed. Second writing: drop speed; work for control.

			Words
1	SS	*Very often, it is the things we think we know that stump us!*	12
2		*This work will be easy if you will just put your mind to it.*	12
3		*Keep in mind that the best mirror you have is an old friend.*	12
4		*Looking at work for hours is a poor way to show love for it.*	12

Prepare the Title Page and Bibliography. Long, formal reports usually have a title page and bibliography. The title page contains the name of the report and its writer. The bibliography contains titles of references that have been consulted.

It will pay you to learn how to write clear, interest-holding papers. It's not an easy job, but with a plan to guide you and some practice, you can turn out good work on your typewriter.

[1] T. F. James, "Hemingway at Work," Cosmopolitan (New York: Hearst Corporation), Vol. CXLIII (August, 1957), p. 54.

[2] David A. Conlin and George R. Herman, Modern Grammar and Composition (New York: American Book Company, 1965), p. 250.

[3] Ibid., p. 251.

• Lesson 98 • *70-space line*

98a • Keyboard Review • Each line at least three times

5 minutes

All letters	SS	Three plucky ushers quenched a major fire blazing above the west exit.
Figure		His address is 932 West 15th Street; his new phone number is 468-7038.
Long words		Andromeda is also the remotest heavenly body visible to the naked eye.
Easy		When the road on which you go is straight, it is not easy to get lost.

Eyes on this copy

| 1 | 2 | 3 | 4 | 5 | 6 | 7 | 8 | 9 | 10 | 11 | 12 | 13 | 14 |

98b • Speed Stretcher • As directed in 78b, page 133

10 minutes

GWAM
1' 5'

All letters

¶ 1
65 words
1.3 si

DS   Do you know what a mollycoddle is? This is the name Teddy Roosevelt   14 3 37
gave to any who lacked the willpower to fight for a good cause. It   28 6 40
denotes weakness of character. Many of today's men have not heard of the   43 9 43
term. Even worse, many do not mind the label. A day's work wears them   57 11 45
out; a tough problem stops them cold.   65 13 47

¶ 2
65 words
1.3 si

Teddy Roosevelt was weak and frail as a small boy, but he made up   13 16 50
his mind to make the most of himself. He rode untamed broncos, climbed   28 18 52
rugged peaks, and hunted wild animals in the jungle. He built himself   42 21 55
into a strong man and leader. Few could match his physical strength.   56 24 58
No one could equal his strength of character.   65 26 60

¶ 3
40 words
1.3 si

Can you spot a mollycoddle? You may discover one in any class.   13 29 63
He needs somebody to coax him before he can do his lessons. He becomes   27 31 65
a class clown to cover up the fact that he is too lazy to work.   40 34 68

All ¶'s
1.3 si

1' | 1 | 2 | 3 | 4 | 5 | 6 | 7 | 8 | 9 | 10 | 11 | 12 | 13 | 14 |
5' | | 1 | | 2 | | 3 | |

98c • Problem Typing

30 minutes

Directions – Continue typing the manuscript of the formal library report started in Lesson 97. Keep the margins and spacing uniform throughout the manuscript.

Problem 1—Personal Note in Modified Block Style

Half sheet
60-space line
Open punctuation

Directions – Type the personal note that follows. The dateline and complimentary close start at the center point of the paper. Type the salutation on the 4th line space from the date.

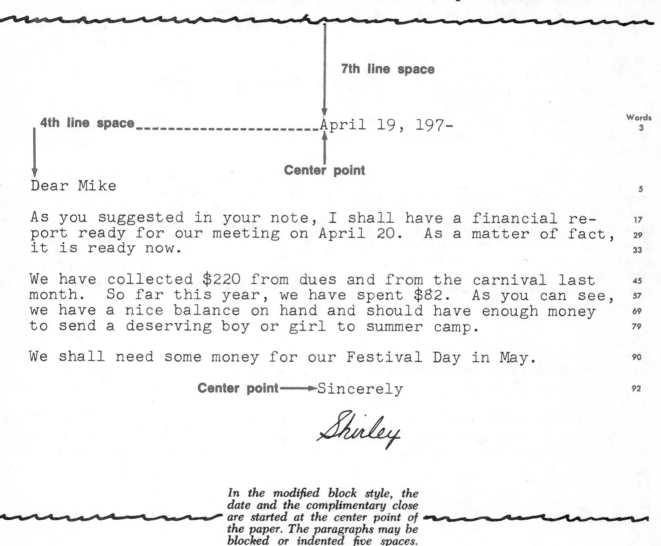

7th line space

4th line space _____ April 19, 197-

Words
3

Center point

Dear Mike   5

As you suggested in your note, I shall have a financial re-   17
port ready for our meeting on April 20. As a matter of fact,   29
it is ready now.   33

We have collected $220 from dues and from the carnival last   45
month. So far this year, we have spent $82. As you can see,   57
we have a nice balance on hand and should have enough money   69
to send a deserving boy or girl to summer camp.   79

We shall need some money for our Festival Day in May.   90

Center point ——►Sincerely   92

Shirley

In the modified block style, the date and the complimentary close are started at the center point of the paper. The paragraphs may be blocked or indented five spaces.

Personal note in modified block style

Problem 2—Personal Note in Modified Block Style

Half sheet
60-space line
Open punctuation

Directions – Type the personal note on the next page in modified block style, with indented paragraphs. Type the salutation on the 5th line space from the date.

WRITING A FORMAL LIBRARY REPORT

"The test of a book," said Ernest Hemingway, "is how much good stuff you can throw away."[1] He added that anything that does not have the ring of hard truth, that seems the least bit overdone, must go into the wastebasket. Deep feelings about something written in words that stick— these are the things a writer must get.

We can't all gain the fame that Hemingway gained as a writer. He worked hard and long at perfecting his skill. We can all learn how to write a short paper, however, long before we get into Hemingway's class. Almost anyone can learn to write a clear, interesting account about something he has read, heard, or seen. Let's see how you might go about this job.

Choose the Right Subject. To begin with, you have to write about something that intrigues you and about which you know. This is basic, says one authority on writing.[2] You can't write about the growing of figs unless you know how figs are grown. You can get your information from books, from talks with fig growers, or from growing figs yourself. The more information you get, the better your paper.

Limit Your Subject. Don't try to cover too much ground in your paper. More than one young writer has butted his head against this wall without getting anything more than a sore head for his trouble. As Conlin says, "Limit your topic, and make yourself an authority on it."[3]

Narrow your subject down. Write about the kind of soil fig trees like or how figs are prepared for the market. You can't cover the whole life of a fig, from seedling to fig sauce, in two hundred words, no matter how skilled you become as a writer.

Prepare a Preliminary Outline. Jot down the major topics you expect to cover. This is the preliminary outline. It consists only of a number of topic headings. No subpoints need to be included.

Prepare Bibliography Cards. After you select a subject and prepare your preliminary outline, you must find out where you can obtain the information you need. For most students, books and articles will furnish the needed help.

As you find books and articles that appear to be helpful, write their titles on cards. On each card, write complete information about a single reference so the card can be used later to prepare the footnotes and bibliography for your paper.

Read; Take Notes. Start your reading. As you read, take notes. Record important facts, ideas, and quotations on note cards so that you can refer to them as you write your paper.

Each note card should be given a heading which describes the notes. Use one of the main headings of your preliminary outline, if you can, to identify each card. Write each note on a separate card. In every case, indicate the page number and reference from which the note was taken.

Prepare the Final Outline. When you have taken notes on all your readings, organize your cards in some order. This will usually be determined by the order of the points in the preliminary outline. You may find that some of the main points should now be changed. Try to group the cards under each major point into two or more subgroups. These will make up the subpoints of your outline.

Remember that an outline shows clearly what points are the most important as well as those that are less important. The Roman numerals show the chief ideas. The capital letters and arabic numerals give details under the main points.

Write the First Draft. The first writing of a paper will usually not be the final one. Present the material you have collected. Don't worry too much about words, spelling, and typing mistakes.

Revise the First Draft. When the first draft has been completed, check it for wording and mistakes. Mark your corrections with a pen or pencil. Careful writers read and correct their copy two or three times to make sure that their papers read well. It is recommended that you do this too.

Prepare the Final Copy. Good appearance in papers is important. Follow accepted rules for typing the final copy. Pay close attention to margins, placement of footnotes, and other similar details.

March 25, 197—

Dear Lori 5

Indent ¶'s ——————→ Thank you so much for your invitation to the game and 16
dance this Friday. I've read about your great team and am 28
looking forward to seeing them in action. 36

I shall come on the train which arrives at your station 47
at 5:30 p.m. I'll plan on returning home Saturday noon. 59

Thanks again for the invitation. I'll see you Friday. 70

Sincerely 72

Mary Lou

Problem 3—Personal Note Typed Lengthwise on 5½- by 8½-inch Paper

Directions – 1. Type the note in Problem 2 on 5½- by 8½-inch paper inserted lengthwise. This note is shown at the right.

2. Start typing the name and address of the writer one-half inch (4th line space) from the top. Set off the return address by typing a line of hyphens from the left to the right edge of the paper, a line space or two below the return address.

3. Use a 40-space line. This will give you left and right margins of about one inch on both pica and elite machines.

4. Type the date at the center point of the paper on the 3d line space below the hyphens under the return address.

   • *To find the center point, refer to page 68; or fold your paper to bring left and right edges together. Crease lightly at the top.*

5. Type the salutation on the 6th or 7th line space from the date.

6. Start the complimentary close at the center point of the paper.

Note typed on personal stationery

96e • Creative Typing

10 minutes

Half sheet
Double spacing
60-space line

Directions – Type the following quotation; then, add a few sentences telling what the quotation means to you. Correct your copy; retype. Give your short report a title. Center it on the half sheet. Use a 60-space line.

Alternate Suggestion

With your teacher's approval, type a summary of the article in 96c, page 163. Use the directions given at the left.

Charles E. Hughes said, "A man has to live with himself, and he should see to it that he always has good company."

• Lesson 97 • *70-space line*

97a • Keyboard Review • Each line at least three times

5 minutes

All letters SS We made expensive jacks of high quality, but they were the wrong size.

Figure-Symbol Pat actually delivered all 104 newspapers before 6:30 a.m. on July 24!

Vowels—e, i Their retired neighbors tried hard to remain silent on certain issues.

Easy Your smile is one thing that is worth more when it is given to others.

Wrists low and still

| 1 | 2 | 3 | 4 | 5 | 6 | 7 | 8 | 9 | 10 | 11 | 12 | 13 | 14 |

97b • Paragraph Skill Builder

10 minutes

Directions – Type a 1-minute writing to determine your goal word. Then type a 5-minute writing. The return will be called at the end of each minute. Try to reach your goal word.

DS   You may be the type of person who likes to sit along the side-
lines rather than play in the game. You should weigh quite carefully
the ideas of others. However, you must also reserve the right to do
your own thinking. Your mind can be most effective when it is active.
Keep your mind in the game.

60 words
1.3 si

Blend fast and slow stroking for flowing rhythm

97c • Problem Typing

30 minutes

Problem—Formal Library Report with Footnotes

Directions – 1. Prepare a manuscript of the following report. Follow the directions for typing bound manuscripts given on page 152.

2. In the problem which follows, the footnotes are placed at the end of the report. Type them at the bottom of pages on which reference is made to them.

• *You will not be able to type the entire report in this lesson. Type as far as you can. You will be given time to complete the manuscript in Lessons 98 and 99. In Lesson 100, you will type a title page and bibliography for this report; then bind it at the left.*

• Lesson 44 • *60-space line*

44a • **Keyboard Review** • Each line three times

7 minutes

All letters   SS   Jack Gates will quiz the vast number of excess people today.

Figure-Symbol   Venezuela's Angel Falls (highest in world) drops 3,312 feet.

"br" reach   Brad Brill may bring his bright brother to the broad bridge.   *Elbows in*

Hyphen   He gave a one-hour talk on his coast-to-coast study of zoos.

Easy   The reason we fail to learn is that we stop before we start.

| 1 | 2 | 3 | 4 | 5 | 6 | 7 | 8 | 9 | 10 | 11 | 12 |

44b • **Paragraph Guided Writings** • As directed in 36d, page 61

15 minutes

• All letters are used in these paragraphs

| | G W A M |
| | 1'   3' |

¶ 1
36 words
1.3 si   DS

Some say the giraffe looks as if it were put together   11   4   40

by a committee. All the members got the same plans, but   22   7   43

what they heard was something else. The queer giraffe is   34   11   47

the result.   36   12   48

¶ 2
36 words
1.2 si

We have the vile habit of hearing only the things we   47   16   52

want to hear. We miss much that we should get. Our views   58   19   55

resemble the zany giraffe. They are short on fact, long on   70   23   59

fiction.   72   24   60

¶ 3
36 words
1.2 si

When something is explained to you, listen carefully.   83   28   64

Get all the facts. Train your mind to catch every detail.   95   32   68

This, after all, is the way to be sharp in school and on   106   35   71

All ¶'s
1.2 si   the job.   108   36   72

| 1' | 1 | 2 | 3 | 4 | 5 | 6 | 7 | 8 | 9 | 10 | 11 | 12 |
| 3' | | 1 | | 2 | | 3 | | 4 | |

44c • **Problem Typing**

23 minutes

• *Cut two sheets of 8½ by 11-inch paper in two so that each of the four pieces measures 5½ by 8½ inches. Type your name and address at the top. Use clever wording or arrangement if you wish. Set off the return address by a line of hyphens as shown on page 75. You will use these sheets in typing the following problems.*

• *The lines in the problems are not set line-for-line the way you will type them. Set the margin stops properly; return your carriage with the bell.*

GWAM
1' 5'

All letters
¶ 1
40 words
1.3 si

DS

Soccer, the world's most popular sport, may soon become one of our   13 3 51

nation's newest pastimes. Players on each team bat a medium-sized ball   28 6 54

around with their heads and feet rather than with their hands.   40 8 56

¶ 2
44 words
1.4 si

Views on soccer's spectator appeal differ. A few sports fans say   53 11 59

there is too much frantic running around without enough scoring. Those   68 14 62

who enjoy the game are quick to point out the fact that it is a most   82 16 64

exciting one.   84 17 65

¶ 3
48 words
1.4 si

In some countries to the south of the U.S., soccer arouses such   97 19 67

passions that the half-time entertainment is often a riot. In a stadium   112 22 70

in Brazil the playing field has a moat on both sides to keep fans and   126 25 73

players from each other's throats.   132 26 74

¶ 4
52 words
1.4 si

So far, the sport has not really caught on big in this country.   145 29 77

Here, the old standbys like baseball, football, and hockey can keep   159 32 80

the fans pretty well occupied. Lack of star players is a problem, too.   174 35 83

Soccer backers now say, though, that America is ready.   184 37 85

¶ 5
56 words
1.3 si

To prove it, they can tell you how soccer already has made its   197 39 87

mark on the city of San Francisco. Without a doubt, some fans have   211 42 90

been caught up in the real spirit of the game. At one amateur match   224 45 93

played there, the referee's call sent hundreds of spectators into a   238 48 96

All ¶'s
1.4 si

brief melee.   240 48 96

1' | 1 | 2 | 3 | 4 | 5 | 6 | 7 | 8 | 9 | 10 | 11 | 12 | 13 | 14 |
5' | 1 | 2 | 3 |

96d • Correcting Errors — Spreading Letters   *5 minutes*

Directions – 1. Type the sentence below just as it appears; then erase the *tra* in *exttra*.

2. Move carriage to the second space following *ext*. Depress the backspace key half way. Type *r*.

3. Release the backspace key. Depress the backspace key half way; type *a*.

The error –   Correct the exttra letter.

The correction – Correct the extra letter.

Problem 1—Personal Note in Modified Block Style

Directions – Modified block style; blocked paragraphs; today's date.
Type the salutation on the 6th line space from the date.

Dear Pat

Are you going to attend the Madison County Coin Show next week?

Mr. Clauson, our Vice Principal, is going to take his station wagon; and there will be plenty of room for you.

Since coin collections from all over the state will be on display, it would be well worth your time to attend.

Write to me immediately, or call if you wish to go with us.

Sincerely

Problem 2—Personal Note in Block Style

Directions – Block style; today's date. Decide for yourself where to type the salutation.

Dear Henry

I am returning the booklet on rare stamps you so kindly sent to me. Thanks for letting me read it.

I have a fairly large collection of stamps. None are so rare as the British Guiana, dated 1856, which, as your booklet states, is now insured for $100,000. And to think it was originally bought from a schoolboy for $1.20!

I find stamp collecting to be great fun. In addition, I have learned a lot about foreign countries. I hope that you enjoy it, too.

Sincerely

Problem 3—Creative Typing

Directions – Compose and type a reply to the personal note in Problem 1. Use the modified block style with indented paragraphs. Arrange the note neatly on your personal stationery. Date your letter three days from today.

Alternate Suggestion
Type the note in Problem 1 in modified block style, indented paragraphs.

44d • Extra-Credit Typing

Directions – Use the choice you did not select in typing Problem 3. Use a sheet of personal stationery of the same size used in typing the three problems in this lesson.

• Lesson 45 • *60-space line*

45a • Keyboard Review • Each line three times

5 minutes

All letters   SS   Please pack my boxes with five dozen jugs of liquid varnish.

Figure-Symbol   George is almost 5'6", Peter is 5'9", while Michael is 6'1".

Eyes on this copy

Easy   To gain from sound advice takes more wisdom than to give it.

| 1 | 2 | 3 | 4 | 5 | 6 | 7 | 8 | 9 | 10 | 11 | 12 |

SECOND CARD

Heading – Introduction

Notes – "The test of a book is how much good stuff you can throw away." Anything that does not have the ring of hard truth, that seems the least bit overdone, must go into the wastebasket. Deep feelings about something written in words that stick—these are the things a writer must get.

Reference and page number – James, p. 54.

THIRD CARD

'*Heading* – Writing effectively

Notes – Descriptive paragraphs:
1. Concentrate upon words that make appeals to our senses.
2. Describe how things appear to us.
3. Put us in touch with the physical world.
4. Let us sense (experience) what is being related.

Reference and page number – Conlin, p. 304.

FOURTH CARD

Heading – Prepare the final outline

Notes – An outline shows what points are most important as well as those that are less important. It is a plan of relationships. The Roman numerals in your outline show the chief ideas. The capital letters and arabic numerals give details under the main points.

Reference and page number – Green, p. 251.

• Lesson 96 • *70-space line*

96a • Keyboard Review • Each line at least three times   5 minutes

All letters	SS	Five or six quarters, won as prize money, jingled in the boy's pocket.
Figure		Over 45,780 attended the fair during the weeks of April 9, 16, and 23.
Long reach		bright bray bring brought bride braid bread brain bran break brilliant
Easy		Those with one-track minds may find that they have no station in life.

Hold wrists steady

| 1 | 2 | 3 | 4 | 5 | 6 | 7 | 8 | 9 | 10 | 11 | 12 | 13 | 14 |

96b • Number Expression Guides — Typing Fractions   5 minutes

Directions – Read the explanation; then type each line twice.

Line 1 – Use the figure keys and the diagonal for typing fractions not on the keyboard ("made" fractions).

Line 2 – Space between whole numbers and "made" fractions.

Line 3 – Be uniform when you type fractions: ½ and ¼, but 1/2 and 2/5.

1	SS	"Made" fractions should be made in this way: 2/3, 3/5, 5/6.
2		They will need 5 2/3 yards of red nylon cloth to do the job.
3		Try to give her 7 2/5 yards of wool for 6 1/2 yards of silk.

Wrists and elbows still

| 1 | 2 | 3 | 4 | 5 | 6 | 7 | 8 | 9 | 10 | 11 | 12 |

45b • Timed Writings

Directions – Type two 3-minute writings on 44b, page 76. Compute *gwam*. Submit the better of the two writings.

45c • Problem Typing

Problem 1—Message Typed on Postal Card

Directions – 1. Insert card; determine horizontal center; set margin stops for a 48-space line.

2. Type the date on Line 3; then type the remaining lines as directed on the card.

3. The complimentary close is omitted because of limited space for the message.

• *Use paper cut to postal card size (5½ by 3¼ inches) if cards are not available.*

Card holders

• *When you insert the card into your typewriter, adjust the card holders, as shown above, and use the paper bail to keep the card from slipping.*

Problem 2—Addressing a Postal Card

Directions – 1. Type the return address and address on the card typed in Problem 1.

2. Type the return address on Line 2 from the top and 3 spaces from the left edge.

3. Type the address about 2 inches from the top and 2 inches from the left edge. Use the block style and single spacing for all addresses. The city and state names and ZIP Code must be typed on one line in that order.

4. The new 2-letter state abbreviations (typed in capital letters without a period or space between) may be used, or the state name may be typed in full or in the standard abbreviation. The 2-letter state abbreviations are shown on page 117.

• *ZIP Code numbers are typed 2 spaces after the state name.*

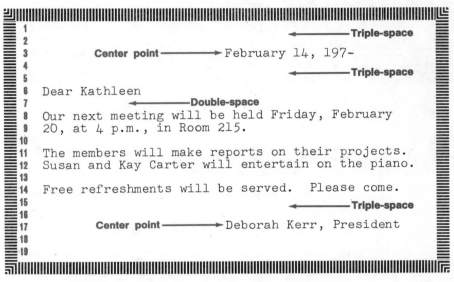

1
2   ←————— Triple-space
3 Center point ——→ February 14, 197-
4   ←————— Triple-space
5
6 Dear Kathleen
7 ←————— Double-space
8 Our next meeting will be held Friday, February
9 20, at 4 p.m., in Room 215.
10
11 The members will make reports on their projects.
12 Susan and Kay Carter will entertain on the piano.
13
14 Free refreshments will be served.   Please come.
15   ←————— Triple-space
16
17 Center point ——→ Deborah Kerr, President
18
19

Postal card in modified block style

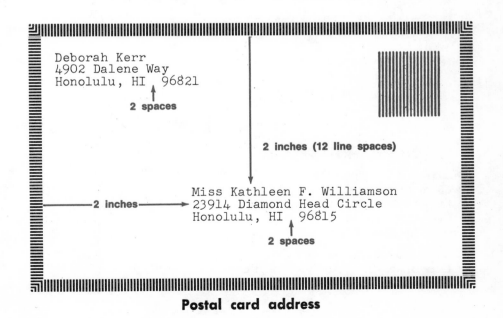

Deborah Kerr
4902 Dalene Way
Honolulu, HI   96821
↑
2 spaces

2 inches (12 line spaces)

→ **2 inches** →

Miss Kathleen F. Williamson
23914 Diamond Head Circle
Honolulu, HI   96815
↑
2 spaces

Postal card address

Author – Giles, Carl H.

Title – The Student Journalist and Feature Writing

Publication information – New York: Richards Rosen Press, Inc., 1969

Short description – New book in the Student Journalist series. It gives a complete guide to the place of feature writing in school publications and explains how to approach and write this type of article.

Library call number – 070.1
H714

Author – Post, Homer A. and Harold R. Snodgrass

Title – News in Print

Publication information – Boston: Allyn and Bacon, Inc., 1967

Short description – Designed for use in almost any situation which includes the publication of a school newspaper. Organization of the newspaper is explained.

Library call number – PN
4775

• Lesson 95 • *70-space line*

95a • Keyboard Review • Each line at least three times   5 minutes

All letters	SS	I was quite lucky that my jams won five prizes at today's big exhibit.	
Figure-Symbol		On more than 290 invoices he typed the following: 16 doz. @ 18¢ each.	Feet on
Balanced- and one-hand		and the date, and the case, and the only, and the rest, and the faster	the floor
Easy		They who spend their leisure time in the right way are sure to profit.	

| 1 | 2 | 3 | 4 | 5 | 6 | 7 | 8 | 9 | 10 | 11 | 12 | 13 | 14 |

95b • Timed Writings   10 minutes

Directions – Type a 1- and a 5-minute writing on 91d, page 156. Circle errors. Compute *gwam*.

95c • Problem Typing

• *Note cards contain ideas, facts, and quotations to be used in preparing the body of a formal report or speech. A note card is illustrated below. Study it carefully.*   30 minutes

Problem—Note Cards

Directions – 1. Prepare four note cards on 5- by 3-inch card stock. Prepare the first card from the illustration at the right. Prepare the other cards from the information that follows.

2. Type the heading on each card about three spaces from the top and three spaces from the left edge.

Heading

Notes

Reference and page number

```
Rules for making note cards

    A note card should carry only one idea.

    The topic heading for each card should
appear in the upper left-hand corner.

    Topic headings are usually taken from the
tentative outline.

    Make reference to the source in the lower
left-hand portion of the card.

Sigband, pp. 39-40.
```

Note card

Problem 3—Message Typed on a Postal Card

48-space line
Single spacing
Open punctuation

Directions – Type the following message on a postal card in modified block style. The return address is Lester Partridge / 395 Clark Street / your city, state, and ZIP Code. Address the card to Mr. Mark Seeley / 315 Avon Way / your city, state, and ZIP Code.

Current date

Dear Mark

The annual barbecue will be held in Cuesta Park next Wednesday, (*give the date*) at 7 p.m.

Pass the word around to all the students to bring their own silverware. Everything else will be furnished.

Lester Partridge
Student Body President

Problem 4—Message Typed on a Postal Card

48-space line
Single spacing
Open punctuation

Directions – Type this message on a postal card in block style. Correct as indicated. The return address is Rod Sinclair / 416 Dexter Avenue / your city, state, and ZIP Code. Address the card to your name / street address / city, state, and ZIP Code.

Current date

Dear (*Your name*)

Single space

I ^have^ ~~got~~ five tickets ^to^ the television program, The Tonight Show, which will ^#^ be telecast by station KTTV next tuesday night at 9:30 p.m. if ^you^ would like to ~~see~~ this show, i'll save one ~~one~~ of the ~~show~~ tickets for you. Write or call right ^#^ away so I can ^let^ ~~leave~~ you know about arrangements.

Rod Sinclair

45d • Extra-Credit Typing

Directions – Compose and type a reply to the message in Problem 4. Arrange the message neatly on a postal card. Address the card to Rod Sinclair / 416 Dexter Avenue / your city, state, and ZIP Code. Type your name and address in the upper left corner of the address side of the card.

• Lesson 94 • *70-space line*

94a • Keyboard Review • Each line at least three times

5 minutes

All letters	SS	Everybody expected a big kid my size to qualify for the javelin throw.
Figure		Kennedy was our President from January 20, 1961, to November 22, 1963.
Long reach		The mayor announced the results of the voting. An unknown doctor won.
Easy		There will be more people left if we will all remember to drive right.

Sit erect

| 1 | 2 | 3 | 4 | 5 | 6 | 7 | 8 | 9 | 10 | 11 | 12 | 13 | 14 |

94b • Correcting Errors — Squeezing Letters

5 minutes

Directions – 1. Type the line just as it appears below.

2. Erase the *ed* in *omited*. The correct spelling is *omitted*.

3. Move the carriage to the space immediately following *omit*.

4. Depress the backspace key half way. Hold it. Type the second *t*.

5. Release the backspace key; depress it half way. Hold it. Type *e*.

6. Release the backspace key; depress it half way. Hold it. Type *d*.

The error — A letter has been omited in the middle of a word.

The correction — A letter has been omitted in the middle of a word.

94c • Speed Ladder Sentences • Type each sentence for 1 minute. The guide will be called at 15-, 12-, or 10-second intervals.

5 minutes

			GWAM 15" 12" 10"
1	SS	Always use a quick, sharp stroke as you type.	36 45 54
2		Curve the fingers and hold them close to the keys.	40 50 60
3		Keep your wrists and elbows steady as you hit the keys.	44 55 66
4		Just try to think and type the short, easy words as a whole.	48 60 72

| 1 | 2 | 3 | 4 | 5 | 6 | 7 | 8 | 9 | 10 | 11 | 12 |

94d • Problem Typing

• *Bibliographical cards contain information about references you expect to use in preparing formal reports. Note the information that is included by referring to the illustration that follows.*

Problem—Bibliographical Cards   *30 minutes*

Directions – 1. Prepare three bibliographical cards on 5- by 3-inch card stock. Prepare the first card from the illustration at the right. Prepare the second and third cards from the information that follows.

2. Type the first entry on the card about three spaces from the top and three spaces from the left edge. To keep the card from slipping, adjust the card holders to hold the card firmly against the cylinder.

Author	Reddick, DeWitt C.
Title	<u>Journalism and the School Paper</u>, Fifth Edition
Publication information	Boston: D. C. Heath and Company, 1963
Short description	This book stresses the work of the reporter. Many kinds of publications are covered. All aspects of writing for newspapers and magazines are included.
Library call number	LB3621 R24j

Bibliographical card

• **Lesson 46** • *60-space line*

46a • **Keyboard Review** • Each line three times

5 minutes

All letters	SS	Peg and Mary will quickly adjust five bird boxes at the zoo.
Figure-Symbol		These pens will sell for $2.75 each, less a discount of 10%.
Easy		In life we must all be able to do, as well as to do without.

| 1 | 2 | 3 | 4 | 5 | 6 | 7 | 8 | 9 | 10 | 11 | 12 |

Wrists low and still

46b • **Spelling and Proofreading Aid** • Each line three times

5 minutes

• *Study carefully the spelling of each word as you type it.*

1	SS	villain prosperous oxygen misspell jealously eligible enemies
2		adjoining partial autumn descent between hastily ninety paid
3		rival dining annoy worried hurried absence brilliant silence

Fingers deeply curved

46c • **Timed Writings**

15 minutes

Directions – 1. Type a 3-minute writing. Compute your *gwam*.
2. Type two 1-minute writings on each paragraph; the first for speed, the second for control.

3. Finally, type another 3-minute writing on all paragraphs. Compute your *gwam*. Compare the *gwam* and number of errors for the 3-minute writings.

• All letters are used in these paragraphs

	G W A M
	1' 3'

			1' 3'
¶ 1 36 words 1.2 si	DS	The first rule of getting along with others is so simple	11 4 43
		that it is amazing more of us do not observe it. People will	24 8 47
		pay you back. They will treat you as well as you treat them.	36 12 51
¶ 2 38 words 1.2 si		If you like people, they will like you. If you respect	47 16 55
		them, they will respect you. If you are courteous to them,	59 20 59
		they will be courteous to you. The rule works. People will	71 24 63
		pay you back.	74 25 64
¶ 3 44 words 1.2 si		Experts say that courtesy pays off. It makes work more	85 28 67
		fun. You can get things done with less effort, and you can	97 32 71
		get them done more quickly. Give praise to those who de-	109 36 75
All ¶'s 1.2 si		serve it. Just praise usually works both ways.	118 39 78

| 1' | 1 | 2 | 3 | 4 | 5 | 6 | 7 | 8 | 9 | 10 | 11 | 12 |
| 3' | | 1 | | 2 | | 3 | | 4 | |

93c • Problem Typing

• *In this lesson, you will start preparing some of the materials used in writing the formal library report that you will type in Lessons 97–100. A preliminary outline, bibliography cards, note cards, and a final outline are usually prepared before a* report *is written. These, then, are the items you will type in Lessons 93, 94, and 95. With your teacher's approval, keep these items until you finish typing the formal report so that you can refer to them.*

Problem 1—Preliminary Outline for Formal Library Report

• *A preliminary outline is a mere listing of the topics you expect to treat in a report.*

Directions – Use a 40-space line. Center the entire outline vertically on a full sheet. The outline below is set in problem form. Double-space the items in the outline. Arrange it correctly.

WRITING A FORMAL LIBRARY REPORT

1. Prepare introduction.
2. Choose subject.
3. Prepare preliminary outline.
4. Collect reading references.
5. Read; take notes.
6. Prepare final outline.
7. Prepare first draft.
8. Correct and revise first draft.
9. Prepare final copy.
10. Prepare title page and bibliography.

Problem 2—Final Outline for Formal Library Report

Directions – Use a 60-space line and the standard 2-inch margin at the top of a full sheet.

WRITING A FORMAL LIBRARY REPORT

I. STEPS TO TAKE BEFORE WRITING STARTS.

  A. Choose the right subject.
    1. Choose a topic that intrigues you.
    2. Choose a topic about which you know something.
  B. Limit your subject.
  C. Prepare a preliminary outline.
    1. Jot down the major points only.
    2. This outline acts as a guide in your search for information.
  D. Prepare bibliography cards.
    1. The cards should contain information on your readings.
    2. The data recorded should be complete and accurate.
  E. Read; take notes.
    1. Use note cards.
    2. Record important facts, opinions, and quotations.
  F. Prepare the final outline.
    1. Organize the information collected.
    2. Group note cards under topics used in the preliminary outline.

II. STEPS TO TAKE IN WRITING THE PAPER.

  A. Write the first draft.
    1. The explanations should be clear, complete, to the point, and accurate.
    2. The sentences should be in logical order.
    3. Illustrate points by references to personal experiences.
    4. Compare your topic with one that is more familiar to the reader.
  B. Revise the first draft.
    1. Check the first draft for wording, spelling, and typographical errors.
    2. Make pencil or pen corrections.
  C. Prepare the final copy.
    1. Good appearance is important.
    2. Use standard rules on arrangement of reports.
  D. Prepare the title page and bibliography.
    1. A title page contains the name of the report and its writer.
    2. The bibliography names the references consulted.

46d • Technique Builder — Carriage Return

46d • Technique Builder — Carriage Return   *10 minutes*

Directions – 1. Type the first line of the paragraph three times as your teacher gives the signal each 20 seconds. Return quickly; resume typing at once.

2. Repeat for lines 2, 3, and 4.
3. Finally, type a 1-minute writing without the call of the guide. Determine your *gwam*.

		Words in Para.	GWAM 20″ Guide

DS *We should tackle some problems that tax our minds, not* — 11 — 33

**47 words
1.2 si** *just those that are easy for us. We are not educated until* — 23 — 36

we do the things we ought, whether we like them or not. We — 35 — 36

learn only when we take on tough jobs and meet new hurdles — 47 — 36

46e • Capitalization Guides   *10 minutes*

Directions – The following are the capitalization guides that you are to study *prior* to typing the lines. Study the guide; then type the line applying the guide. Type each line twice.

Line 1 – Capitalize the first word of a complete sentence.

Line 2 – Capitalize the first word of a quoted sentence. (A period or comma is typed before the ending quotation mark.)

Line 3 – The names of school subjects, except languages and numbered courses, are not capitalized.

Line 4 – Do not capitalize a quotation resumed within a sentence.

Line 5 – Capitalize the pronoun *I*, both alone and in contractions.

Line 6 – Capitalize titles of organizations, institutions, and buildings.

1   SS   Electronics is a growing field with many rich opportunities.

2   An old proverb says, "Kind words don't wear out the tongue."

3   George is taking English, Music 2, Spanish, and bookkeeping.   Eyes and mind on copy as you type

4   "The danger," an author said, "lies in giving up the chase."

5   Yes, I plan to go to the show, but I'll have to leave early.

6   The students of Westlake School saw a play at Ripon College.

| 1 | 2 | 3 | 4 | 5 | 6 | 7 | 8 | 9 | 10 | 11 | 12 |

• Lesson 47 • *60-space line*

47a • Keyboard Review • Each line three times   *5 minutes*

All letters   SS   The quiz show Jack Palm entered had six boys and five girls.

Figure-Symbol   Model 196-52 will be reduced by 3 1/3 if Berle's plan works.   Space quickly

Easy   Wait for your ship to come in only if you have sent one out.

| 1 | 2 | 3 | 4 | 5 | 6 | 7 | 8 | 9 | 10 | 11 | 12 |

Problem 2—Sentence Outline

Directions – Set the margin stops for a 60-space line. Type the outline in the exact center on a half sheet. The copy is set in problem form. Space and arrange the outline correctly.

SAFETY RULES FOR BICYCLES

I. WHAT ARE COMMON CAUSES OF ACCIDENTS?

    A. Two or more riders on a bicycle ranks first.
    B. Bicycle hitchhiking ranks second.
    C. Riding too closely behind other vehicles ranks third.

II. OBSERVE THESE COMMON-SENSE RULES.

    A. Obey all traffic laws.
        1. Make all necessary arm signals.
        2. Use lights for night riding.
    B. Do not be a show-off trick rider.
    C. Avoid riding in heavy traffic.
    D. Do not make sudden turns or stops.

• Lesson 93 • *70-space line*

93a • Keyboard Review • Each line at least three times   *5 minutes*

All letters	SS	Joyce knew exactly why she received a bad grade on the final map quiz.
Figure-Symbol		Though 1,493 students took the 20 tests, only 76 scored more than 85%.
Long reach		The humble drummer stumbled as he jumped to avoid the other musicians.
Easy		It is tough for us to keep our minds and mouths open at the same time.

Space quickly

| 1 | 2 | 3 | 4 | 5 | 6 | 7 | 8 | 9 | 10 | 11 | 12 | 13 | 14 |

93b • Speed Stretcher • As directed in 78b, page 133   *10 minutes*

All letters

¶ 1
54 words
1.4 si   DS

It is such a simple matter these days to hop on a giant jet and zip from coast to coast in just a few hours. The vast plains, rushing rivers, and rocky peaks below provide majestic views. Flying along at top speeds, one can easily forget the hardships of early travel.

¶ 2
55 words
1.3 si

A century ago these wonders of nature caused major problems that had to be solved if the country was to be linked by the iron horse. In fact, many said the task of tying east to west with a ribbon of rails was too great. Squabbles over the proposed route hindered progress.

¶ 3
55 words
1.3 si

The bulk of the work began after the Civil War. The job of laying track across the vast expanse of land was finished in less than three years. Thousands of men labored diligently for their dollar a day by

All ¶'s
1.3 si

struggling over mountains and toiling in heat, cold, rain, and snow.

	GWAM		
	1'	5'
	13	3	36
	27	5	38
	41	8	41
	54	11	44
	13	13	46
	27	16	49
	41	19	52
	55	22	55
	13	24	57
	27	27	60
	41	30	63
	55	33	66

1' | 1 | 2 | 3 | 4 | 5 | 6 | 7 | 8 | 9 | 10 | 11 | 12 | 13 | 14 |
5' | 1 | 2 | 3 |

47b • Typing from Dictation and Spelling Checkup

5 minutes

Directions – Your teacher will dictate the words in 46b, page 80. Type the words from dictation. Check for correct spelling. Retype words in which you made an error.

47c • Continuity Practice from Rough Draft

5 minutes

Directions – At least twice. Make the corrections as you type.

	Words
DS The personal letters you write should look neat and fresh.	12
make them them look as smart as you your self would like	22
48 words 1.2 si to look when you meet your friends face to face. write clearly	35
and correctly, of course, but keep the the wording warm and	46
friendly.	48

TYPING PERSONAL BUSINESS LETTERS

• *The most commonly used form for a personal business letter is illustrated on page 83. The typewritten name of the sender below the complimentary close is optional.*

Step 1 – Set the machine for single spacing for all except very short letters.

Step 2 – Set the margins. (The margins vary according to the length of the letter.)

Step 3 – Start typing the return address on the 10th line space. For a modified block style letter, start the return address at the center point of the paper. For a block style letter, position the return address at the left margin.

Step 4 – Space down for the address. (The number of lines varies with the letter size. The longer the letter, the fewer the number of spaces.)

Step 5 – Type the salutation a double space below the address.

Step 6 – Start the body a double space below the salutation.

Step 7 – Type the complimentary close a double space below the body. For a modified block style letter, start at the center point. For a block style letter, type it at the left margin.

Step 8 – Type the name of the writer on the 4th line space from the complimentary close.

47d • Problem Typing

30 minutes

Problem 1—Personal Business Letter in Modified Block Style

Full sheet
50-space line
Open punctuation

Directions – Type the letter on the next page. Follow the directions given for typing personal business letters. Type the address on the 10th line space from the date.

• *ZIP Code numbers are typed two spaces after the state name or abbreviation.*

Problem 2—Modified Block Style with Paragraph Indentions

Full sheet
50-space line
Open punctuation

Directions – Type the letter in Problem 1 again. Use today's date in the heading. Indent the first line of each paragraph 5 spaces.

Lesson 92 • *70-space line*

92a • Keyboard Review • Each line at least three times

All letters SS The judge will request several dozen back copies of my deluxe edition.

Figure   On December 16, 1903, Orville Wright made the very first plane flight.   Type with-

Long words   The study of a file of correspondence will yield valuable information.   out pauses

Easy   Big problems in the world are often caused by a lot of small problems.

| 1 | 2 | 3 | 4 | 5 | 6 | 7 | 8 | 9 | 10 | 11 | 12 | 13 | 14 |

92b • Paragraph Skill Builder

10 minutes

Directions – 1. Type a 1-minute writing. Remember the last word you typed; it is your goal word.

2. Type a 5-minute writing on the same material.

At the end of each minute, the return will be called. Try to reach the goal word at each 1-minute goal signal.

DS   Many men are filled with the desire to get ahead. Some of them
get over the feeling in thirty minutes or less. Some of them have it

60 words   for thirty days, or perhaps a little longer. Those who want to get

1.3 si
ahead for thirty years, though, are the ones who become successful.
They find that patience pays.

Quick carriage return

92c • Problem Typing

30 minutes

Problem 1—Topic Outline

Directions – 1. Set the margin stops for a 60-space line. Type the main points at the left margin. Set and use tabulator stops for subpoints.

2. Use a standard 2-inch top margin.

3. Indent, space, capitalize, and punctuate exactly as shown in the problem. Two spaces follow the period after all numbered or lettered divisions.

• *Align Roman numerals in the outline at the period.*

TYPING BOUND MANUSCRIPTS

I. MARGINS

A. Left margin of 1½ inches
B. Right margin of 1 inch
C. Top margin of first page of 2 inches
D. Top margin of subsequent pages of 1 inch
E. Bottom margin of all pages of at least 1 inch
  1. At least 2 lines of paragraph at bottom of page
  2. At least 2 lines of paragraph carried forward to new page

II. SPACING

A. Double spacing of contents
B. Single spacing of quoted materials of 4 lines or more, footnotes, and bibliographical items
C. Triple spacing after the title

III. PAGE NUMBERS

A. Centered ½ inch from bottom of first page
B. Aligned with right margin ½ inch (4 line spaces) from top for pages following the first

			Words
Return address ——— Center point ——→	5883 Glaspell Street		4
	Davenport, Iowa 52804		9
Dateline ————————————→	February 16, 197-		12

		Words
Address	School of Journalism	17
	Drake University	20
	Des Moines, Iowa 50317	25
Salutation	Gentlemen	27

	Words
Will you please send copies of any booklets or	36
articles you may have on careers for reporters.	46

		Words
	Our general business class is making a study of	56
	careers, and I am definitely interested in becoming	66
Body	a newspaper reporter. I would like to know about	76
	the duties of a reporter, the training he needs,	87
	and the salary he can expect to receive.	94

	Words
I shall appreciate any help you can give me in	104
preparing for a career as a reporter.	111

		Words
Complimentary close ——— Center point ——→	Yours very truly	115
	Janet Taylor	
4th line space	Janet Taylor ←—— **Typed name**	117

This style, with minor variations, is used in almost all personal business letters. Open punctuation is used. Marks are omitted after the lines of the date, address, salutation, and complimentary close unless an abbreviation is used, in which case the period is typed as part of the abbreviation. A man should not use Mr. in his typed or handwritten name at the end of a letter. A woman may add her personal title to her signature. The title need not be used and is most often omitted.

Personal business letter in modified block style

91d • Speed Ladder Paragraphs • As directed in 76c, page 131

As directed in 76c, page 131

20 minutes

All letters

¶ 1 DS
36 words
1.3 si

Dune buggies are one of the latest fads to bloom in the desert sunshine. The frisky new sport of piloting a homemade jalopy over hill and dale can put some added zip in your life.

¶ 2
40 words
1.3 si

Buggies are put together from odds and ends of other vehicles. Some of them are long and pointed in shape. They may have fat airplane tires on the rear with extra-thin motorcycle tires in the front.

¶ 3
44 words
1.3 si

Drivers include youngsters as well as people in their sixties. Many dune buggy buffs bring the wife and kids to roam the sandy hills. Every buggy carries a flag on a pole to make it easy for drivers to spot each other.

¶ 4
48 words
1.3 si

The buggies come in quite a number of sizes, shapes, and colors. Their events include dune climbing and drag racing. Many provide jump seats behind mom and dad where children can scream in joyful terror as the bug roars down a steep dune.

¶ 5
52 words
1.3 si

Lovers of the new sport claim it's an ideal way to cure freeway frustrations. There are no traffic jams or signal lights. It's safe, too. The major danger is a collision with another bug, but this is

All ¶'s
1.3 si

unlikely as the flag pole can be seen even behind a dune.

GWAM	1'	5'
	13	3 47
	27	5 49
	36	7 51
	49	10 54
	63	13 57
	76	15 59
	89	18 62
	103	21 65
	117	23 67
	120	24 68
	133	27 71
	147	29 73
	162	32 76
	168	34 78
	181	36 80
	195	39 83
	209	42 86
	220	44 88

1' | 1 | 2 | 3 | 4 | 5 | 6 | 7 | 8 | 9 | 10 | 11 | 12 | 13 | 14 |
5' | 1 | 2 | 3 |

91e • Continuity Practice from Script • Type as many times as possible in the time that remains.

10 minutes

DS

All letters
60 words
1.3 si

There is a well-known quotation that tells us that we have not lived a full day unless we have done something for someone who will not be able to repay us. For a full life, just remember this old motto; live by it. Do something for somebody without expecting a prize of any kind for your efforts.

Words
12
25
37
50
60

48a • Keyboard Review • Each line three times
5 minutes

All letters   SS   Bob Jade was given extra maps quickly as he was in a frenzy.

Figure   The United States has a land area of 3,022,387 square miles.

Easy   Try using your head at a job before you try your hand at it.

| 1 | 2 | 3 | 4 | 5 | 6 | 7 | 8 | 9 | 10 | 11 | 12 |

Quick, sharp strokes

48b • Paragraph Guided Writings
10 minutes

Directions – 1. Set a speed goal for a 1-minute writing. Type three 1-minute writings. Try to type your goal word just as time is called. Type no faster or no slower than the goal you select.

2. Raise your goal by 8 words. Type three additional 1-minute writings. Try to reach your new goal as time is called. Your teacher may call the quarter- or half-minutes to guide you.

DS   Set a goal that is within your easy reach; try to hit

that goal exactly as the time is called. No need to type

40 words
1.3 si   any faster, but do not type any slower either. Merely set a

goal; hit it on the letter.

Read words
Think words
Type words

48c • Problem Typing
30 minutes

Full sheet
50-space line
Current date

Directions – Type the address on the 10th line space from the date. Use your address in the return address. Sign the letter.

• *When you supply the information, 11 words are counted for the heading, which includes the return address and date.*

Problem 1—Personal Business Letter in Modified Block Style

	Words
Coach Earl M. Dollahan	11
East High School	16
Your city, state, and ZIP Code	19
	25
Dear Coach Dollahan	29
As chairman of our Career Day, I wish to thank you	39
again for coming to our school to speak on "Health	49
Education as a Career."	54
We enjoyed hearing about the humorous events that	64
have occurred during your many years of coaching	74
as well as the sound advice you gave us about doing	85
well in our schoolwork. I am certain that all the	95
students at Paul Revere School now have a far better	105
understanding of the field of health education	115
than they did before you met with us.	123
Yours very truly	126

~~~~~~

BIBLIOGRAPHY

Triple-space ————————————————————————→

5-space ——→ Blough, Margaret, et al. Guide to Modern English 7. Glenview: Scott,
indention   Foresman and Company, 1968.
                                                            ←—————————————Double-space

Conlin, David A., George R. Herman, and Jerome Martin. Our Language
    Today 8. New York: American Book Company, 1966.

Mower, M. L., and L. Barney. "Which Are the Most Important Dictionary
    Skills?" Elementary English, (April, 1968), 468-71.

Warriner, John E., and Francis Griffith. English Grammar and Compo-
    sition, Grade 10. New York: Harcourt, Brace & World, Inc., 1963.

~~~~~~

Bibliography

• Lesson 91 • *70-space line*

91a • Keyboard Review • Each line at least three times   *5 minutes*

All letters SS Dozens of bombs exploded high over the quaint city just as dawn broke.
Figure-Symbol   Check #3904 (dated June 27) for $68 was sent to Brown & Son yesterday.   Type steadily
Adjacent keys   Their newer engineers were prepared there before November or December.
Easy   You have to use the right touch if you want to do good work in typing.
                 | 1 | 2 | 3 | 4 | 5 | 6 | 7 | 8 | 9 | 10 | 11 | 12 | 13 | 14 |

91b • Correcting Errors — Squeezing Letters   *5 minutes*

> • *If a letter has been omitted from the end of a word and no space has
> been allowed for it, you may make the correction by squeezing letters.*

Directions – 1. Type the line just as it appears   3. Depress the backspace key half way. Hold it.
below.   Type *n*.
2. Move the carriage to the space following *bee*.   4. Repeat the problem.

The error   - A letter has bee omitted at the end of a word.

The correction - A letter has been omitted at the end of a word.

91c • Number Expression Guides — Review   *5 minutes*

Directions – Type each sentence twice. The first line
gives the rule. The remaining lines apply it.

1   SS You must type all numbers used at the beginning of a sentence in full.
2   Thirty-six of our states now grow choice eating apples for the market.   Even stroking
3   Twenty-five thousand carloads are shipped from Washington in one year.
         | 1 | 2 | 3 | 4 | 5 | 6 | 7 | 8 | 9 | 10 | 11 | 12 | 13 | 14 |

Problem 2—Addressing Small Envelope

Directions – Address a small envelope for the letter on page 83. Fold the letter; insert it. Refer to the illustration below.

• *Use paper cut to envelope size (6½ by 3⅝ inches) if envelopes are not available.*

ADDRESSING A SMALL ENVELOPE

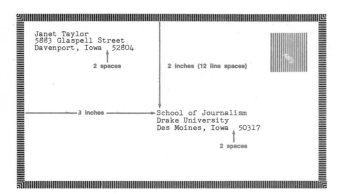

Janet Taylor
5883 Glaspell Street
Davenport, Iowa   52804

2 spaces

2 inches (12 line spaces)

3 inches

School of Journalism
Drake University
Des Moines, Iowa   50317

2 spaces

1. Type the writer's name and his return address in the upper left corner as shown in the illustration. Begin on the second line space from the top edge and 3 spaces from the left edge.
2. Type the receiver's name about 2 inches (12 line spaces) from the top of the envelope. Start about 3 inches from the left edge.
3. Use the block style and single spacing for all addresses. City and state names and ZIP Code (see p. 117) must be typed on one line in that order.
4. The new 2-letter state abbreviations may be used, or the state name may be typed in full or in the standard abbreviation.

FOLDING LETTERS FOR SMALL ENVELOPES

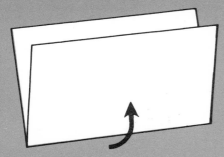

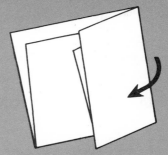

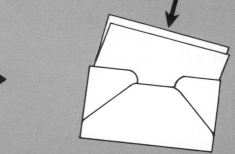

Step 1 – Fold the lower edge of the letter to within half an inch of the top.

Step 2 – Fold from right to left making the fold about one third the width of the sheet.

Step 3 – Fold from left to right, leaving about a half-inch margin at the right in order that the letter may be opened easily.

Step 4 – Insert the letter into the envelope so that the left-hand creased edge is inserted first and the last side folded is toward the backside of the envelope.

90a • Keyboard Review • Each line at least three times

5 minutes

All letters	SS	Very few citizens objected to our making plaques for the fall exhibit.
Figure		Mariner 4 flew a total distance of 325 million miles in only 228 days.
Shift		Mr. and Mrs. Carl Nelson and Dr. and Mrs. L. Dean Whitlow are in Reno.
Easy		A man has to give some thought to his work if he is to profit from it.

Cut out waste movements

| 1 | 2 | 3 | 4 | 5 | 6 | 7 | 8 | 9 | 10 | 11 | 12 | 13 | 14 |

90b • Timed Writings

10 minutes

Directions – Type a 1- and a 5-minute writing on 86d, page 147. Circle errors. Compute *gwam*.

90c • Problem Typing

30 minutes

Problem 1—Title Page

Directions – 1. Type the title page in the illustration at the right. It is a title page for the report that you typed in Lesson 89.

2. Follow the directions given on the illustration at the right. The data on the title page are given in larger print below. Type from the larger print.

USING THE DICTIONARY

By

Your name
Typewriting II

Current date

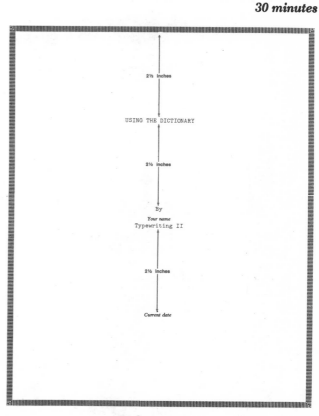

2½ inches

USING THE DICTIONARY

2½ inches

By
Your name
Typewriting II

2½ inches

Current date

Title page

Problem 2—Bibliography

Directions – 1. Type the bibliography shown on the next page. Use the same margins used in the body of the report. Start typing 2 inches from the top.

2. This is the bibliography for the report you typed in Lesson 89. Number this page as page 3. Place the title page you prepared in Problem 1 on top. Staple the entire report at the left.

Problem 3—Addressing Small Envelopes

Directions – 1. On six envelopes or paper cut to envelope size (6½ x 3⅝ inches), type the addresses below.

2. Learn to place the address on envelopes by sight.

Use spacing directions given on page 85 for the first three envelopes. Estimate the placement of the address on the last three envelopes.

3. Type your name and address as the sender.

Miss Dottie Davis
5588 Gulf Shores
Corpus Christi, TX   78411

Mr. James Hosler
15 Griffith Avenue
Memphis, Tenn.   38107

Leger Gallaries, Ltd.
13 Old Bond Street
London, W.1
ENGLAND

Mr. Raymond White
2199 Iroquois Avenue
Flint, Mich.   48503

Dr. Michael Wunsch
14477 Willmohr Street
Brooklyn, New York   11212

Foothills Sportswear
1200 First Street, S.W.
Calgary, Alberta
CANADA

• Lesson 49 • *60-space line*

49a • Keyboard Review • Each line three times

5 minutes

All letters   SS   Will paused to see the fox, jaguar, and zebras move quickly.

Figure-Symbol   The book, Phil's Hard Times, costs $5.70 at Brooking's Shop.

Easy   Tact is the knack of letting the other fellow have your way.

| 1 | 2 | 3 | 4 | 5 | 6 | 7 | 8 | 9 | 10 | 11 | 12 |

Type with your fingers

49b • Paragraph Guided Writings • As directed in 48b, page 84

10 minutes

DS   It has been said that a self-made man is the product of unskilled labor. True, some men achieve greatness without going to school very long. These men are the first to admit that they learned much from others and applied it to their jobs.

48 words
1.2 si

Quick, crisp, short strokes

49c • Problem Typing

30 minutes

Problem 1—Personal Business Letter in Modified Block Style, Paragraph Indentions, and Mixed Punctuation

Full sheet
50-space line
Mixed
    punctuation

Directions – 1. Type the letter on the next page in modified block style. Type the address on the 8th line space from the date.

2. Address an envelope. Fold and insert the letter.

• *In mixed punctuation, a colon follows the salutation; a comma follows the complimentary close. Other parts are punctuated as they are in open punctuation.*

USING THE DICTIONARY

The prime function of the dictionary, of course, is to promote accuracy—in spelling, pronunciation, and word division. According to authorities in the field, the dictionary provides a reliable way of getting answers to questions about words. You know that you will find the answers you need, and you will be sure they are right.[1]

Warriner says that the dictionary helps us in the following ways: [2]

Words printed in italics are underlined when typed

Spelling. The dictionary is the authority on correct spelling. If there are two spellings for a word, the preferred one is given first.

Capital Letters. The dictionary indicates when a word should or should not be capitalized.

Syllables. Dots or small dashes are used to divide a word into syllables.

Pronunciation. Special marks, usually explained at the bottom or top of each page, show how a word should be pronounced.

Part of Speech. An abbreviation after each word tells what part of speech the word is.

Derivation. The dictionary gives the origin of a word or the language from which it has come.

Meaning. Most words have several different meanings. You must seek out the particular one that fits the sentence in which you have found the word.

Slang, Colloquial, Obsolete, etc. When words are not considered in good usage, they are referred to as *slang*; *colloquial* means that the word may be used only in conversation or informal writing; a word no longer in common use is considered *obsolete*.

Synonyms and Antonyms. A *synonym* is a word which has nearly the same meaning as the word being defined. An *antonym* has the opposite meaning.

Illustrations. Pictures of the thing you are looking up may be shown if the object cannot be easily described.

Single-space ——
Double-space ——

[1]Margaret Blough, Mary Linehan MacKinnon, H. Alan Robinson, and Charlotte Wilson, Guide to Modern English 7 (Glenview: Scott, Foresman and Company, 1968), p. 66.

[2]John E. Warriner and Francis Griffith, English Grammar and Composition, Grade 10 (New York: Harcourt, Brace & World, Inc., 1963), pp. 285-91.

Word counts column: 17, 30, 44, 58, 71, 85, 100, 114, 130, 136, 151, 153, 169, 180, 196, 201, 217, 222, 236, 250, 253, 273, 291, 305, 315, 332, 347, 351, 367, 376, 380, 392, 412, 417, 435, 452, 454

Winthrop Junior High School 6
New Haven, Connecticut 06511 12
November 15, 197— 15

Dr. William Gibbs, Chairman 21
Christmas Fund Drive 25
1913 Whittlesey Avenue 30
New Haven, Connecticut 06514 36

Dear Dr. Gibbs: 39

This is an offer on the part of the Teen-Age 48
Club of our school to help you in the Christmas 58
Fund Drive this year. 62

We are aware of the fine reputation the Drive 72
has earned under your leadership. There is a lot of 82
hard work involved, and our club can do a great deal 93
to ease the burden of busy people such as yourself. 103

Perhaps we could best serve in the sorting and 113
packaging phase of the drive since we could not take 123
part in soliciting funds. However, we shall do what- 134
ever you think we could best do. 141

Please let me know if we can help you. 149

Yours very truly, 152

Wilmert Perkins, President 158
Teen-Age Club 160

Problem 2—Personal Business Letter from Unarranged Copy

Full sheet
50-space line
Indented ¶'s
Mixed punctuation
Current date

Directions – Type the letter in modified block style. Type the address on the 8th line space from the date. Address an envelope. Fold and insert the letter.

• *The lines in the problem are not set line-for-line the way you will type them. Set the margin stops properly; return your carriage with the bell.*

Return Address—Madison School / Selma, Alabama 36701
Address—Mr. Russell Duval / President, Hi-Y Club / Ashton School / Selma, Alabama 36701

Dear Russell:

Plans are going ahead for the Hi-Y Conference to be held at Bragg Park next weekend.

Will you please send the name of the luncheon chairman and the name of the person who will be in charge of the games in the afternoon. We shall need this information for the printing of the program.

Six schools are now signed up to send delegates. Each one will have at least eight members in attendance. It looks like a good conference, and we all appreciate the time and work you are putting into this meeting.

Sincerely,

Art Godfrey

89a • Keyboard Review • Each line at least three times

All letters	SS	Jasper seized an extra arrow from my quiver and shot at the big flock.
Figure		One man hit 199 out of 200 tries in the 1934 clay target championship.
Long words		This was a challenging message, representing another appeal to thrift.
Easy		Remember that no person can be blamed for advice that he did not give.

| 1 | 2 | 3 | 4 | 5 | 6 | 7 | 8 | 9 | 10 | 11 | 12 | 13 | 14 |

Elbows in

89b • Skill Comparison

Directions – Type two 1-minute writings on each sentence. Try to type all sentences at the rate set on the first one.

Easy	SS	It is said by many that I have but to start a job to get it half done.
Figure-Symbol		V. Brumel holds the world's record high jump (at 7 feet 5 3/4 inches).
Shift		Henry D. Holden visited the Smithsonian Institute in Washington, D. C.
Rough draft		Only the man who is abel to see teh invisable will the impossibly.

| 1 | 2 | 3 | 4 | 5 | 6 | 7 | 8 | 9 | 10 | 11 | 12 | 13 | 14 |

Think as you type

DIRECTIONS FOR TYPING BOUND MANUSCRIPTS

• *The directions given here apply to typing theses, formal reports, and other manuscripts bound at the left. Use these directions in typing the reports and compositions that follow.*

1. Set margin stops for a 1½-inch left margin (pica, 15 spaces; elite, 18 spaces) and a 1-inch right margin (pica, 10 spaces; elite, 12 spaces).

   • *Move the center point 3 spaces to the right to allow for the wider left margin.*

2. On all but the first page, leave 1-inch top and bottom margins.

3. Type the title in all capital letters 2 inches from the top of the first page. Triple-space after it.

4. Long quotations (4 line spaces), footnotes, and bibliographical items should be single spaced.

Long quotations should be indented 5 spaces from each margin. Double-space the remainder of the report.

5. If the first page is numbered, center the number ½ inch from the bottom. The following pages are numbered ½ inch (4 line spaces) from the top of the page and aligned with the right margin. Triple-space after typing the page number; type the body of the report.

6. At least 2 lines of a paragraph must appear at the bottom of a page, and at least 2 lines of a paragraph should be carried forward to a new page.

89c • Problem Typing

Problem—Two-Page Report to Be Bound at the Left

Directions – 1. Type the following two-page report. Use the directions given above; number both pages.

2. Type the footnotes at the bottom of the first page of your typed report.

50a • **Keyboard Review** • Each line three times

5 minutes

All letters	SS	Rex Walters may give the quaint box to Jack for third prize.
Figure-Symbol		They bought the costumes from Henry Flood & Son for $160.25.
Easy		Remember that the kind words we use are seldom used in vain.

| 1 | 2 | 3 | 4 | 5 | 6 | 7 | 8 | 9 | 10 | 11 | 12 |

Type steadily

ADDRESSING LARGE ENVELOPES

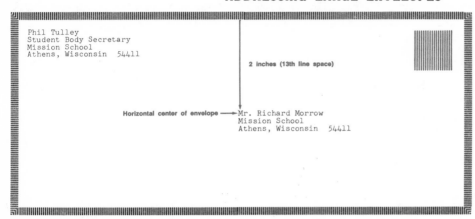

Phil Tulley
Student Body Secretary
Mission School
Athens, Wisconsin 54411

2 inches (13th line space)

Horizontal center of envelope ──► Mr. Richard Morrow
Mission School
Athens, Wisconsin 54411

A large envelope (9½ by 4⅛ inches) is usually typed for business letters with enclosures, or for letters of more than one page. Type the address 2 inches from the top and at the horizontal center of the envelope. Directions for spacing the address and using abbreviations for the state name and the ZIP Code are given on page 78.

FOLDING LETTERS FOR LARGE ENVELOPES

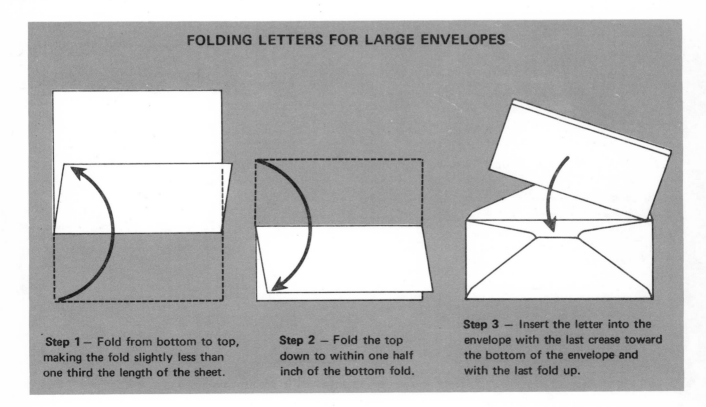

Step 1 — Fold from bottom to top, making the fold slightly less than one third the length of the sheet.

Step 2 — Fold the top down to within one half inch of the bottom fold.

Step 3 — Insert the letter into the envelope with the last crease toward the bottom of the envelope and with the last fold up.

HOW TO MAKE AN OUTLINE

"The first step in organizing your report," says a recent

English book, "is to think carefully about the subject you have

selected and to jot down a rough outline or list of the main

topics you think you will want to cover."[1] Making an outline is

a way of organizing your information into a logical sequence.

Outlines may be one of two kinds--a topic outline or a

sentence outline. In a topic outline each part is a word, phrase,

or clause. In a sentence outline the topics and subtopics are

expressed in a complete sentence.

USING GOOD ENGLISH presents a list of helps for preparing an

outline.[2] The following points are included:

1. Use Roman numerals to designate the main topics in
   your outline.

2. Use capital letters in alphabetical order to designate
   the subtopics under a main topic.

3. Use Arabic numerals to designate points under the
   topics that are marked with capital letters.

4. Use small letters to designate subpoints under points
   that are marked with Arabic numerals.

5. Whenever you divide a topic or subtopic, be sure you
   have at least two items under the topic you are
   dividing.

[1]Mildred A. Dawson, Eric W. Johnson, Marian Zollinger, and
M. Ardell Elwell, Language for Daily Use (New York: Harcourt,
Brace & World, Inc., 1966), p. 223.

[2]Harold G. Shane, Kathleen B. Hester, Mary York, Marion L.
Street, and Stanley Peterson, Using Good English, Junior High
School Book Two (River Forest: Laidlow Brothers, 1967), p. 312.

First page of theme with footnotes

50b • Problem Typing

Problem 1—Personal Business Letter in Block Style

50-space line
Open punctuation

• *The symbol (¶) stands for a new paragraph.*

Directions – Type the address on the 9th line space from the date. Address a large envelope with a return address in the upper left corner as shown on page 88.

• *An enclosure notation is used when a paper (or papers) is sent with the letter. Type the notation at the left margin a double space below the name of the sender or his title. Use the plural, Enclosures, if two or more items will be enclosed.*

Return address—Mission School / Athens, Wisconsin   54411 / January 6, 197—
Address—Mr. Richard Morrow / Mission School / Athens, Wisconsin   54411

Dear Coach Morrow

Congratulations! We have just received word that our team won the Soroka Sportsmanship Trophy at the Christmas Holiday Tournament in Madison. (¶) The student body is very proud of our team and of you, the coach. The students, teachers, and others who saw our boys play in Madison are still talking about the team's hard, clean play. (¶) I saw the game with Monroe and took a number of pictures. Prints of three of them are enclosed. I think that they are quite good. Sincerely yours

Phil Tulley
Student Body Secretary
                Double-space
Enclosures

Personal business letter in block style

Problem 2—Personal Business Letter in Block Style

Block style
50-space line
Open punctuation

Directions – Type the address on the 9th line space from the date. Address a large envelope. Type the return address on the envelope. Fold and insert the letter.

Return address—914 State Street / Rutland, Vermont   05701 / May 1, 197—
Address—Mr. John Hart / 920 Camden Drive / Rutland, Vermont   05701

Dear Mr. Hart

I am applying for a job at Bishop Lodge in Newport for the summer months and need three letters of reference. (¶) Will you please write one of these letters. As you know, I have been delivering the *Rutland Times* to your home for the past year. I would like to spend the summer at Bishop Lodge and need the job to go there. (¶) The letter should be sent to Mr. Ted Barnes, Manager, Bishop Lodge, Newport, Vermont   05855. I am enclosing a copy of the letter received from Mr. Barnes and shall appreciate your writing to him.

Yours very truly / Michael Agnew / Enclosure

				G W A M
				1' 5'

All letters
¶ 1
60 words
1.3 si

DS   Perhaps you don't think you could ever be tempted by a bargain   13   3 38

that seems just too good to pass up or be deceived by a fast-talking   26   5 40

salesman. Do not be too sure about that. Neither did thousands of   40   8 43

others who each year have had to make complaints to better business   54 11 46

bureaus or chambers of commerce.   60 12 47

¶ 2
60 words
1.3 si

    How can you keep from becoming the victim of a gyp artist? The   13 15 50

most important rule is to deal only with salesmen or stores that are   27 17 52

familiar to you, your neighbors, or your friends. If you don't know   40 20 55

a man who calls on you, question what he says. Be extremely wary if   54 23 58

your questions go unanswered.   60 24 59

¶ 3
55 words
1.3 si

    You should also realize the dangers in buying or in signing for   13 27 62

something before you have had time to check out the firm with which you   27 29 64

All ¶'s
1.3 si

are dealing. Try not to take needless chances. A good plan is not to   41 32 67

buy until you have compared prices for the same kind of merchandise.   55 35 70

1' | 1 | 2 | 3 | 4 | 5 | 6 | 7 | 8 | 9 | 10 | 11 | 12 | 13 | 14 |
5' | 1   2   3 |

DIRECTIONS FOR TYPING FOOTNOTES

- *All important statements of fact or opinion and all direct quotations that are taken from books or articles for use in a theme must have footnotes. Footnotes give complete information about the references from which materials were taken.*

1. Make a light pencil mark in the margin to indicate where the divider line will be typed.

- *Although footnotes vary in length, in general the following system works well for determining where the divider line should be typed: (a) make a light pencil mark for the 1-inch bottom margin, (b) from this pencil mark space up 3 line spaces for each footnote and once for the divider line, (c) make a second light pencil mark—the point at which the divider line should be typed.*

2. After typing the last line of a full page of copy, space once; then use the underline key to type a 1½-inch divider line.

3. After typing the divider line, double-space; type the footnote reference.

4. Single-space the footnotes and place a double space between them.

- *On a page only partially full, the footnotes appear at the bottom of the page.*

88d • Problem Typing

25 minutes

Problem—First Page of Theme with Footnotes

Directions – Type the first page of the theme illustrated on page 151. Use theme style. Follow the form shown in the illustration.

50c • Timed Writings

15 minutes

Directions – 1. Type a 3-minute writing. Compute your *gwam*.
2. Type two 1-minute writings on each paragraph; the first for speed, the second for control.

3. Finally, type another 3-minute writing on all paragraphs. Compute your *gwam*. Compare the *gwam* and number of errors for the two 3-minute writings.

	GWAM 1'	3'

All letters
¶ 1   DS   Being courteous does not mean that you must always agree — 1⅓ 4 45
36 words
1.3 si   with others. You have a mind, and you are expected to use it. — 24 8 49

Keep in mind though that others must enjoy the same chance. — 36 12 53

¶ 2   You must learn to state your own views correctly. Do — 11 16 57
42 words
1.2 si   not call another who does not see things as you do a zany — 22 19 60

fool, a bully, or a liar. That's the quickest way to declare — 35 24 65

a war and the surest way to lose it. — 42 26 67

¶ 3   Learn to admit that the ideas of others may have some — 11 30 71
46 words
1.3 si   merit. Be willing to listen to them. Don't quibble over — 22 33 74

small points. If you have some facts to support your ideas, — 35 38 79

All ¶'s
1.3 si   give them. Few men will question your right to be heard. — 46 41 82

1' | 1 | 2 | 3 | 4 | 5 | 6 | 7 | 8 | 9 | 10 | 11 | 12 |
3' | 1 | 2 | 3 | 4 |

50d • Extra-Credit Typing

Problem 1

Directions – 1. Type the timed writing in 50c as a short report. Provide a title; type it in all capital letters.

2. Use a 60-space line; double-space the body.
3. Center the entire report vertically on a full sheet.

Problem 2

Directions – 1. Assume that you are John Hart in the letter in Problem 2, page 89. Write the kind of letter about Michael Agnew (the writer of the letter in the problem) that you would like to have written about you if you were applying for the job.

2. Type the letter in modified block style, blocked paragraphs, mixed punctuation. Date it for May 5, 197–. Use personal titles as needed.
3. Address a small envelope. Fold and insert the letter.

Problem 3

Directions – 1. Address large envelopes for each of the addresses given in Problem 3, page 86.

2. Type your name and address as the sender on all the envelopes.

Problem 2—Short Report with Indented Items

Directions – Set the margin stops for a 60-space line. Double-space the report; single-space numbered paragraphs. Indent numbered paragraphs 5 spaces from each margin and double-space between them. Spread the heading.

IMPROMPTU SPEAKING

You will be called upon many times to give a talk on the spur of the moment. You might be asked to give a short report on a book, trip, or play. You might be called upon to make an announcement or present a gift to a teacher. If you found yourself on one of these spots, could you deliver?

A plan for an impromptu talk is always helpful. Here is such a plan:

1. Make a statement that gets attention. If you can't think of anything else, tell your group that you are glad to tell them about your subject. Being glad in this situation is unique enough to draw some attention.

2. Explain why your subject is important to the group.

3. Make two or three general statements about your subject. Illustrate each with a few examples. Cite interesting cases. Describe them vividly.

4. Summarize your ideas. Do this quickly. Don't let your talk drag—especially at the end.

The ability to give a brief talk on almost any subject on short notice can be very profitable to you. You will be envied by everyone. Practice giving this type of talk. Collect your wits; think fast; organize your ideas. Prepare your talk along the lines suggested in the plan just described.

• Lesson 88 • *70-space line*

88a • Keyboard Review • Each line at least three times   *5 minutes*

All letters SS   The objective was to organize and make plans for an exquisite display.

Figure-Symbol   They should have purchased a Model #7F-205 for less than $314 in 1968.   Quick, crisp, short strokes

Vowels—o, i   The anxious seniors outside noticed commotion coming from his offices.

Easy   They cannot stop men and women from thinking, but they can start them.

| 1 | 2 | 3 | 4 | 5 | 6 | 7 | 8 | 9 | 10 | 11 | 12 | 13 | 14 |

88b • Correcting Errors — Squeezing Letters   *5 minutes*

• *This problem shows you how to add an omitted letter to the beginning of a word when no space has been allowed for it.*

Directions – 1. Type the line just as it appears below.

2. Move the carriage to the *m* in *mitted*.

3. Depress the backspace key half way. Hold it. Type *o*.

4. Repeat the problem.

The error   - A letter has been mitted at the beginning of a word.

The correction - A letter has been omitted at the beginning of a word.

Typing Themes and Outlines

General Directions • Lessons 51 – 60

Machine Adjustments – Except as otherwise directed, use a 60-space line. Single-space lines of words and sentences, but double-space between repeated groups of lines. Double-space paragraph copy.

Erasing Errors – Your teacher will tell you if you are to erase and correct errors on problem typing.

• Lesson 51

51a • Keyboard Review • Each line three times

5 minutes

All letters	SS	Bud Roper may take this quiz next week if Jack will give it.
Figure-Symbol		Send us 4,500 copies of Form #39. We need them by March 27.
Easy		It will pay you to learn what you are to do before you type.

| 1 | 2 | 3 | 4 | 5 | 6 | 7 | 8 | 9 | 10 | 11 | 12 |

Type steadily

51b • Spelling and Proofreading Aid • Each line three times

5 minutes

1	SS	opera naughty double quality really battery calendar foreign
2		abrupt similar report told affect magnet tongue succeed toll
3		hostile elastic loose truly desire plum grammar sought cries

Wrists and elbows still

51c • Technique Builder — Stroking • Each line three times

5 minutes

One-hand	SS	Fred gave Lynn Waters a red scarf. John Holly was defeated.
Balanced-hand		Do sign the eight forms so the busy men may handle this job.
Long reach		Brad Browne hunted in the humid brush for a mysterious bird.

| 1 | 2 | 3 | 4 | 5 | 6 | 7 | 8 | 9 | 10 | 11 | 12 |

Quick, sharp strokes

51d • Paragraph Guided Writings

10 minutes

Directions – 1. Set a speed goal for a 1-minute writing. Type three 1-minute writings. Try to type your goal word just as time is called. Type no faster or no slower than the goal you select.

2. Raise your goal by 8 words. Type three additional 1-minute writings. Try to reach your new goal as time is called. Your teacher may call the quarter- or half-minutes to guide you.

DS

An expert is someone who can call his shot and make it. He hits his mark every time. How about trying the same stunt in typing? Can you type at your goal rate? If you can, you can do what the expert does. He hits the target every time.

48 words
1.2 si

Flowing, rhythmic stroking

• Lesson 87 • *70-space line*

87a • Keyboard Review • Each line at least three times

5 minutes

All letters	SS	Lee knew my expensive habits jeopardized chances for making the quota.
Figure		Ted Williams, who hit .406 in 1941, was the last player to reach .400.
Double letters		Bill succeeded in getting the committee's message to the office staff.
Easy		Now is the time for more of them to make their plans for their future.

Fingers deeply curved

| 1 | 2 | 3 | 4 | 5 | 6 | 7 | 8 | 9 | 10 | 11 | 12 | 13 | 14 |

87b • Control Ladder Paragraphs

10 minutes

Directions – Type 1-minute writings on the paragraphs in 86d, page 147. When you can type a paragraph without error, move to the next one. Type with control.

87c • Problem Typing

30 minutes

Problem 1—One-Page Report

Directions – Type the report in regular theme style. Set the margin stops for a 60-space line. Follow spacing directions given on the illustration below.

A BOOK TO SETTLE ARGUMENTS

You may find it hard to believe that the fastest time for demolishing an upright piano and passing the entire wreckage through a ring nine inches in diameter is just under five minutes. Believe it or not, two college fraternity members turned the trick way back in 1963.

Such interesting, if somewhat impractical, bits of information are contained in the GUINNESS BOOK OF WORLD RECORDS, a publication that lists almost every conceivable type of record that might have been set anywhere by anybody.

Take the world's record for continuous talking, for instance. According to this book, an Irishman by the name of Kevin Sheehan once talked for 133 hours straight. Interestingly enough, the women's record for a similar feat is under 96 hours. Even the longest political speech required less than 30 hours.

Since the record book was first published, more than two million copies have been sold. Because records change so often, many revised editions have had to be printed. One of the editions, for example, listed the world teeter-totter record as only 101 hours. A reader was quick to point out that a community college team from Michigan really deserves the credit for their 121 hours of non-stop seesawing.

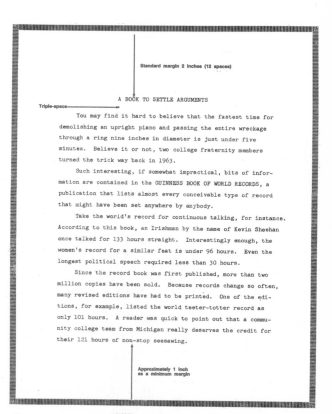

One-page report

51e • Timed Writings

Directions – Type 1-, 2-, and 3-minute writings on the copy below. Repeat. Try to equal your 1-minute rates on the longer writings.

Technique Goals – Feet on the floor; body relaxed, but erect. Fingers deeply curved; wrists low and still. Keep your eyes on the copy.

• *For the 2-minute rate, divide the 1-minute GWAM by 2.*

		GWAM		
		1′		3′

DS

Benjamin Franklin is well known for his common-sense **11 4 44**
"quotable quotes." They are often used. For example, he **22 7 47**
once wrote that we should beware of little expenses, for a **34 11 51**
small leak would sink a big ship. We learn every day that **46 15 55**
it is the little things in life that count. We are what we **58 19 59**
are because of a great many little things we do—or forget **70 23 63**
to do. **71 24 64**

He who turns his lessons in late is known as a poor stu- **82 27 67**
dent. A few misspelled words in a theme are certain to bring **94 31 71**
a low grade to an otherwise good report. It is indeed true **106 35 75**
that a small-sized leak will sink a big ship—or damage one's **119 40 80**
career. **120 40 80**

All letters
120 words
1.3 si

```
1' |  1  |  2  |  3  |  4  |  5  |  6  |  7  |  8  |  9  | 10  | 11  | 12  |
3' |        1        |        2        |        3        |        4        |
```

51f • Control Practice

Directions – 1. Type the last paragraph of 51e, above, as many times as you can in the time that remains.

2. Circle your errors. Place a check mark (√) in the margin of each paragraph in which you made no more than one error.

• Lesson 52 • *60-space line*

52a • Keyboard Review • Each line three times

All letters   SS   By having zeal, Jan Frame gets her expert work done quickly.

Figure-Symbol   Don't type the decimal point and zeros in a sum like $8,572.

Easy   If you wish to think well of yourself, think well of others.

Fingers
deeply
curved

52b • Typing from Dictation and Spelling Checkup

Directions – Type the words in 51b, page 91, from your teacher's dictation. Check for correct spelling. Retype any words in which you made an error.

86d • Speed Ladder Paragraphs • As directed in 76c, page 131

		GWAM
		1' 5'

All letters

¶ 1
36 words
1.3 si

DS Today it seems quite natural for us to shake hands when we greet   13 3 47

a person. Like lots of things that we do without thinking, such an   27 5 49

action at one time likely symbolized something.   36 7 51

¶ 2
40 words
1.3 si

In primitive life the hand was probably a symbol of power. It   49 10 54

was used to fight enemies and to make spears. When extended, the hand   63 13 57

might have meant good will by showing that a person was not armed.   76 15 59

¶ 3
44 words
1.3 si

We know that the hand played a major role in early religions. The   89 18 62

Greeks prayed to their gods with raised hands. Presenting the hands,   103 21 65

palm to palm, was at one time how an inferior person paid homage to a   117 23 67

superior one.   120 24 68

¶ 4
48 words
1.3 si

In these days there are still a number of different ways to shake   133 27 71

hands throughout the world. Among certain groups, one rubs his palms   147 29 73

together. There are chiefs in some African tribes who snap the middle   161 32 76

finger three times when greeting.   168 34 78

¶ 5
52 words
1.3 si

We can easily see that the hand, and what was done with it, has   181 36 80

been full of meaning all through the ages. Although today it is very   195 39 83

common for most of us to shake hands without even thinking, we are   208 42 86

\lll ¶'s
.3 si

really carrying on a custom handed down from ancient times.   220 44 88

```
1' |  1  |  2  |  3  |  4  |  5  |  6  |  7  |  8  |  9  | 10  | 11  | 12  | 13  | 14  |
5' |        1        |        2        |        3        |
```

86e • Continuity Practice from Script • Type the paragraph as many times as you can in the time that remains.

	Words
DS A sign in a big city zoo informs visitors that it would be possible	14
to build one more needed monkey house with the money it takes just to	28
60 words pick up litter. This sum is peanuts compared to the millions of dollars	42
1.3 si it costs to scoop up litter from our streets, parks, beaches, and public	57
areas each year.	60

52c • Paragraph Skill Builder from Rough Draft

5 minutes

Directions – Type the paragraph once for practice; then type three 1-minute writings on it. Circle your errors; figure the *gwam*. Compare your best rate with the highest rate reached on 51d, page 91.

		Words	
DS	Teh most harm ful things man has ~~yet~~ invented todate is	11	62
All letters	the excuse. if your question ~~these~~ this points of view, just size up	24	75
51 words	the man who is ~~good~~ adept at making them. You will ~~then~~ soon agree that	36	87
1.3 si	he lacks skil in any thing else; but he is always rady--with an	49	100
	exucse.	51	102

VERTICAL CENTERING SHORTCUT

1. Insert paper to Line 33, the vertical center. Roll the cylinder back (toward you) once for each two lines in the copy to be typed. This will place the copy in *exact vertical center*.
2. To type a problem in *off-center* or *reading position*, roll the cylinder back three more times.

3. If you wish, you can square the edges of the paper from top to bottom and make a slight crease at the right edge. The crease will be at the vertical center (Line 33). Insert the paper to the crease, roll back once for each two lines to the position for typing.

52d • Problem Typing

30 minutes

Problem 1—Poem Typed in Centered Position

Directions – 1. Full sheet. Center the poem vertically. Double-space after each 2 lines. Center the poem horizontally by the 4th line, which is the longest.

2. Type the author's name to end at the right margin with the longest line.

Problem 2—Poem Typed in Reading Position

Directions – Type the poem in Problem 1 again. This time type it in *reading position*.

Trees

Triple-space

I think that I shall never see
A poem lovely as a tree.

Double-space

A tree whose hungry mouth is pressed
Against the earth's sweet flowing breast;

A tree that looks to God all day,
And lifts her leafy arms to pray;

A tree that may in summer wear
A nest of robins in her hair;

Upon whose bosom snow has lain;
Who intimately lives with rain.

Poems are made by fools like me,
But only God can make a tree.

Double-space

-- Joyce Kilmer

Typing School Reports

General Directions • Lessons 86 – 100

Machine Adjustments – For the lessons in this unit, use a 70-space line. Single-space lines of words and sentences, but double-space between repeated groups of lines. Double-space paragraph copy.

Erasing Errors – Your teacher will tell you whether or not you are to erase and correct errors on the problems of this unit. She will also tell you whether or not you may use the suggestions presented in this unit for correcting errors by "squeezing" and "spreading" letters and typing insertions.

• Lesson 86

86a • Keyboard Review • Each line at least three times

5 minutes

All letters SS The jovial banquet speaker excited and amazed a large crowd of youths.

Figure Charles Lindbergh crossed the Atlantic in 33 hours 39 minutes in 1927.

Quick, sharp strokes

4th finger lamp palm quiz zipper pail lap soap group pupil people palace pit quit

Easy Wise men are like pins; their heads will keep them from going too far.

| 1 | 2 | 3 | 4 | 5 | 6 | 7 | 8 | 9 | 10 | 11 | 12 | 13 | 14 |

86b • Alignment of Paper — Horizontal and Vertical

5 minutes

Directions – 1. Type the following sentence.

This job requires high skill.

2. Note the relationship of the top of the aligning scale to the bottom of the letters. Note also how the white lines on the scale line up with the letters "i" and "l" in the typewritten matter.

3. Remove the paper from the machine and reinsert it in position to type over the first typing.

4. Align horizontally first by using the paper-release lever and moving the paper to the left or right until the lines on the scale are brought into alignment with the letters "i" and "l."

5. Align vertically using the variable line spacer.

6. Retype the sentence over the first writing.

7. Repeat the problem.

86c • Typing "Spread" Headings

5 minutes

Directions – Spread and center each heading given at the right. The first line is typed in correct form.

1. Backspace from the midpoint once for each letter, except the last one in the line, and once for each space between words.

2. Type the heading. Space once between letters and three times between words.

```
T Y P I N G   H E A D I N G S

THE FIRST PHOTOGRAPH

A VACATION TRIP

THE SPACE AGE

APRIL FOOL
```

• Lesson 53 • *60-space line*

53a • Keyboard Review • Each line three times

All letters   SS   Four experts quickly amazed the crowd by juggling five axes.

Figure   Type distances in figures: I drove 8,634½ miles in 27 days.   Space quickly

Easy   It is easy to fight for ideals, but hard to live up to them.

| 1 | 2 | 3 | 4 | 5 | 6 | 7 | 8 | 9 | 10 | 11 | 12 |

53b • Paragraph Guided Writings • As directed in 51d, page 91

10 minutes

DS   To err is human, but when the eraser wears out before

48 words
1.2 si   the pencil, beware! Always do your work as well as you can   Quick carriage return

do it. You must know that smart people are the ones who have

short pencils with long erasers. They can think as they work.

53c • Problem Typing

30 minutes

Problem—One-Page Report or Theme

Directions – 1. Type the report on page 95. Use a 60-space line. Indent paragraphs five spaces.

2. Double-space the body of the report. Center the report vertically on a full sheet.

• Lesson 54 • *60-space line*

54a • Keyboard Review • Each line three times

5 minutes

All letters   SS   Jack Paxton might visit the quiet city of Bern, Switzerland.

Figure   An 8½ by 11-inch sheet contains 85 pica or 102 elite spaces.   Elbows in

Easy   Be alert! Do not miss out while the others are finding out.

| 1 | 2 | 3 | 4 | 5 | 6 | 7 | 8 | 9 | 10 | 11 | 12 |

54b • Technique Builder — Stroking • Each line three times

10 minutes

Hyphen   SS   The left-handed pitcher can be sure-footed and clear-headed.

One-hand   saw him, refer you, we are, look upon, as you are, my grades

Weak fingers   Zane Pepper will acquire the apparatus for the player piano.

Balanced-hand   they may, with them, for the, and then, if she, and did work   Type with your fingers

Combination   and see, the case, with only, for him, may look, he saw them

Double letters   I shipped the books to the committee that equipped the room.

| 1 | 2 | 3 | 4 | 5 | 6 | 7 | 8 | 9 | 10 | 11 | 12 |

• Lesson 85 • *70-space line*

85a • Keyboard Review • Each line at least three times

All letters	SS	Johnny quickly vowed never to forget his ZIP Code or box number again.
Figure-Symbol		Maps on pages 434 & 435 use the asterisk (*) to denote state capitals.
Home keys		Older hardware dealers definitely declined to indicate delivery dates.
Easy		Always keep your goal in view, and you can reach the top in your work.

Instant release

| 1 | 2 | 3 | 4 | 5 | 6 | 7 | 8 | 9 | 10 | 11 | 12 | 13 | 14 |

85b • Timed Writings

10 minutes

Directions – Type a 1- and a 5-minute writing on 81d, page 138. Circle errors. Compute *gwam*.

85c • Problem Typing

30 minutes

Problem—Club Schedule

Directions – Type the following club schedule on a half sheet. Center the main heading one inch from the top. Use double spacing. Leave eight spaces between columns.

• *You may need to review the steps in arranging tables, page 109, and the steps for centering columnar headings, page 118.*

BRIDGE CLUB SCHEDULE

Month	Hostess	Co-hostess
October	Madeline Swanson	Ellen Sloan
November	Ruby Jones	Grace Naakes
December	Jean Strong	Jean Hull
January	Louise Murphy	Sally Hagen
February	Marian Kremen	Carol Lippey
March	Barbara Dodds	Audrey Brewer
April	Valerie Camegys	Dorothy Coe
May	Shirley Donald	Ann Van Velder

85d • Extra-Credit Typing

Problem 1

Directions – Assume that you were a weekend guest in a friend's home. On 4¼- by 5½-inch stationery, write a "bread and butter" note to your friend's mother.

Problem 2

Directions – Type the letter in Problem 1, page 142, in modified block style with indented paragraphs and mixed punctuation on 8½- by 11-inch paper. Arrange the letter neatly.

Problem 3

Directions – Type the letter in Problem 1, page 140, in modified block style with indented paragraphs and mixed punctuation on a full sheet. Arrange it neatly.

TYPING A SHORT REPORT OR THEME

Triple-space ⟶

Short reports or themes of one page or less may be typed   18
with a 60-space line. If the number of lines can be counted   30
easily, center the copy vertically; if not, use a standard   42
margin of 2 inches (12 line spaces) at the top.   51

Double spacing is usually used in themes and reports.   62
Class notes, book reviews, and minutes are usually single-   74
spaced to provide better groupings of information.   84

Every report should have a title which is typed in all   95
capital letters. It is always separated from the body by a   107
triple-space.   110

Longer reports or papers are usually typed with side   121
margins of 1 inch. When the paper is to be bound at the   132
left, however, an extra one-half inch must be provided in   144
the left margin for binding.   150

The heading is typed 2 inches from the top of the first   161
page. All pages after the first have a top margin of 1 inch.   174
The bottom margin should not be less than 1 inch. The copy   186
usually looks better if this margin runs an extra one-half   198
inch.   199

◄─────────── 60-space line ───────────►

One-page theme

Problem 2—Order Letter in Modified Block Style

Full sheet
50-space line
Indented ¶'s
Mixed punctuation

• *See page 89 for the correct placement of the enclosure notation.*

Directions – 1. Type the letter as a personal business letter in modified block style. Type the address on the 9th line space from the date.

2. Type the ordered items as a table in a 40-space line. (Merely set the left margin stop in 5 spaces. Set the carriage at the right margin less 5 spaces; then backspace once for each letter in the longest item in the second column. Set the tab stop at this point for the second column.)

3. Prepare a carbon copy. Address a large envelope. Fold the letter; insert it into the envelope.

Return address—450 Elwood Drive / Moorhead, Minnesota 56560 / November 29, 197—

Address—Weber & Byde, Inc. / 3819 Herndon Avenue / St. Paul, Minnesota 55110

Gentlemen

Please send me the following tools you have advertised in the December issue of <u>Shop News</u>. I understand that by ordering now I can be sure of having them in time for Christmas.

Crosscut saw	$10.25
Keyhole saw	1.65
Curved claw hammer	2.40
Deluxe hand drill	5.85
Total	$20.15

Enclosed is a check for $20.15. According to your advertisement, the postage on these items will be prepaid.

Sincerely yours

Andy Houtz

Enclosure

Order form

Problem 3—Order

Directions – 1. Type a copy of the order exactly as it appears in the illustration above.

2. Use the variable line spacer and the top of the alignment scale to adjust the paper correctly for each line of copy. An order form is included in your workbook.

Alternate Suggestion

If a workbook is not available, order the items in Problem 3 by order letter similar to the one typed for Problem 2.

Carbon Copies

To make carbon copies, place the carbon paper (with glossy side down) on a sheet of plain paper. The paper on which you will prepare the original is then laid on the carbon paper, and all the sheets are inserted into the typewriter. The *dull* surface of the carbon sheet should be toward you when the sheets have been rolled into the typewriter. Erasing on carbon copies is explained on page xii.

> • *Carbon copies are called for in this lesson. Your teacher will tell you if you are to prepare carbon copies in any other lessons in this unit.*

54c • Spelling and Proofreading Aid   5 minutes

1   ss   develop liable safety replies film urge across memory lesson

2   changing doctor budget piece laborer color suing mining omit   Think as you type

3   awkward weather guess occupy knowledge fourth familiar ghost

54d • Problem Typing   25 minutes

Problem—Short Report or Theme

60-space line
Double spacing

Directions – Use a standard 2-inch top margin (12 line spaces). Make one carbon copy.

	Words
HOW TO GET HIGHER GRADES IN YOUR CLASSES	8

Ask questions. If you don't understand an explanation, get help from your teacher, either in class or after classes are over. Teachers often wonder why students don't ask for help when they need it.   21 / 36 / 49

Raise your hand. Take an active part in class discussions. You may not always be right, but it is better for you to test your views than it is to sit in complete silence.   62 / 77 / 83

Get assignments straight. Teachers are always amazed at the number of students who turn in wrong assignments. Write them down. If you have any doubts, check with your teacher.   97 / 112 / 119

Make up missed work. Teachers are always puzzled by the great number of students who don't turn in late assignments or those that are missed during an absence. A few zeros are bound to pull a grade down quickly.   133 / 148 / 162

Do a little more than is required. Read ahead; work extra problems. Bring in outside reports about the topics you are discussing. These small extras pay off in higher grades.   176 / 190 / 198

Do these hints help students earn higher grades? The students who have tried them say they do. Why don't you try them, too?   212 / 223

84a • Keyboard Review • Each line at least three times

5 minutes

All letters SS Mickey won big prizes for diving in the last exciting junior aquatics.

Figure-Symbol In the 1820's good Texas farm land was selling for only 12½¢ per acre.

Think letters

Long reach numb debit sum any zebra hunt myself nut nurse mystery style zany mute

Think words

Easy We can do good work if we have a goal for each bit of work that we do.

| 1 | 2 | 3 | 4 | 5 | 6 | 7 | 8 | 9 | 10 | 11 | 12 | 13 | 14 |

84b • Punctuation Guides — Comma • Each sentence twice

10 minutes

Line 1 – Use a comma after each item in a series, except the last.

Line 2 – Use a comma to separate consecutive adjectives when the *and* has seemingly been omitted. Do not use the comma when the adjectives do not apply equally to the noun they modify.

Line 3 – Use a comma to separate a dependent clause that precedes the main clause.

Line 4 – Use a comma to separate the independent parts of a compound sentence joined by *and, but, for, or, neither, nor.*

Line 5 – Use a comma to prevent misreading or confusion.

Line 6 – Use a comma to set off a direct quotation from the rest of the sentence.

Line 7 – Do not set off an indirect quotation from the rest of the sentence.

1 SS Most of our players can hit, catch, and throw the ball extremely well.

2 You will enjoy this new, useful book. I like its light blue sketches.

Sit erect

3 Whenever you type personal papers, you will want to type with control.

4 Gayle worked the problems he assigned, but she did not write the poem.

5 In 1970, 364 were sold. Compared to Ruth, Amy cannot dance very well.

Feet on the floor

6 I thought it was Franklin who said, "A penny saved is a penny earned."

7 Mrs. Brock said I could leave when I had finished the math assignment.

| 1 | 2 | 3 | 4 | 5 | 6 | 7 | 8 | 9 | 10 | 11 | 12 | 13 | 14 |

84c • Problem Typing

30 minutes

Problem 1—Typing on Ruled Lines

Half sheet
40-space line
Triple spacing
2" top margin

Directions – 1. Using the underline, type three lines across the page. Note the position of the line in relation to the top of the alignment scale.

2. Remove the paper; then reinsert it.

3. Align the paper, using the variable line spacer, to type on the first line.

4. Type the lines shown at the right.

Mr. Gordon Scott

2614 Oak Ridge Avenue

Jackson, Mississippi   39216

• Lesson 55 • *60-space line*

55a • Keyboard Review • Each line three times

5 minutes

All letters	SS	Van Mudge will quickly explain the fire hazards of this job.
Figure-Symbol		There is no space between the # and a number: Order #13478.
Easy		Use well the gift of learning to add to the things you know.

Type without pauses

| 1 | 2 | 3 | 4 | 5 | 6 | 7 | 8 | 9 | 10 | 11 | 12 |

55b • Timed Writings • As directed in 51e, page 92

15 minutes

GWAM
1' 3'

¶ 1
42 words
1.2 si

DS

Have you ever noticed that busy people are the ones who   11 4 49

are asked to do important jobs? That's because they have   23 8 53

learned how to organize their work, lay out a plan, and stick   35 12 57

to it. When they work, they work.   42 14 59

¶ 2
44 words
1.3 si

Thinking and studying go hand in hand. If you want to   53 18 63

cut down on the time you spend on homework, you can do it   65 22 67

all right. The formula is quite simple. Give your mind a   76 25 70

chance to think by closing out everything else.   86 29 74

¶ 3
48 words
1.3 si

Have a definite time for study. When that time comes,   97 32 77

plunge right in. Do not find excuses for doing something   108 36 81

else. Keep your mind fixed on the task at hand. Close out   120 40 85

confusion. Ideas will come to you only if you give them a   132 44 89

All ¶'s
1.3 si

chance.   134 45 90

1' | 1 | 2 | 3 | 4 | 5 | 6 | 7 | 8 | 9 | 10 | 11 | 12 |
3' | 1 | 2 | 3 | 4 |

55c • Problem Typing

25 minutes

Problem—Two-Page Theme

Directions – 1. Type the theme on page 98. Use theme style, double spacing.

2. Top margins—
   First page: 2 inches (13th line space).
   Second page: 1 inch (7th line space).

3. Set stops for 1-inch side margins.

• *As is illustrated on page vi, there are 10 spaces per inch on a pica typewriter and 12 spaces per inch on an elite typewriter.*

• *For pica typewriters, the side margins should each contain 10 horizontal spaces. For elite typewriters, the side margins should each contain 12 spaces.*

83d • Problem Typing

Problem 1—Personal Business Letter in Block Style with Quoted Paragraphs

Full sheet
60-space line
Open punctuation

Directions – 1. Type the letter below as a personal business letter in block style. Type the address on the 6th line space from the date. Indent the quoted paragraphs 5 spaces from each margin.

2. Address a small envelope. Fold the letter; insert it into the envelope.

2579 Wilson Road
Council Bluffs, Iowa   51501
October 18, 197—

Mr. Paul Aldrich
Student Body President
West High School
Omaha, Nebraska   68128

Dear Paul

The two paragraphs quoted below were taken from the brochure Mr. Taylor left at our school:

> The student from whom you receive this note is engaged in a school project intended to earn money for a worthy purpose. This project will help him or her develop poise, confidence, and good manners. It provides a work experience that can be valuable in later life.

> You can make an important contribution to the success of our project by choosing from this list of magazines and by encouraging the student to call on other prospects.

The remainder of the brochure contains the price list as well as a sample order form. If you will let me know how many you need, I can get a supply from Mr. Taylor next week.

Sincerely yours

Robin Peterson

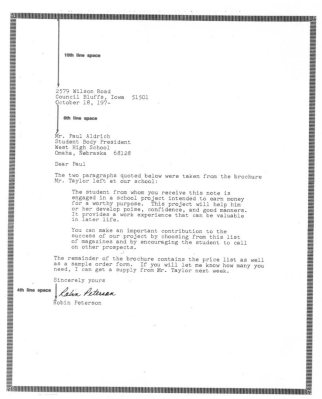

Personal business letter in block style

Problem 2—Personal Business Letter in Block Style

Directions – 1. Type the letter in Problem 1 again. This time, however, address the letter to Miss Barbara Harris, Student Body Vice President. Type the address on the 5th line space from the date.

2. Use your own address and today's date in the return address. Type your name at the end of the letter; sign it.

Miniature models of both pica and elite solutions of the first page are shown below. Do not type from the models; work from the copy at the bottom of the page.

Leave a margin of at least one inch at the bottom of the first page. A bottom margin of 1½ inches is preferred. Before inserting your paper, draw a light pencil line in the horizontal center of your paper, 1½ inches from the bottom edge as a warning.

For the page number on the second page, type 2 on the 4th line space from the top, at the right margin.

PATENTS

Since Congress passed the Patent Act in 1790, the Patent Office has issued more than four million patents. This office maintains a huge room in Washington, which is open to the public. Here drawings of new products can be seen, and descriptions can be read. What an interesting room! It contains a record of man's inventive genius in every field from bubble gum to computers.

Most products that are patented serve a real need, like the self starter for cars or the camera that turns out a finished picture in 60 seconds or less. People invent some strange things, too. Take the case of the farmer who invented a pair of glasses for a nearsighted rooster. Another man invented a ladies' hat that blows soap bubbles. Another invented a fly-swatter pistol guaranteed to bring down the elusive fly, no matter how tricky.

There is no record that the inventors of these odd-ball devices ever got rich. On the other hand, some men who have invented highly useful devices never got rich either. Take the case of Walter Hunt, who invented the safety pin. By the time the public caught on to its value, his patent expired. He made no money from it. Hunt decided that Americans did not really know what they wanted, so he invented a pair of shoes "for walking up walls." Nobody wanted his shoes either.

The Patent Office was barely four years old when Eli Whitney patented his cotton gin. Later, patents went to Cyrus McCormick for his reaper; to Samuel Colt for his revolving gun—the original six shooter; to Samuel Morse for his telegraph; to Joseph Glidden for barbed wire; and to the Wright brothers for a flying machine.

Many years ago, Abraham Lincoln noted that "the patent system added the fuel of interest to the fire of genius." The demand for new products keeps growing. With the help of the fuel provided by the patent system, Americans seem to be inventing more than ever to satisfy this demand.

• **Lesson 83** • *70-space line*

83a • **Keyboard Review** • Each line at least three times
5 *minutes*

All letters   SS   The King and Queen brought dozens of expensive jewels from the colony.

Figure-Symbol   My projector has f/1.2 lens, 406-foot take-up reel, and costs $375.98.

Adjacent keys   Some seventh graders dashed madly for class seconds ahead of schedule.

Eyes on this copy

Easy   Men should be at work today trying to solve the problems of the world.

| 1 | 2 | 3 | 4 | 5 | 6 | 7 | 8 | 9 | 10 | 11 | 12 | 13 | 14 |

83b • **Speed Stretcher** • As directed in 78b, page 133
10 minutes

GWAM
1'   5'

All letters
¶ 1
60 words
1.3 si

DS   A new era began not long ago with man's first step on the moon.   13   3   37

Many who witnessed the televised image of a foot being placed on lunar   27   5   39

soil had the feeling that their lives would never be quite the same   41   8   42

again. Today, the moon is no longer merely a subject of myth in the   55   11   45

sky; instead, it's a place.   60   12   46

¶ 2
56 words
1.3 si

From early times the moon has been one heavenly body that men have   13   15   49

aspired to visit. The sun appeared a searing ball of fire. The stars   28   18   52

and planets were nothing more than points of light. Those who imagined   42   20   54

man might some day fly, however, often dreamed of zooming to the moon.   56   23   57

¶ 3
54 words
1.3 si

Of what use is the moon? No one knows for sure, of course, but   13   26   60

some believe it has potential value for many things. Perhaps it will   27   29   63

be used as a space lab or as a base for further explorations. Possibly   41   31   65

All ¶'s
1.3 si

it can serve as a refueling stop and launching site for rockets.   54   34   68

1' | 1 | 2 | 3 | 4 | 5 | 6 | 7 | 8 | 9 | 10 | 11 | 12 | 13 | 14 |
5' | | 1 | | 2 | | 3 |

83c • **Skill Builder** • Two 1-minute writings on each sentence
5 minutes

1   SS   It is better to know where you are going than to get there in a hurry.

2   Remember that although he may eat the canary, a cat still cannot sing.

Quiet wrists and arms

| 1 | 2 | 3 | 4 | 5 | 6 | 7 | 8 | 9 | 10 | 11 | 12 | 13 | 14 |

Lesson 56 • *60-space line*

56a • Keyboard Review • Each line three times

5 *minutes*

All letters	SS	Jack Howe can mix five quarts of gray paint for Liz and Bud.
Figure-Symbol		Mr. Gay's students collected $53.80 in the membership drive.
Easy		The right angle to use in solving problems is the try angle.

| 1 | 2 | 3 | 4 | 5 | 6 | 7 | 8 | 9 | 10 | 11 | 12 |

Quick, firm
reach to the
shift key

56b • Paragraph Guided Writings • As directed in 51d, page 91

10 minutes

DS

All letters
52 words
1.3 si

The best thing about the future is that it comes only
one day at a time. Keep this simple text in your quest for
typing speed. Just add a word a day to your speed, and very
soon you will have the ability to whiz through copy on your
typewriter in record time.

Read words
Think words
Type words

56c • Timed Writings

15 minutes

Directions – Type 1-, 2-, and 3-minute writings on the copy below. Repeat. Try to equal your 1-minute rate on the longer writings.

Technique Goals – Fingers deeply curved; wrists low and still. Use quick, short, sharp strokes. Type at a steady pace—without pauses.

	GWAM
	1' 3'

DS	Genius, it has often been said, is the ability to evade	11 4 44
	work by doing it right the first time it is done. We know that	24 8 48
	it is not the man who works the hardest or longest who gets the	37 12 52
	most completed. That prize goes to the man who knows how to	49 16 56
	organize his work. He knows exactly what must be done.	60 20 60
	A man does not need to have genius to learn how to plan	71 24 64
	his work. All he needs is some common sense. He must know	83 28 68
	enough to get the directions for doing a job clearly in mind	95 32 72
	before he jumps into it. Yes, common sense is all that is re-	108 36 76
	quired, all right; and if one has enough of it, he has genius.	120 40 80

All letters
120 words
1.2 si

| 1' | 1 | 2 | 3 | 4 | 5 | 6 | 7 | 8 | 9 | 10 | 11 | 12 |
| 3' | | 1 | | 2 | | 3 | | 4 | |

82c • Problem Typing

30 minutes

Problem 1—Personal Business Letter in Modified Block Style

Full sheet
50-space line
Blocked paragraphs
Open punctuation

Directions – 1. Type the letter below as a personal business letter in modified block style. Type the address on the 10th line space from the date.
2. Address a small envelope. Fold the letter; insert it into the envelope.

• *See page 82 for directions on typing personal business letters.*

Personal business letter in modified block style

327 Monroe Avenue
Mason City, Iowa   50434
Current date

First National Bank
317 North Broadway
Mason City, Iowa   50406

Gentlemen

While listening to the radio yesterday, I heard about your Christmas Club savings plan. I am a Wilson School student and earn a weekly allowance. I would like to have a regular savings plan, and your Christmas Club sounds like a good one.

Will you please send me any information you have explaining the plan of the Christmas Club. I would like to become a member as soon as possible. I am looking forward to hearing from you soon.

Sincerely yours

Miss Jane Biel

Problem 2—Personal Business Letter in Modified Block Style

Directions – 1. Follow the directions given in Problem 1. Type the address on the 7th line space from the date.

2. Use your own address and today's date in the return address.

Fay's Fabric Supply / 29 Erie Lane / Topeka, KS   66684 / Gentlemen / Mr. Allen Smith, Manager of the Modern Fabric Center in Salina, suggested that I write and explain to you our urgent need for orange fringe. Mr. Smith sent an order to you on August 23, but he says shipments sometimes take as long as two weeks. (¶) We will have to receive the material by September 2 if we are to complete making our pep girl uniforms in time for orientation. If you can possibly speed up delivery of Mr. Smith's order for the additional fringe, all the pep girls at Washington Junior High School will be grateful. We hope you won't let us down! Sincerely yours, Kathy Burcell

Problem 3—Personal Business Letter in Modified Block Style

Directions – Type the letter in Problem 2 again. This time, use mixed punctuation. Indent the paragraphs 5 spaces.

56d • Composing at the Typewriter

5 minutes

Directions – Type answers to as many of these questions as time permits. Use complete sentences.

1. Name a nationally prominent person in politics and the office he holds or has held.
2. Name one of the United States senators from your state.
3. Name the capital city of the state in which you are now living.
4. What nationally prominent person would you most like to meet in person? Why?

56e • Capitalization Guides

10 minutes

Directions – Read the explanation carefully; type the line to which it applies twice.

Line 1 – Capitalize days of the week, months of the year, and holidays, but not seasons.

Line 2 – Capitalize names of rivers, oceans, and mountains.

Line 3 – Capitalize *North, South,* etc., when they name particular parts of the country, but not when they refer to directions.

Line 4 – Capitalize names of religious groups, political parties, nations, nationalities, and races.

Line 5 – Capitalize adjectives that come from a proper name.

Line 6 – Capitalize the names of stars, planets, and constellations, except *sun, moon, earth,* unless these are used with other astronomical names.

Line 7 – Capitalize the title of a person when used with his name.

1 SS The Fourth of July falls on Monday this summer, does it not?

2 Ralph crossed the Columbia River and soon saw Mount Rainier.

3 From Tacoma, I drove east on the Northwest's newest highway.

4 The Norwegian people gave the French books to the Democrats.

Quick, firm reach to the shift key

5 I bought a Swiss watch, a Hawaiian shirt, and an Indian rug.

6 I saw Mercury and Mars in relation to the Earth and the Sun.

7 Senator Jones, Governor Brown, and Judge King spoke briefly.
| 1 | 2 | 3 | 4 | 5 | 6 | 7 | 8 | 9 | 10 | 11 | 12 |

• Lesson 57 • *60-space line*

57a • Keyboard Review • Each line three times

5 minutes

All letters SS Van, Joe, and Larry saw the six men picked for the big quiz.

Figure The longest swim on record was 292 miles; it took 87½ hours.

Eyes on this copy

Easy Everything comes to him, though, who hustles while he waits.
| 1 | 2 | 3 | 4 | 5 | 6 | 7 | 8 | 9 | 10 | 11 | 12 |

81e • Punctuation Guides — Period, Question Mark, and Exclamation Point

10 minutes

Directions – Read the explanation carefully; type each line to which it applies twice.

• *A space follows each period after initials. No space is needed after a period within an abbreviation. Space once after a period that ends an abbreviation unless that period also ends a sentence, in which case, space twice.*

Line 1 – Use a period after a sentence making a statement or giving a command.
Line 2 – Use a period after initials.
Line 3 – Nicknames are not followed by periods.
Line 4 – Use a period after most abbreviations.

Line 5 – Use a question mark after a question.
Line 6 – After requests and indirect questions, use a period.
Line 7 – Use an exclamation point to express strong or sudden feeling.

1 SS Frank told the class that we bought Alaska for only two cents an acre.
2 The new members are E. T. Austin, Harry G. Costis, and J. Perry Dodds.
3 Ed told me that he and Al would get together with Marv later that day.
4 We will leave at 11:15 a.m. and arrive in Washington D.C. at 1:10 p.m.
5 How many tickets have been sold for the variety show on Tuesday night?
6 I asked Fran how she remembered. Will you please let me know at once.
7 Hurrah! Your team won the game! Congratulations! What a great gang!

| 1 | 2 | 3 | 4 | 5 | 6 | 7 | 8 | 9 | 10 | 11 | 12 | 13 | 14 |

Cut out waste movements

• Lesson 82 • *70-space line*

82a • Keyboard Review • Each line at least three times

5 minutes

All letters SS Don is explaining why he believes I must acquire a jackal for the zoo.
Figure While Maury Wills stole 104 bases in 1962, he was thrown out 13 times.
Balanced- and one-hand We saw him there. Read my theme at noon. I saw my men work and rest.
Easy I know that one way to get rid of an enemy is to make him your friend.

| 1 | 2 | 3 | 4 | 5 | 6 | 7 | 8 | 9 | 10 | 11 | 12 | 13 | 14 |

Resume typing at once

82b • Speed Builder

10 minutes

Directions – 1. Type a 1-minute writing. The last word typed will be your goal word.

2. Type a 5-minute writing. At the end of each minute, the return will be called. Try to reach your goal.

	Words
DS Some may not know that the typical neckties men wear today are	13
often called four-in-hand. They received this name from a group of	26
60 words 1.3 si nineteenth century carriage drivers who were noted for holding the	40
reins of four horses in one hand. When most people were wearing bow	53
ties, the drivers wore long ones.	60

57b • Spelling and Proofreading Aid • Each line three times   5 minutes

1   ss   ancient athletics aviator condemn disappear governor freight

2   exceed neighbor address vehicle process chief column worried   Wrists and elbows still

3   experience recipe paid dissolved shield equally subtle local

57c • Skill Comparison • 1-minute writing on each sentence. Compare gwam.   5 minutes

Words

Goal sentence   ss   Truth has to change hands but a few times to become fiction.   12

One hand   Fred Polk erected seats in a vast cave. Jim Lyon ate beets.   12

Script   *Write out the chief ideas of a lesson, using your own words.*   12

Rough draft   Arrange the points of a lesson in some order that make sense.   12

| 1 | 2 | 3 | 4 | 5 | 6 | 7 | 8 | 9 | 10 | 11 | 12 |

57d • Problem Typing   30 minutes

Problem 1—Sentence Outline

Directions – 1. Set margin stops for a 60-space line. Type the main points at the left margin. Set and use tabulator stops for subpoints.
2. Type the outline in reading position on a full sheet.

3. Indent, space, capitalize, and punctuate exactly as shown in the problem. Two spaces follow the period after all numbered or lettered divisions in an outline.

• *Note that complete sentences are used. Each is followed by a period.*

```
                        GUIDES FOR STUDYING
                                                    ←——————— Triple-space

     I.   STUDYING IS A SKILL, LIKE READING AND WRITING.
                                                    ←——————— Double-space
4-space          →A.   Learn how to study.
indention         B.   Develop correct study habits through practice.

Align Roman——→
numerals at      II.   OBSERVE THESE GUIDES IN DEVELOPING STUDYING SKILL.
right
                  A.   Set up a schedule with definite study periods.
8-space          →1.   Do not let anything change this schedule.
indention         2.   Find a quiet place to study.
                  3.   Have needed materials available before you start.
                  4.   Start at once; don't find excuses for delaying.
                  B.   Study with a purpose.
                  1.   Copy your assignments accurately; know what you
                       are to do.
                  2.   Search for ideas; think as you read or solve
                       problems.
                  C.   Practice remembering the main points of a lesson.
                  1.   Ask yourself questions on what you have studied.
                  2.   Take brief notes.
```

Sentence outline

81c • Technique Builder — Stroking

5 minutes

Directions – Type each line three times.   Technique Goal – Finger-action stroking.

1	SS	Try never to confuse keeping your chin up with sticking your neck out.
2		It is best to borrow from a pessimist as he thinks he won't be repaid.
3		A secret is what a person tells someone else because he can't keep it.
4		It doesn't pay to brood——after all, only the chickens get paid for it.

Resume typing at once

| 1 | 2 | 3 | 4 | 5 | 6 | 7 | 8 | 9 | 10 | 11 | 12 | 13 | 14 |

81d • Speed Ladder Paragraphs • As directed in 76c, page 131

15 minutes

GWAM
1' 5'

¶ 1
36 words
1.3 si

Edison once said that everything comes to him who hustles while he   13 3 47
waits. Time alone will bring you nothing. All gain requires some   27 5 49
effort. Know what you want; then work for it.   36 7 51

¶ 2
40 words
1.3 si

Experts claim that the reason we dislike some people is that we   49 10 54
see in them our defects. We dislike them for our weaknesses. If this   63 13 57
be true, we can use others as a mirror to uncover our own faults.   76 15 59

¶ 3
44 words
1.3 si

Everybody wants to improve the world, but no one thinks of improv-   89 18 62
ing himself. The world is the people who live in it. What you do in   103 21 65
a small way the world does in a big one. Begin with yourself if it   117 23 67
needs improving.   120 24 68

¶ 4
48 words
1.3 si

The trouble with being a good sport is that one has to lose to   133 27 71
prove it. Nobody likes to lose; everybody likes to win. We must remem-   147 29 73
ber, however, that all winners lose at times. Thus, good winners must   161 32 76
know how to take a loss in stride.   168 34 78

¶ 5
52 words
1.3 si

In the long history of law and order, early man took his longest   181 36 80
step forward when the tribe to which he belonged sat down in a circle   195 39 83
and permitted but one man to talk at a time. Any group to which you   209 42 86

All ¶'s
1.3 si

belong would get more done if it adopted a similar rule.   220 44 88

1' | 1 | 2 | 3 | 4 | 5 | 6 | 7 | 8 | 9 | 10 | 11 | 12 | 13 | 14 |
5' | 1 | 2 | 3 |

Problem 2—Topic Outline

Directions – 1. Set margin stops for a 40-space line. Type the problem in reading position on a full sheet. 2. The outline is set in two columns. Type it in a single column. Space between parts as illustrated in Problem 1.

• *Topic statements are used; omit ending periods.*

LEARNING TO WRITE SUMMARIES

I. REASONS FOR SUMMARIZING
   A. Getting ideas from your lessons
   B. Expressing ideas concisely
II. GUIDES FOR WRITING SUMMARIES
   A. Reading the lesson
   B. Finding the central idea
   C. Finding supporting ideas
   D. Writing down ideas
      1. Writing briefly
      2. Using nouns and verbs
      3. Using your own words
   E. Editing your first draft
      1. Eliminating minor details
      2. Arranging ideas in logical order
      3. Omitting your own opinions
   F. Writing summary in final form
      1. Using proper form
      2. Writing or typing neatly

• Lesson 58 • *60-space line*

58a • Keyboard Review • Each line three times   5 minutes

All letters	SS	Joy Brave will squeeze six big limes for the drink of punch.
Figure		1 and 2 and 3 and 4 and 5 and 6 and 7 and 8 and 9 and 10 and
Easy		The greatest homage that we can pay to truth is to reuse it.

Resume typing at once

| 1 | 2 | 3 | 4 | 5 | 6 | 7 | 8 | 9 | 10 | 11 | 12 |

58b • Paragraph Guided Writings   10 minutes

Directions – Three 1-minute writings on each paragraph. Try for no more than two errors on the first writing; one error on the second; no errors on the third. Compute *gwam* on the three writings.

			GWAM 1′	3′
¶ 1 58 words 1.3 si	DS	Does the invention of new machines put men out of work?	11 4	43
		This is a commonly held belief. A power shovel will dig as	23 8	47
		much dirt in a day as a hundred men can by hand all right.	35 12	51
		A truck can haul as many sacks of cement as dozens of men	47 16	55
		can carry on their backs—without getting sore muscles.	58 19	58
¶ 2 58 words 1.3 si		Because we have power shovels, trucks, and other equip-	11 23	62
		ment, we can build roads for cars. Think of the new jobs	23 27	66
		created by the car industry. Millions of men are needed to	35 31	70
		make, sell, paint, and fix them and work in gas stations.	46 35	74
		Machines destroy some jobs, but they also create new ones.	58 39	78

1′ | 1 | 2 | 3 | 4 | 5 | 6 | 7 | 8 | 9 | 10 | 11 | 12 |
3′ | 1 | 2 | 3 | 4 |

Problem 2—Personal Letter in Semibusiness Form

Directions – Follow the directions given in Problem 1.

10219 Palm Drive
Miami, Florida   33155
May 27, 197——

Dear Mrs. Smith

Greetings to all of you as we go forward to another great year! It is a challenge to be president of such an outstanding group of people. Thank you again for the honor.

Your entire board will be working all summer formulating plans for next season. Please share in these plans by sending us any suggestions you feel will be of benefit in our goal of making the Saturday Morning Club the most outstanding club in this city. We ask you to share your talents and enthusiasm with us.

Sincerely

Mrs. Ronald Smith
513 Parrish Drive
Miami, Florida   33155

• Lesson 81 • *70-space line*

81a • Keyboard Review • Each line at least three times   *5 minutes*

All letters   SS   James knew by the quizzical expression on my face that I had given up.

Figure-Symbol   Invoice #3845 lists this charge: 167 gallons of oil @ 29¢ per gallon.

Right-hand   In my opinion, you imply I pull my plump, lion puppy upon Poplin Hill.

Even stroking

Easy   It is better to get in the first thought than to get in the last word.
| 1 | 2 | 3 | 4 | 5 | 6 | 7 | 8 | 9 | 10 | 11 | 12 | 13 | 14 |

81b • Speed Ladder Sentences   *10 minutes*

Directions – Type each sentence for 1 minute. Your teacher will call the guide at 15-, 12-, or 10-second intervals. Return the carriage quickly. Start typing immediately. Repeat sentences on which you were not able to type a complete line with the call of the guide.

			GWAM 15"	12"	10"
1	SS	You should think about the future today.	32	40	48
2		It will pay you to build strong study habits.	36	45	54
3		Choose all your classes with a great deal of care.	40	50	60
4		See if you can find where your own special talents lie.	44	55	66
5		Every student is a problem in search of some good solutions.	48	60	72
6		Learn all you can about those fields which interest you the most.	52	65	78
7		When you are older, you will be very glad that you heeded this advice.	56	70	84

| 1 | 2 | 3 | 4 | 5 | 6 | 7 | 8 | 9 | 10 | 11 | 12 | 13 | 14 |

Problem—Typing Class Notes in Final Form

Directions – 1. Assume that the following notes have been prepared from those taken sketchily in class. They appear here in final form. Prepare a type-written copy of them.

2. Use regular theme style. Type the date 1 inch from the top of the page and the heading 2 inches from the top.

3. Assume, too, that these notes are to be placed in a notebook; thus, the copy requires a wider left than right margin so that it will have a centered appearance when placed in the notebook.

  a. Set the margin stops for a 1½-inch left margin and a 1-inch right margin.

  ● *As is illustrated on page vi, there are 10 spaces per inch on a pica typewriter and 12 spaces per inch on an elite typewriter.*

  ● *For pica typewriters, the left margin should contain 15 horizontal spaces; the right margin, 10 horizontal spaces. For elite typewriters, the left margin should contain 18 horizontal spaces; the right margin, 12 horizontal spaces.*

  ● *In setting the right margin stop, 5 to 8 spaces are added for the bell.*

  b. Because of the wider left margin, the center point will be 3 spaces to the right of the point normally used.

Today's date

                    TAKING NOTES

Notes on What You Hear

    1. Don't try to write everything down. Get only the important
        facts and ideas.

    2. Relate what you know to what you hear. In this way you will
        get a better understanding of the topics discussed.

    3. If the speaker says something is important, put it down.

    4. If the speaker dwells on a fact or point, put it down.

Notes on What You Read

    1. Get the major points in mind by reading an article that gives
        you a broad view of the subject in which you are interested.

    2. Summarize. Don't try to copy everything you read.

    3. If a statement is made that you wish to quote, put quotation
        marks around it. Get the complete source.

Preparing Notes in Final Form

    1. If you have taken the notes hurriedly, the sooner you type them
        in final form, the better.

    2. Type your notes in complete sentences. Add details that you
        remember from your reading or from listening to a discussion
        so that your notes will be meaningful to you when you read them
        later.

    3. Type your notes in good form. Space them so they will be easy
        to read. Put a heading on them. Date them.

• Lesson 80 • *70-space line*

80a • Keyboard Review • Each line at least three times

All letters SS	I know it is an expensive job to organize and equip the men carefully.
Figure-Symbol	Dan's note for $3,270 (due June 15) bears interest at the rate of $6\frac{1}{4}\%$.
Left-hand	We saw brave crews steer fast craft as great westward breezes started.
Easy	Men who learn from their failures often make their names in the world.

Feet on
the floor

| 1 | 2 | 3 | 4 | 5 | 6 | 7 | 8 | 9 | 10 | 11 | 12 | 13 | 14 |

80b • Timed Writings

5 minutes

Directions – Type a 1- and a 5-minute writing on 76c, page 131. Circle errors. Compute *gwam*.

80c • Problem Typing

30 minutes

Problem 1—Personal Letter in Semibusiness Form

Directions – 1. Type the letter below as illustrated at the right on half-size stationery (5½ by 8½ inches).

2. Start typing the return address on the 7th line space from the top.

3. Use a 40-space line. Type the salutation on the 8th line space from the date. Paragraph indentions: 10 spaces.

1385 North Cedar Street
Muncie, Indiana   47332
April 23, 197—

Dear Mr. Anderson

You will be happy to learn that our program plans for the coming school year are now complete. Two evening meetings are planned in addition to the annual Back-to-School Night in October. Afternoon meetings will be held in November and March.

Mrs. Nancy Elias has done an outstanding job as chairman of the program committee. Her enthusiasm for the work of the Tioga Junior High School PTA should make this our best year ever.

Sincerely

Mr. David Anderson
155 Barstow Avenue
Muncie, Indiana   47314

• *Note the placement of the address at the left margin at the end of the letter.*

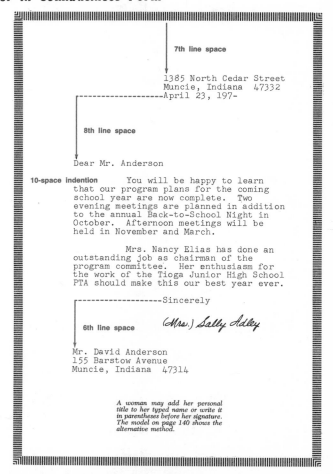

Personal letter in semibusiness form

• Lesson 59 • *60-space line*

59a • Keyboard Review • Each line three times

5 minutes

All letters	SS	May Dick will give the puzzle to Jess Quinn for the old box.
Figure-Symbol		Check #590 for $32.67 was sent to his store at 98 Elko Road.
Easy		Time can take care of more problems than most men can solve.

Instant release

| 1 | 2 | 3 | 4 | 5 | 6 | 7 | 8 | 9 | 10 | 11 | 12 |

59b • Typing from Dictation and Spelling Checkup

5 minutes

Directions – Type 57b, page 101, from your teacher's dictation. Check for correct spelling. Retype any words in which you made an error.

59c • Skill Comparison

5 minutes

Directions – Type a 1-minute writing on each sentence. Compare *gwam* rates. Try typing all sentences at the rate made on the first one.

			Words
Easy	SS	We prove what we really are by what we do with what we have.	12
Long reach		My young brother may bring the extra money that Myron needs.	12
Script		*The prize goes to the man who knows how to do some job well.*	12
Rough draft		the print ing of money does not create the wealth of a nation.	12

| 1 | 2 | 3 | 4 | 5 | 6 | 7 | 8 | 9 | 10 | 11 | 12 |

59d • Problem Typing   Problem 1—Assignment Paper

30 minutes

Directions – 1. Assume that you are preparing this problem as an assignment paper for a class. Use a 60-space line, a 2-inch top margin, and double spacing.

2. As you type the sentences, capitalize the words that should be capitalized. Capitalization rules are summarized on page xiv. Refer to them if necessary.

APPLYING THE CAPITALIZATION RULES

1. he will spend this fall and winter in denver, colorado
2. he visited miami junior high school on friday morning
3. we saw senator percy in a school in gary on labor day
4. an indian from asia stayed at the hilton hotel in omaha
5. the danish reporters attended a meeting of republicans
6. he read a paper on venus and mars in his english class
7. the mayors may tour damaged areas of the south this fall
8. from tulsa, he drove east until he crossed the river
9. dale smith belongs to the boy scouts of america
10. the meeting is set for friday in the methodist church
11. the senators will study pollution of the atlantic ocean
12. the irish and french teams will meet on thursday, may 1

79a • **Keyboard Review** • Each line at least three times

5 minutes

All letters	SS	Jack got zero on his final exam simply because we gave hard questions.
Figure-Symbol		The admission for adults was $1.50; children 5-11, 75¢; under 5, free.
Adjacent keys		Terry wrote three other letters reporting the threats to their resort.
Easy		People, like ships at sea, always toot loudest when they are in a fog.

Space quickly

| 1 | 2 | 3 | 4 | 5 | 6 | 7 | 8 | 9 | 10 | 11 | 12 | 13 | 14 |

79b • **Control Builder**

5 minutes

Directions – Use Speed Stretcher 78b, page 133, for four
1-minute writings. Type at your control rate.

79c • **Number Expression Guides — Time of Day**

5 minutes

Directions – Type each sentence three times. The first line
gives the rule; the remaining lines apply it.

1	SS	With "o'clock," spell out the hour. Use figures with "a.m." or "p.m."
2		Our Glee Club will sing in the library at eleven o'clock this morning.
3		When it is 10:15 a.m. in Long Beach, it is 1:15 p.m. in New York City.

Think as you type

| 1 | 2 | 3 | 4 | 5 | 6 | 7 | 8 | 9 | 10 | 11 | 12 | 13 | 14 |

79d • **Problem Typing**

30 minutes

Problem 1—Postal Card Announcement

Directions – 1. Start typing on the third line space
from the top. Triple-space between the date and
the salutation. Double-space between paragraphs.

2. Address the card to Mr. Paul Lange / 736 Grand
Street / Scottsdale, Arizona   85251.

• *A postal card address and message are illustrated on page 78.*

• *Use paper cut to postal card size (5½ by 3¼ inches) if cards are not available.*

241 Bond Drive
Scottsdale, Arizona   85252
May 21, 197—

48-space line
Single spacing

Dear Mr. Lange

The Hoover Dads Club will hold its final meeting of the year on Thursday, June 1, in the Hoover multi-purpose room. Dinner will be served promptly at 7 p.m. The program will begin at 8:15. (¶) Please make your reservation by calling Ray Harrison at 439-0759 before next Friday.

Bob Carr, President

Problem 2—Postal Card Announcements

Directions – Type the message in Problem 1 to the names at the right. Address the cards. Use appropriate salutations.

Mr. Wayne Brooks
118 Rural Road
Scottsdale, Arizona   85252

Dr. Charles E. Swanson
2476 West Alamos Avenue
Scottsdale, Arizona   85264

Problem 2—Outline of Directions for Typing Book Reviews

Directions – Set the margin stops for a 60-space line. Use a standard 2-inch top margin. Indent, space, capitalize, and punctuate the outline correctly.

Directions for Writing a Book Review *) all caps*

Triple space ——→

I. Items to ~~be~~ Included in Review *) all caps*

    A. Title *and name* of author *the*
    B. central theme of book *characters*
    C. Some of tah important ~~people~~
    D. Setting for the story *interesting*
    E. Brief summary of some incidents
    F. comments on and opinion of the book ~~itself~~

II. General Guides ~~which are~~ to be Followed *) all caps*

    A. Should arouse reader's interest
    B. Should be well written
    C. Should contain examples to *support* comments

III. Typing Guides to ~~be~~ Observed *) all caps*

    A. Typed in regular theme *style* ~~form~~
    B. Single spaced with double spacing between parst
    C. Extra spaces in left margin for binding
    D. heading typed in off-centered position

• Lesson 60 • *60-space line*

60a • Keyboard Review • Each line three times   *5 minutes*

All letters	SS	Jack Walder bought five exquisite topaz pins in Mexico City.
Figure-Symbol		The largest gold nugget ever found: 7,560 ounces (in 1872).
Easy		You win when you get your mind to stick to a job to the end.

    | 1 | 2 | 3 | 4 | 5 | 6 | 7 | 8 | 9 | 10 | 11 | 12 |

Elbows in

60b • Timed Writings   *10 minutes*

Directions – Type two 3-minute writings on 58b, page 102. Compute *gwam*. Submit the better of the two writings.

60c • Problem Typing — Book Review   • On next page   *30 minutes*

Directions – Use regular theme style with the heading typed 2 inches from the top. Single-space the copy, but double-space before and after capitalized headings and between paragraphs. As this book review is to be placed in a notebook, use a 1½-inch left margin and a 1-inch right margin.

• *Directions for 58c, page 103, explain how to set 1½-inch left and 1-inch right margins.*

INVITATIONS, ACCEPTANCES, AND THANK YOU NOTES

Invitations, acceptances, "bread and butter" notes, thank you notes, and similar letters vary greatly in wording and form. Formal notes are usually printed. Informal notes may be handwritten or typewritten. As a rule, they are written without an address on personal-size stationery (usually 5½ by 8½ inches or 4¼ by 5½ inches). Only a handwritten signature is used.

78c • Problem Typing

30 minutes

Problem 1—Informal Invitation

Directions – 1. Type the informal invitation shown in the model illustration at the right. Use 4¼- by 5½-inch stationery. Allow a margin of about 1 inch at the top and ¾ inch in each side margin.

2. Begin the return address, date line, and complimentary close at the horizontal center of the paper.

3. Allow from 2 to 4 line spaces between the date and the salutation.

• *The number of line spaces which should be left between the date and the salutation is determined by the length of the message (in Problem 1 you are instructed to allow 2 to 4 line spaces). For shorter messages, increase this amount of space.*

```
                        717 Grand Avenue
                        Ada, Ohio  45810
                        April 15, 197-


Dear Ruth

     Will you and Ernest dine
with us next Monday, the twenty-
second, at seven o'clock, and
then go with us afterwards to
the symphony at the Carlyle
Auditorium?

     I know that Ernest is a very
busy man these days, but we are
hoping that he will enjoy a break
from his heavy schedule.

                    Very sincerely

                    Mary
```

Typewritten informal invitation

Problem 2—Informal Acceptance

Directions – 1. Type the informal acceptance below.

2. Follow the directions given for Problem 1.

694 Ashton Place / **Ada, Ohio 45810** / **April 17, 197—**

Dear Mary

Ernest and I both say "yes" to your nice invitation to dinner and the symphony. We are thrilled at the thought of hearing the Chicago Symphony with you. I understand that it's excellent.

We shall be with you at seven. Thanks so much for thinking of us.

Very sincerely

Problem 3—"Bread and Butter" Note • As directed in Problem 1

37 East Shaw / **Austin, Texas   78744** / **May 9, 197—**

Dear Marilyn

Thank you for a most relaxing weekend in your lovely new home. All of us thoroughly enjoyed the chance to talk over old times again.

Please don't forget your promise to come out our way next year. We'll certainly do our best to repay your many kindnesses. Thanks again.

Sincerely

BOOK REVIEW: DR. OX'S EXPERIMENT

Triple-space

THE AUTHOR

9

Double-space

Jules Verne

11

Double-space

THE STORY AND ITS SETTING

16

Jules Verne was the top fiction-science writer of his day (1828-   29
1905). He had a fantastic imagination that he used in telling some of the   44
wildest stories ever written. The report of a new oxygen discovery pro-   59
vides the plot for this book. The story is set in the small village of   73
Quiquendone.   76

Double-space

Quiquendone is a dead town. As one of the characters in the book   89
says, it is a town "where the coachmen do not insult each other, where   103
horses do not run away, where dogs do not bite, and where the cats do   117
not scratch." Into this dull setting comes Dr. Ox to build a gas plant   132
or so the people think. Actually, Dr. Ox plans to flood the village with   146
oxygen to liven things up a bit. He does, and they do.   158

INTERESTING INCIDENTS

162

A performance at the opera goes wild. Shrubs grow into trees. Cab-   176
bages become bushes. Students throw objects at their teachers. Two men   190
fight a duel. Finally, the people of Quiquendone declare war on a nearby   205
village for something that happened 500 years ago.   216

Luckily for everyone, the "gasworks" blows up before the war gets   229
under way, and the citizens of Quiquendone fall into their old ways.   243

COMMENTS

245

The story is humorous and lively. Anyone who likes adventure stories,   259
especially those written by Jules Verne, will really enjoy this one.   272

60d • Extra-Credit Typing

Problem 1

Directions – Type the two paragraphs in 56c, page 99, in regular theme style, following the guides for typing reports stressed in this unit. Supply an appropriate title for this paper.

Problem 2

Directions – Compose and type a sentence outline on the article in 55c, page 97. Type it on a full sheet; 60-space line; 2-inch top margin.

Problem 3

Directions – Prepare the manuscript of a short article from a current magazine. Type your paper in regular report form, following the guides for typing reports stressed in this unit.

Problem 4

Directions – Compose and type in report form a short report on how to get higher grades. Get ideas from 54d, page 96, but use your own words.

Problem 2—Invitation

Half sheet—Triple spacing—Exact vertical center

DELEGATES TO GIRLS LEAGUE
you are invited to the sponsor's home
for tea
Thursday, November 19, 4:15 p.m.
9900 Riverside Drive, Van Nuys

Problem 3—Announcement

Full sheet—Triple spacing—Reading position

KIWANIS CLUB PICNIC
Sunday, July 15—2:30 p.m.
Swimming and Games for Everyone
Hot Dogs, Potato Salad, Lemonade
Don't Miss the Fun!

• Lesson 78 • *70-space line*

78a • Keyboard Review • Each line at least three times   *5 minutes*

All letters SS   We all realized that even an expert jockey must qualify before racing.

Figure   Two men rowed a boat from New York to England in just 54 days in 1896.   Fingers
deeply
Long reach   debt bet batter bury tub tumble gamble stumble mumble bench turn curve   curved

Easy   Do not tell others of their faults until you have no more of your own.
| 1 | 2 | 3 | 4 | 5 | 6 | 7 | 8 | 9 | 10 | 11 | 12 | 13 | 14 |

78b • Speed Stretcher • Speed Stretchers may be used for 5-minute writings, or each paragraph may be used separately for 1-minute writings.   *10 minutes*

		GWAM 1' 5'

All letters
¶ 1
54 words
1.3 si   DS

Many students and their parents seem to take it for granted today   13 3 35

that after high school comes college. This is quite sensible because   27 5 37

there is no doubt that a need exists for more students who have been   41 8 40

college trained. We need them in key jobs throughout the nation.   54 11 43

¶ 2
53 words
1.3 si

Should everyone go to college? The answer to such a question is   13 13 45

clear. Many will realize that this is the last and perhaps worst place 27 16 48

for them to be. College is a place for people with good reasons for   41 19 51

wanting to be there and with sufficient talents to succeed.   53 21 53

¶ 3
55 words
1.3 si

Are you college material? You are if you're going to college for   13 24 56

the right reasons and if you have what it takes to succeed there. Go   27 27 59

because you want to go. Go to prepare yourself for a career. College 41 30 62

All ¶'s
1.3 si

may be a place where you will discover what you really want in life. 55 32 64

1' | 1 | 2 | 3 | 4 | 5 | 6 | 7 | 8 | 9 | 10 | 11 | 12 | 13 | 14 |
5' | 1 | 2 | 3 |

Learning to Type Tables

General Directions • Lessons 61 – 70

Machine Adjustments – Single-space sentences and drill lines. Double-space between repeated groups of lines. Double-space paragraph copy. Set a tabulator stop for a 5-space paragraph indention.

Erasing Errors – Your teacher will tell you if you are to correct errors in the problems in this unit.

• *Use a 60-space line for all lessons in this unit.*

• Lesson 61

61a • Keyboard Review • Each line three times
5 *minutes*

All letters	SS	Tommy Planck will squeeze five or six juice oranges by hand.
Figure-Symbol		We saw "Fantastic Voyage" on November 28, 1970, at Warner's.
Easy		Thus, we must never let someone else do our thinking for us.

Quick, firm reach to the shift key

| 1 | 2 | 3 | 4 | 5 | 6 | 7 | 8 | 9 | 10 | 11 | 12 |

61b • Fluency Practice
5 *minutes*

Directions – Type each line three times.   **Technique Goal** – Think the words as you type.

• The vertical lines indicate brief reading stops

1	SS	and he │ and if he │ and if he is │ and if he is to do the work
2		and go │ with us │ and go with us │ and go with us to the right
3		if they │ and if they │ and if they go │ and if they go to this
4		and show │ and to show │ and to show it │ and to show it to the

Even stroking

61c • Technique Builder — Stroking • Each line three times
10 *minutes*

Hyphen	SS	This well-known actor-singer won the coast-to-coast contest.
Double letters		The assessor called a committee meeting on the small matter.
Long reach		Myron Bray may bring a number of jumpers to the annual hunt.
One-hand		Jump up, Estes Weaver! Look at my car race on Cascade Hill.
Balanced-hand		Is this the form she is to sign so that she can do the work?
Balanced- and one-hand		Jim West is to sign the form so that he can enter the races.

Wrists and elbows quiet

| 1 | 2 | 3 | 4 | 5 | 6 | 7 | 8 | 9 | 10 | 11 | 12 |

61d • Skill Comparison • Type 57c, page 101, as directed
5 *minutes*

76d • Spacing Guides — Review

10 minutes

Directions – Type each line twice. Read the explanation for each line before you type it.

Line 1 – Space twice after the period at the end of a sentence.

Line 2 – Space once after a semicolon or comma.

Line 3 – Space twice after a question mark at the end of a sentence.

Line 4 – Space twice after a colon.

Line 5 – Space twice after an exclamation point that ends a sentence.

Line 6 – Type the dash with hyphens, without spacing before or after.

1   SS   Please pay attention. Directions are not repeated. Listen carefully.

2   Tomorrow is the assembly; remember that your schedule will be changed.

3   What time is it? Can I get there in an hour? Who will drive the bus?   **Think as you type**

4   Please bring these materials: baseballs, bat, gloves, mitt, and mask.

5   Heads up! Be alert! To learn anything, you must have a zealous mind.

6   Many things can be done in a day——if you don't make that day tomorrow.

| 1 | 2 | 3 | 4 | 5 | 6 | 7 | 8 | 9 | 10 | 11 | 12 | 13 | 14 |

• Lesson 77 • *70-space line*

77a • Keyboard Review • Each line at least three times

5 minutes

All letters   SS   We couldn't give any excuse for most of his crazy quips and bad jokes.

Figure   The Dodgers' Koufax walked only 71 men while striking out 382 in 1965.   **Reach with your fingers**

4th finger   was upon saw polite warm zone zeal police quake quack quit pay pad paw

Easy   We should not spend so much time asking others to do this and do that.

| 1 | 2 | 3 | 4 | 5 | 6 | 7 | 8 | 9 | 10 | 11 | 12 | 13 | 14 |

77b • Control Ladder Paragraphs

10 minutes

Directions – Type 1-minute writings on the paragraphs in 76c, page 131. When you can type a paragraph without error, move to the next one. Type with control.

77c • Problem Typing

30 minutes

Problem 1—Announcement

FEBRUARY MEETING OF WOLTERS SCHOOL PTA MEMBERS

Tuesday, February 10, 7:30 p.m.

School Cafeteria

Panel Discussion on Parent-Teacher Relationships

Mrs. Lynn Arkelian, President

Half sheet
Triple spacing
Exact vertical center

61e • Paragraph Guided Writings

15 minutes

Directions – 1. Type a 3-minute writing. Circle errors. Note your *gwam*.

2. Type each circled word 3 times along with the words preceding and following it.

3. Type two 1-minute writings on each paragraph. Try to add 4 words to your 3-minute *gwam* each time.

4. Type another 3-minute writing. Note your *gwam* and compare it with that of the first writing.

		GWAM		
		1'	3'	

¶ 1
40 words
1.2 si

DS

What we do speaks so loud that no one can hear us speaking. More of us should remember this bit of advice. We talk
too much, yet do too little. Work carefully done has ways
of speaking for itself.

11	4	48
24	8	52
35	12	56
40	13	57

¶ 2
44 words
1.3 si

We complain away many hours telling our friends about
a paper that we must write; then spend a few minutes writing
it. The paper looks it, too. The next time you write a report, write it. Your work speaks for itself.

51	17	61
63	21	65
75	25	69
84	28	72

¶ 3
48 words
1.3 si

An actor proves his worth on the stage or screen. We
can tell in a minute whether or not his performance is genu-
ine. In the same way, the work we do reflects us—it matters

95	32	76
107	36	80
119	40	84

All ¶'s
1.3 si

not whether we are actor or student. Our work has a loud
voice.

| 131 | 44 | 88 |
| 132 | 44 | 88 |

1' | 1 | 2 | 3 | 4 | 5 | 6 | 7 | 8 | 9 | 10 | 11 | 12 |
3' | 1 | 2 | 3 | 4 |

61f • Control Practice

5 minutes

Directions – 1. Type the last paragraph of 61e as many times as you can in the time that remains.

2. Circle your errors. Place a check mark in the margin of each paragraph in which you made no more than one error.

• Lesson 62 • *60-space line*

62a • Keyboard Review • Each line three times

5 minutes

All letters   SS   Major Philips could give the first quiz in botany next week.

Figure   The 23-foot bicycle carries 10 men; it is the longest built.

Flowing rhythm

Easy   The only men to get even with are those who have helped you.

| 1 | 2 | 3 | 4 | 5 | 6 | 7 | 8 | 9 | 10 | 11 | 12 |

Weak finger SS	Pat was quite amazed by the political opinions expressed in the paper.
Weak finger	Paul Quintana always gave pop quizzes in his sixth period law classes.
First row	I cannot exactly blame the men for not moving back into the next zone.
Third row	It is quite true that they were to report to you right after our trip.
One-hand	I'll wager you were aware that my baggage was carried by nonunion men.
One-hand	We think we can get him to look after my puppy and my pony after noon.

Quick, sharp stroking

| 1 | 2 | 3 | 4 | 5 | 6 | 7 | 8 | 9 | 10 | 11 | 12 | 13 | 14 |

76c • Speed Ladder Paragraphs   *20 minutes*

Directions – Type as many 1-minute writings as time permits. When you can type the first paragraph at the rate specified, type the next one. Climb the speed ladder. See if you can reach the top.

Alternate Procedure – If time remains after you reach the top speed, start from the beginning. Move from one paragraph to the next only when you type at the rate specified without error.

			GWAM 1'	5'
¶ 1 36 words 1.3 si	DS	Stick to a job until it is completed. This is the thing that	12	2 36
		people who reach the top in art, music, flying, or education have in	26	5 39
		common. They do not quit; they stick to the job.	36	7 41
¶ 2 40 words 1.3 si		The biggest room in the world, we are told, is the room for improve-	50	10 44
		ment. This being the case, why not study the way you are stroking the	64	13 47
		keys? You can eliminate errors by using quick, sharp strokes.	76	15 49
¶ 3 44 words 1.3 si		One frequently hears that the world is like a jigsaw puzzle. The	89	18 52
		job you do, no matter how small, is related to other jobs. The puzzle	104	21 55
		would not be complete without it. That is precisely why you must do	117	23 57
		your job well.	120	24 58
¶ 4 48 words 1.3 si		No man knows how hard another one works until he tries to do his	133	27 61
		job. We envy the boy who gets high grades. He seems to get them so	147	29 63
		easily. The truth is that he has discovered how to study. All talent	161	32 66
All ¶'s 1.3 si		must be developed through practice.	168	34 68

| 1' | 1 | 2 | 3 | 4 | 5 | 6 | 7 | 8 | 9 | 10 | 11 | 12 | 13 | 14 |
| 5' | | | 1 | | | | 2 | | | | 3 | | |

62b • Sentence Guided Writings

Directions – 1. Type each sentence for 1 minute. Try typing each at least *four* times in the minute.

2. Your teacher will call the return of the carriage each 15 seconds to guide you.

10 minutes

• *The rates at which you will be typing are given in the* first *column at the right.*

			G W A M 15″ Guide	12″ Guide
1	SS	Time will not wait for anyone.	24	30
2		Every day gives you another chance.	28	35
3		You are worth what you make of yourself.	32	40
4		Every time you speak, your mind is on parade.	36	45
5		Do not look for jobs that are equal to your skill.	40	50
6		Look, instead, for skills that are equal to your tasks.	44	55
7		The only time people dislike gossip is when it's about them.	48	60

| 1 | 2 | 3 | 4 | 5 | 6 | 7 | 8 | 9 | 10 | 11 | 12 |

STEPS IN ARRANGING TABLES
Horizontal Placement

1. Center the paper in the machine.
2. Move the left and right margin stops to the ends of the scale. Clear the tabulator rack.
3. Find how many spaces are to be used between the columns. The directions for problems that follow tell how many spaces to use.
4. Move the carriage to the center of the machine.
5. Spot the longest word or entry in each column.
6. Backspace once for each two spaces in the longest word or entry in each column.
7. Backspace once for each two spaces *between* the columns.

8. Set the left margin stop at the point at which you stop backspacing. This is the point where the first column will start.
9. From the left margin, space forward once for each letter, digit, and space in the longest entry in the first column and once for each space between Columns 1 and 2. Set a tab stop for the second column. Continue in this way until stops have been set for all columns.
10. Return the carriage. Operate the tab bar or key to determine whether or not all the tab stops have been set.

Vertical Placement

Vertical placement of material is not new to you. See directions given on page 62.

62c • Problem Typing

30 minutes

Problem 1—Short Trial Table

Directions – 1. Type the table on a half sheet of paper as it appears on page 110.

2. Leave 12 spaces between columns. Set the left margin stop for the first column and a tab stop for the second column, as directed above.

3. Vertical placement directions are given on the table for this problem. This table is placed in *exact vertical center.* In the problems that follow, you will have to plan the vertical placement yourself.

• *A half sheet of paper contains 33 line spaces.*

Cycle 3 •

Preparing Personal Papers

Problem Summary – Using the following summary, look at some of the problems you will prepare in Cycle 3 before you begin your typing:

Announcements, invitations, and thank you notes, pages 132-35.
Letters in semibusiness form, page 136.
Personal business letters, pages 140-42.
Orders and order letters, page 144.
Themes and reports, including outlines, footnotes, title pages, bibliographies, and note cards, pages 148-68.
Agenda and minutes, pages 171-73.
Club tickets and membership cards, page 174.
Postal cards, page 175.
Bar graphs, pages 178-79.
School organization budget, page 180.
Programs of meetings, pages 181-83.
Bulletin board notices, pages 185-86.
Articles and stories for the school newspaper, pages 187-90.
Application letter and other employment papers, pages 192-96.
Student-writer's style guide, pages 197-200.

Improving Your Basic Skills – In addition to the problems, every lesson provides materials for improving your typing accuracy and speed. One lesson in each group of five lessons is entirely devoted to technique refinement and skill building. Continue to improve your speed and accuracy through these drills and lessons.

Emphasis on Related Learnings – Drills stressing capitalization, punctuation, and number expression guides appear throughout the lessons of this cycle. Use these drills to improve the quality of your written work in typewriting and in your other classes.

Measurement – Timed writings to check your progress in typing are scheduled in each group of five lessons. In addition, Unit 15 includes problems typical of those typed earlier in the cycle. Use this unit to check up on your understanding of the different types of problems covered in Cycle 3.

Extra-Credit Assignments – Problems are given at the end of each unit for students who finish assignments ahead of schedule. Type these problems as time permits. Extra credit will be given for them.

• Unit 10

Typing Papers and Reports for Your Family

General Directions • Lessons 76 – 85

Line Length – Use a 70-space line for drills and timed writings. Much of the problem copy that you will type will be set in lines either longer or shorter than those for which your margins are set. It will be necessary for you to listen for the bell, to use the right margin release, and to divide long words coming at the ends of lines.

Identifying Papers – Your teacher will tell you how to identify the papers you prepare.

Erasing – Your teacher will tell you if you are to erase errors made on problem copy.

Spacing – Single-space sentences and drill lines. Double-space between repeated groups of lines. Double-space paragraph copy. Space problem copy as directed.

Margin Stop Reminder – Set the right margin stop 5 to 8 spaces beyond the desired right margin.

• Lesson 76

76a • Keyboard Review • Each line at least three times   *5 minutes*

All letters	SS	Five or six big jet airliners flew quickly overhead at amazing speeds.
Figure		On January 24, 1966, nearly 263 million tons of snow fell on the U. S.
Adjacent keys		Only a long look below the surface will help you locate their problem.
Easy		It is a shame that more folks are not able to laugh at their problems.

Wrists low and still

| 1 | 2 | 3 | 4 | 5 | 6 | 7 | 8 | 9 | 10 | 11 | 12 | 13 | 14 |

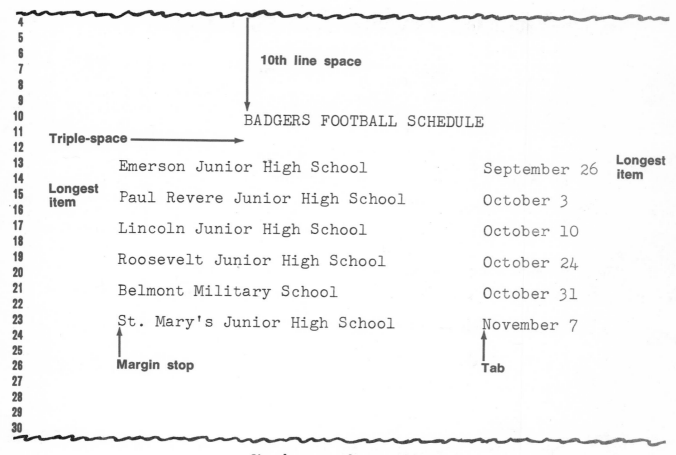

	10th line space	
4		
5		
6		
7		
8		
9		
10	BADGERS FOOTBALL SCHEDULE	
11		
12	Triple-space ⟶	

Longest item

Emerson Junior High School	September 26	Longest item
Paul Revere Junior High School	October 3	
Lincoln Junior High School	October 10	
Roosevelt Junior High School	October 24	
Belmont Military School	October 31	
St. Mary's Junior High School	November 7	

Margin stop   Tab

Simple two-column table

Problem 2—Two-Column Table

Directions – 1. Retype the table in Problem 1, but add another game to the schedule with University Junior High School on November 14.

2. This time type the table on a full sheet in *reading position*. Leave 16 spaces between the columns.

- *Use the vertical centering shortcut explained on page 93. Remember to place the table in reading position.*

• Lesson 63 • *60-space line*

63a • Keyboard Review • Each line three times

5 minutes

All letters	SS	Jacqueline amazed everyone by fixing these packages of bows.
Figure		Mt. Whitney is 14,495 feet, 333 feet higher than Mt. Shasta.
Easy		Anyone would much rather be a good winner than a good loser.

Cut out waste movements

| 1 | 2 | 3 | 4 | 5 | 6 | 7 | 8 | 9 | 10 | 11 | 12 |

75b • Sentence Guided Writings • Type each sentence for one minute. Try typing each at least four times in the minute.

10 minutes

• *The typing rate is in the first column at the right.*

			G W A M 15″ Guide	12″ Guide
1	SS	I sent the bill to Esgro & Son in Omaha.	32	40
2		Jill Drew sewed a pink nylon dress in Joplin.	36	45
3		He should pay $15 on his last month's bill of $45.	40	50
4		We should—and we can—do this job by tomorrow morning.	44	55
5		Anyone reflects what he is by what he does with what he has.	48	60

| 1 | 2 | 3 | 4 | 5 | 6 | 7 | 8 | 9 | 10 | 11 | 12 |

75c • Concentration Practice

10 minutes

Directions – Type the paragraph twice without timing.   Technique Goal – Try typing without errors.

		Words
DS	The Hanging Gardens of Babylon, one of the seven wonders	11
	of the ancient world, were built by Nebuchadnezzar for his	23
	wife Amytis. There were four great terraces with arches and	35
	tunnels through which water could be pumped from the Euphrates	48
	River to keep flowers, trees, and shrubs growing in the midst	60
	of sandy plains.	64

| 1 | 2 | 3 | 4 | 5 | 6 | 7 | 8 | 9 | 10 | 11 | 12 |

75d • Timed Writings from Rough Draft

5 minutes

Directions – Type three 1-minute writings.
Circle errors. Compute *gwam*.

		Words
DS	An typping error is not fa vital. It can be errased. if your	11
	learn the trick of erasing, you r copy work will look fresh and be	23
50 words 1.2 si	tidy. Erasnig will take s time, through, so when you types	34
	some thing you wish want to use type it at a rates at which your feel	47
	sure fo your self.	50

75e • Paragraph Guided Writings • Type 74e, page 128, as directed

15 minutes

63b • Skill Comparison

Directions – Type two 1-minute writings on each sentence. Compare *gwam*.
Try typing all sentences at the rate of the first one.

			Words
Easy	SS	Say what you will, those who learn to study earn top grades.	12
Figure		A boat 14½ feet long crossed the mighty Atlantic in 84 days.	12
Script		*It is a simple fact of life that we do far less than we can.*	12
Rough draft		Believe it not, learning how to study in the school pays off.	12

| 1 | 2 | 3 | 4 | 5 | 6 | 7 | 8 | 9 | 10 | 11 | 12 |

63c • Spelling and Proofreading Aid

Directions – Type each line twice. Study the
words carefully as you type them.

1   SS   altogether committee mischief pamphlet library already style

2   thorough actor eighth ninth surprise assistant depot balloon   *Type letter by letter*

3   dilemma until license newsstand benefited jeopardy all right

63d • Problem Typing

Problem 1—Two-Column Table

Directions – 1. *Center* this table vertically on a half sheet of paper. Leave 20 spaces between columns.

2. Single-space the columnar entries. Triple-space between the heading and the columns.

LEADERS IN PRODUCTION OF FOOD CROPS

Triple-space ———————→

Barley	Soviet Union
Cacao Beans	Ghana
Coffee	Brazil
Corn	United States
Oats	United States
Peanuts	India
Potatoes	Soviet Union
Rice	China
Rye	Soviet Union
Sugar	Soviet Union
Wheat	Soviet Union

Problem 2—Two-Column Table

Directions – 1. Retype the table in Problem 1. Use a full sheet; type the table in *reading position*.

2. Double-space the columnar entries. Leave 24 spaces between columns.

74e • Paragraph Guided Writings

Directions – 1. Type a 3-minute writing. Circle the errors. Note your *gwam*.
2. Type each circled word three times along with the words preceding and following it.
3. Type two 1-minute writings on each paragraph. Try to add four words to your 3-minute *gwam* each time.
4. Type another 3-minute writing. Note your *gwam* and compare it with that of the first writing.

	GWAM	
	1'	**3'**

¶ 1
50 words
1.2 si
DS

The hands of a clock are like the blades of a pair of | 11 | 4 54
scissors. At midnight, they snip off another day; you are one | 23 | 8 58
day closer to your goal, whatever it might be. Time waits for | 36 | 12 62
nobody. It only gives you a chance to tackle the jobs that | 48 | 16 66
await you. | 50 | 17 67

¶ 2
50 words
1.2 si

Before this day is snipped from the clock, ask yourself | 61 | 20 70
what steps you took to reach your goal. If getting an edu- | 73 | 24 74
cation is your goal, just what did you learn today that you | 85 | 28 78
did not know yesterday? What did you do that can make you | 97 | 32 82
a better person? | 100 | 33 83

¶ 3
50 words
1.3 si

The clock passes time by keeping its hands busy. So it | 111 | 37 87
must be with you. You must learn how to solve problems and | 123 | 41 91
enjoy music and art to the full. You cannot learn these things | 136 | 45 95
if you put off until tomorrow the work you should have done | 148 | 49 99

All ¶'s
1.2 si

yesterday. | 150 | 50 100

```
1'|  1  |  2  |  3  |  4  |  5  |  6  |  7  |  8  |  9  |  10  |  11  |  12  |
3'|        1        |        2        |        3        |        4        |
```

• Lesson 75 • *60-space line*

75a • Keyboard Review • Each line three times

All letters   SS   Rex paused to see the wolf, jaguar, and zebras move quickly.

Figure-Symbol   Sue's checks are as follows: #759 for $50.29; #821 for $34.   Sit erect

Easy   A man who empties his purse into his head will lose neither.

```
|  1  |  2  |  3  |  4  |  5  |  6  |  7  |  8  |  9  |  10  |  11  |  12  |
```

• Lesson 64 • *60-space line*

64a • Keyboard Review • Each line three times

5 minutes

All letters	SS	A jury saw Max very quickly analyze the bid forged on paper.
Figure		The first airplane trip ever made covered scarcely 850 feet.
Easy		The way to fail is to do only as much as you must to get by.

| 1 | 2 | 3 | 4 | 5 | 6 | 7 | 8 | 9 | 10 | 11 | 12 |

Quiet wrists
and arms

64b • Typing from Dictation and Spelling Checkup

5 minutes

Directions – Type the words in 63c, page 111, from dictation. Check for correct spelling. Retype any words in which you made an error.

64c • Sentence Guided Writings • Turn to 62b, page 109

10 minutes

Directions – 1. Type each sentence for one minute. Try typing each four times in the minute without error.

2. Your teacher will call the return of the carirage each 15 seconds to guide you.

64d • Problem Typing

25 minutes

Problem 1—Table with Subheading

Full sheet
Double-space column entries

Reading position
24 spaces between columns

• *Space the main heading and sub-heading as shown in the table.*

PRESIDENTS OF THE UNITED STATES

Double-space entries ←————Double-space

Since 1900

←————Triple-space

Theodore Roosevelt	1901 – 1909
William H. Taft	1909 – 1913
Woodrow Wilson	1913 – 1921
Warren G. Harding	1921 – 1923
Calvin Coolidge	1923 – 1929
Herbert C. Hoover	1929 – 1933
Franklin D. Roosevelt	1933 – 1945
Harry S. Truman	1945 – 1953
Dwight D. Eisenhower	1953 – 1961
John F. Kennedy	1961 – 1963
Lyndon B. Johnson	1963 – 1969
Richard M. Nixon	1969 –

Problem 2—Table with Subheading

Full sheet
Double-space column entries

Exact vertical center
18 spaces between columns

• *Space main and subheading as you did in Problem 1.*

NATIVE STATES OF PRESIDENTS

Since 1900

Theodore Roosevelt	New York
William H. Taft	Ohio
Woodrow Wilson	Virginia
Warren G. Harding	Ohio
Calvin Coolidge	Vermont
Herbert C. Hoover	Iowa
Franklin D. Roosevelt	New York
Harry S. Truman	Missouri
Dwight D. Eisenhower	Texas
John F. Kennedy	Massachusetts
Lyndon B. Johnson	Texas
Richard M. Nixon	California

• Lesson 74 • *60-space line*

74a • Keyboard Review • Each line three times

5 minutes

All letters	SS	Walter may give the quaint box to Tex Jacks for third prize.
Figure		On October 1, 1942, the Bell XP59 made our first jet flight.
Easy		All things come to those who wait long enough—even justice.

Cut out waste movements

| 1 | 2 | 3 | 4 | 5 | 6 | 7 | 8 | 9 | 10 | 11 | 12 |

74b Technique Builder — Stroking • Each line three times

10 minutes

3d and 4th fingers	SS	The quince as well as the squash proved to be quite popular.
Third row		I quoted Rip Powers on the value of his trip to the tropics.
Shift		Bob Price may visit Quebec in May and New York City in June.
Balanced- and one-hand		and my, and to do my, and only, and to do the only, and care
Balanced- and one-hand		did see, they did see, they did agree, he did, and he agreed
Balanced- and one-hand		and we, and we saw, and we saw him, they saw, and he saw you

Eyes and mind on copy as you type

| 1 | 2 | 3 | 4 | 5 | 6 | 7 | 8 | 9 | 10 | 11 | 12 |

74c • Concentration Practice • Twice for control

10 minutes

Words

	DS	Work on the statue of the Sioux Indian Chief, Crazy Horse,	12
		located near Mount Rushmore, South Dakota, was begun in 1939.	24
All letters		When completed, it will be the world's largest statue. Reports	37
		say that it will be 561 feet high and 641 feet long. The job	50
		will require the removal of 6 million tons of stone.	60

| 1 | 2 | 3 | 4 | 5 | 6 | 7 | 8 | 9 | 10 | 11 | 12 |

74d • Timed Writings from Script • Type three 1-minute writings. Circle errors. Compute gwam.

5 minutes

Words

	DS	Good writing is like walking, it must get you somewhere.	12
		Write as straight as you can, because that is the best way to	24
56 words 1.3 si		get there. In straight writing, the sentences are usually	36
		short and clear. General nouns and verbs are replaced by	47
		those that have precise, lively meanings.	56

• **Lesson 65** • *60-space line*

65a • **Keyboard Review** • Each line three times

5 minutes

All letters	SS	Jack Kibby will take the next quiz given for camp directors.
Figure-Symbol		Tom, age 14, quoted the March 27 copy of <u>The New York Times</u>.
Easy		Give equal force to the strokes so your typing will be even.

Type steadily

| 1 | 2 | 3 | 4 | 5 | 6 | 7 | 8 | 9 | 10 | 11 | 12 |

65b • **Technique Builder — Stroking** • Each line three times

10 minutes

Home row	SS	Dashing Sir Galahad, with sword and half a flag, flashed by.
First fingers		Tyrus can try to hunt with my gun, as it is not the new one.
Second fingers		Did Dick check Cedric's deck and dice to locate any defects?
Third fingers		Walter Swanson with sixty-six others followed Lloyd to Oslo.
Direct reach		My brother expects to hunt for a diamond mine in the jungle.
Repeated letters		He agreed to call a committee meeting to discuss the matter.

Center stroking in fingers

| 1 | 2 | 3 | 4 | 5 | 6 | 7 | 8 | 9 | 10 | 11 | 12 |

65c • **Timed Writings**

10 minutes

Directions – Type two 3-minute writings on the paragraphs. Circle errors.
Compute *gwam*. Submit the better of the two writings.

	GWAM	
	1'	3'

¶ 1
42 words
1.2 si

DS How many times have you heard people say that they just | 11 4 49
could not write letters? You never hear these same people | 23 8 53
say that they cannot talk to their friends. Still the two | 35 12 57
remarks mean exactly the same thing. | 42 14 59

¶ 2
46 words
1.3 si

Writing a friendly note or letter to someone is like | 53 18 63
having a long cozy chat with him or her. If you find chat- | 64 21 66
ting with someone pleasant, you should not find writing too | 76 25 70
terrifying; for you can just write as if you were talking. | 88 29 74

¶ 3
48 words
1.3 si

Begin your letter by typing the first thought that enters | 100 33 78
your head. Write about what you did, whom you saw, or what | 112 37 82
you read. Very quickly, you will find that one idea leads to | 124 41 86

All ¶'s
1.3 si

another until the page is full of news that sounds like you. | 136 45 90

1' | 1 | 2 | 3 | 4 | 5 | 6 | 7 | 8 | 9 | 10 | 11 | 12 |
3' | 1 | 2 | 3 | 4 |

73b • Technique Builder — Stroking

10 minutes

Directions – Type each line three times.   Technique Goal – Use sharp, even strokes.

4th finger	SS	Paula may apply for this position. A quiz will be required.
Double letters		Allen passed the written test. He must possess a keen mind.
One-hand		we saw, you were, see him, look upon, my regards, as you are
Balanced-hand		for the, to them, do so, and they, did work, go with, may go
Balanced- and one-hand		The great mystery has not been solved by anyone in the army.
Direct reach		Both of the men did see him go to the lake with the baggage.
Direct reach		nu nu nu numb nuts nurse annual nudge numeral nuzzle nucleus

Type with-
out pauses

| 1 | 2 | 3 | 4 | 5 | 6 | 7 | 8 | 9 | 10 | 11 | 12 |

73c • Concentration Practice

10 minutes

Directions – Type the paragraph twice without timing.   Technique Goal – Try typing without errors.

	Words
DS At one time, New Year's Day came on April 1; but a new	11
calendar was made, and this changed the beginning of the new	23
year to January 1. For a long time, people had been saying	35
"Happy New Year" in April. It was difficult to change; so,	47
whenever someone forgot and gave the greeting, "Happy New	59
Year" in April, he was told he was an "April Fool."	69

| 1 | 2 | 3 | 4 | 5 | 6 | 7 | 8 | 9 | 10 | 11 | 12 |

73d • Timed Writings • Type 72d, page 125

15 minutes

73e • Continuity Practice from Rough Draft

5 minutes

Directions – Type as many copies of this paragraph as you can
in the time that remains. Type at a steady pace.

	Words
DS Some one once said that their is to much face finding in	11
47 words	this country world, too little fate facing. this is as true in typ-	24
1.2 si	ing as it is in any thing else you do. It is now time too face the	36
	fact. the only way to improve your skill is to type ringt.	47

65d • Problem Typing

Problem 1—Three-Column Table

Directions – 1. Type the table in *reading position* on a full sheet of paper.
  2. Double-space the columnar entries.
  3. Leave six spaces between the columns.

• *Use the directions on page 109 for setting the left margin stop for the first column and tab stops for the second and third columns.*

GREAT INVENTIONS AND SCIENTIFIC DISCOVERIES

Selected Items

Air Conditioning	Carrier	1911
Airplane, Jet Engine	Whittle	1930
Engine, Automobile	Benz	1897
Meter, Parking	Magee	1953
Movie, Talking	Warner Brothers	1927
Pen, Fountain	Waterman	1884
Piano	Cristofori	1709
Radar	Taylor and Young	1922
Sewing Machine	Thimmonier	1830
Soap, Hard-Water	Bertsch	1928
Telephone	Bell	1876

Problem 2—Two-Column Table from Script

Directions – 1. Type the table in *exact vertical center* on a half sheet of paper.
  2. Single-space the columnar entries.

  3. Leave 8 spaces between columns.
  • *Space the main and subheadings as you did in earlier problems.*

HOW THE AVERAGE FAMILY SPENDS ITS INCOME

After Taxes

Housing	25.1%
Food	21.2
Transportation	13.2
Clothing	8.9
Personal Insurance and Investments	8.6
Medical Care	5.8
Recreation and Education	5.1
Gifts and Contributions	4.8
Miscellaneous	7.3

		GWAM
		1' 3'

¶ 1
50 words
1.2 si

DS   The bark of a cork tree plays an important part in our   11   4   54

daily lives. It is widely used in shoe soles, sun helmets,   23   8   58

paper, floor coverings, and a host of other products. It is   35   12   62

so very light that it floats; yet it is so tough that it stands   48   16   66

hard wear.   50   17   67

¶ 2
50 words
1.2 si

Cork comes from the bark of the cork oak, which is grown   61   20   70

in many parts of the world. Most of our cork, though, comes   74   25   75

from Portugal, Spain, and Algeria. The cork tree is skinned   86   29   79

alive every nine years, an ordeal which it will survive for   98   33   83

many crops.   100   33   83

¶ 3
50 words
1.2 si

When cut, the cork is left in the sun to dry; then it   111   37   87

is placed into vats and boiled to remove the sap and tannic   123   41   91

acid. When this job is completed, the cork is bound into   134   45   95

bales and transported on the backs of mules to Lisbon or   146   49   99

All ¶'s
1.2 si

Seville for shipment.   150   50   100

1' | 1 | 2 | 3 | 4 | 5 | 6 | 7 | 8 | 9 | 10 | 11 | 12 |
3' | 1 | 2 | 3 | 4 |

72e • Corrective Practice   *5 minutes*

Directions – Choose the better of the two writings on the paragraphs in 72d and type the paragraph in which you made the most errors at least twice. Submit this paper with your timed writing.

• Lesson 73 • *60-space line*

73a • Keyboard Review • Each line three times   *5 minutes*

All letters   SS   Clement gave Kip exquisite old jewelry for the bazaar today.

Figure-Symbol   Joe's company has been in business for 91 years (1880-1971).   Instant release

Easy   Thus, he who falls in love with himself will have no rivals.

| 1 | 2 | 3 | 4 | 5 | 6 | 7 | 8 | 9 | 10 | 11 | 12 |

• Lesson 66 • *60-space line*

66a • Keyboard Review • Each line three times

All letters   SS   Marvel Jackson was requested to pay a tax for the big prize.

Figure   The United States has a land area of 3,022,387 square miles.   Instant release

Easy   Wisdom is knowing what to do, and virtue is getting it done.

| 1 | 2 | 3 | 4 | 5 | 6 | 7 | 8 | 9 | 10 | 11 | 12 |

66b • Capitalization Guides — Typing Titles

5 minutes

- Capitalize first words and all other words in titles of books, articles, periodicals, headings, and plays, *except* words which are articles, conjunctions, and prepositions.

- *The title of a book may be underscored or typed in all capital letters.*

Directions – Type each line twice. The sentences illustrate the capitalization rule given above.

1   SS   He is playing a small part in the musical, "Sound of Music."

2   I took the notes from an article, "Africa's Garden of Eden."   Think as

3   DELOS is the name of Nelson's book on the islands of Greece.   you type

4   He reported on Durrell's book, Birds, Beasts, and Relatives.

| 1 | 2 | 3 | 4 | 5 | 6 | 7 | 8 | 9 | 10 | 11 | 12 |

66c • Control Ladder Sentences

15 minutes

Directions – Type 1-minute writings on each sentence. Try typing each four times without error. Your teacher will call the return of the carriage each 15 seconds to guide you.

- The rate increases 4 words a minute with each succeeding line

GWAM 15" Guide

1   SS   Wear a smile and have friends.   24

2   Wear a scowl and have bad wrinkles.   28

3   You must believe in yourself, of course.   32

4   Great jobs are performed by sticking to them.   36

5   No problem we face is as big as the ones we dodge.   40

6   *Are the fingers deeply curved for quick, sure streaking?*   44

7   Do you keep your arms in and your wrists low and quiet?   44

8   *Make a study of the errors you make so you can correct them.*   48

9   A smart person makes errors; a dull one goes on making them.   48

| 1 | 2 | 3 | 4 | 5 | 6 | 7 | 8 | 9 | 10 | 11 | 12 |

71d • Timed Writings • Type 70c, page 121, as directed *15 minutes*

71e • Continuity Practice from Script *5 minutes*

Directions – Type as many times as you can in the time that remains.

	Words
SS *Our goal is not in doing what we want to do but in being*	11
what we ought to be. Keep this thought in mind, for the best	24
lessons you will learn in school are those that teach you to do	37
the things you should whether you like to do them or not.	48

• Lesson 72 • *60-space line*

72a • Keyboard Review • Each line three times *5 minutes*

All letters	SS	Jeff expects to have two dozen big aprons made very quickly.	
Figure-Symbol		Did you know that 80.6% of all car trips are under 10 miles?	Elbows in
Easy		The report says that most hard-boiled people are half-baked.	

| 1 | 2 | 3 | 4 | 5 | 6 | 7 | 8 | 9 | 10 | 11 | 12 |

72b • Concentration Practice • Twice for control *10 minutes*

	Words
DS The Temple of Diana at Ephesus, an ancient wonder of the	11
world, was first built in the seventh century B.C. The temple	24
was destroyed by fire in 356 B.C. by Herostratus. It was re-	36
placed by a more marvelous one by the indignant Ephesians.	48

| 1 | 2 | 3 | 4 | 5 | 6 | 7 | 8 | 9 | 10 | 11 | 12 |

72c • Paragraph Guided Writings *10 minutes*

Directions – Set goals of 40, 44, and 48 words a minute. Type two 1-minute
writings at each rate. Try to hit your goal just as time is called.

DS Believe in luck, but keep in mind that luck only gives
you an opportunity to get what you want. It does not replace

**48 words
1.3 si**

the hard work needed to gain an end. Luck comes to those
willing to try, never to those who only wait, postpone, and
wish.

Eyes on copy
as you return
the carriage

66d • Paragraph Guided Writings • As directed in 61e, page 108

• All letters are used in these paragraphs

GWAM
1' 3'

¶ 1
48 words
1.3 si

DS   We envy the batter who can hit the ball out of the park,   11 4 52

the swimmer who has the title for fancy diving, or the artist   24 8 56

who can give life to colors on canvas. What we fail to see   36 12 60

is the long hours these experts spent acquiring their skill.   48 16 64

¶ 2
48 words
1.3 si

One must get quite a thrill when he learns for the first   59 20 68

time that he is endowed with raw talent. He can sing, write a   72 24 72

story, or jump higher than anybody else in his class. But   84 28 76

talent has its price. Unless it is developed, it is useless.   96 32 80

¶ 3
48 words
1.2 si

Practice is a potent learning aid. All experts know this   107 36 84

secret, and they use it to perfect their craft. Why not use   120 40 88

this secret, too? Prize good work highly; practice. It is   132 44 92

All ¶'s
1.3 si

great to have the power to learn; it is tragic not to use it.   144 48 96

```
1' | 1 | 2 | 3 | 4 | 5 | 6 | 7 | 8 | 9 | 10 | 11 | 12 |
3' |     1     |     2     |     3     |     4     |
```

66e • Control Practice

Directions – 1. Type the last paragraph of 66d, above, as many times as you can in the time that remains.

2. Circle your errors. Place a check mark in the margin of each paragraph in which you made no more than one error.

• Lesson 67 • 60-space line

67a • Keyboard Review • Each line three times

All letters   SS   Zelda expects to be in Quincy for a visit with Jack Goodman.

Figure-Symbol   He paid $7.00 for books, $1.20 for paper, and 75¢ for a pen.

Easy   All work that is well done has a way of speaking for itself.

```
| 1 | 2 | 3 | 4 | 5 | 6 | 7 | 8 | 9 | 10 | 11 | 12 |
```

Type with
your fingers

Improving Your Basic Skills — Measurement

General Directions • Lessons 71 – 75

Machine Adjustments – For the lessons in this unit, use a 60-space line. Single-space lines of words or sentences, but double-space between repeated groups of lines. Double-space paragraph copy.

Adapting the Lessons to Your Needs – The plan of these lessons is suggestive and aimed at improving many basic skills. Take additional time for practice on lesson parts on which you need special help.

• Lesson 71

71a • **Keyboard Review** • Each line three times

• *If time permits, type 1-minute writings on the keyboard reviews in the lessons of this unit.*

5 minutes

All letters	SS	Pack the seven dozen boxes of quince jam on the yellow rigs.
Symbol		He read "How We Mapped the Moon" in the <u>National Geographic.</u>
Easy		The man who knows but little—and knows it—knows very much.

Quick, sharp strokes

| 1 | 2 | 3 | 4 | 5 | 6 | 7 | 8 | 9 | 10 | 11 | 12 |

71b • **Concentration Practice**

10 minutes

Directions – Type the paragraph twice without timing.   **Technique Goal** – Try typing without errors.

Words

DS   The pyramids of Egypt, wonders of the modern and ancient   11

worlds, are the oldest structures in the world. Herodotus,   23

the "father of history," tells us that the Great Pyramid was   36

built by Cheops. One hundred thousand men, working for twenty   48

years, were needed to complete this great pyramid.   58

| 1 | 2 | 3 | 4 | 5 | 6 | 7 | 8 | 9 | 10 | 11 | 12 |

71c • **Technique Builder — Stroking** • Each line three times

10 minutes

3d and 4th fingers	SS	What sizes are the zinc plates? Are the zinc plates square?
Double letters		The class may meet the girl who worked the difficult puzzle.
Balanced- and one-hand		did see, they did see, they did agree, he did, and he agreed
Shift		Fred saw Pikes Peak. Ben fished in Lake Erie. Leo paid Al.
Direct reach		br br br bride brush brings bright brace broom brought brief
Direct reach		ce ce ce center certain cents accept niece mice piece police
Direct reach		Cecil Hunter may bring his musical group to the opera house.

Reach with your fingers

| 1 | 2 | 3 | 4 | 5 | 6 | 7 | 8 | 9 | 10 | 11 | 12 |

67b • Spelling and Proofreading Aid • Each line three times

5 minutes

1   ss   financial forgave mortgage enthusiasm imitate attempt nephew

2   wreck promptly weary statue campaign privilege doubted debts

*Type letter
by letter*

3   bureaus often travelers courteous muscles completely easiest

67c • Paragraph Guided Writings

5 minutes

Directions – 1. Turn to ¶ 1, 66d, page 116.
2. Set a goal of 40, 44, or 48 words a minute on the paragraph.

3. Type three 1-minute writings. Try to hit your goal word just as time is called. The quarter- or half-minutes will be called to guide you.

67d • Problem Typing

30 minutes

Problem—Four-Column Table

Directions – 1. Type the table in *reading position* on a full sheet of paper.
2. Single-space the columnar entries.
3. Leave six spaces between the columns.

• *Use the directions on page 109 for setting the left margin stop for the first column and tab stops for the second, third, and fourth columns.*

TWO-LETTER ABBREVIATIONS FOR THE STATES

Recommended by the U.S. Post Office Department

Alabama	AL	Montana	MT
Alaska	AK	Nebraska	NE
Arizona	AZ	Nevada	NV
Arkansas	AR	New Hampshire	NH
California	CA	New Jersey	NJ
Colorado	CO	New Mexico	NM
Connecticut	CT	New York	NY
Delaware	DE	North Carolina	NC
Florida	FL	North Dakota	ND
Georgia	GA	Ohio	OH
Hawaii	HI	Oklahoma	OK
Idaho	ID	Oregon	OR
Illinois	IL	Pennsylvania	PA
Indiana	IN	Rhode Island	RI
Iowa	IA	South Carolina	SC
Kansas	KS	South Dakota	SD
Kentucky	KY	Tennessee	TN
Louisiana	LA	Texas	TX
Maine	ME	Utah	UT
Maryland	MD	Vermont	VT
Massachusetts	MA	Virginia	VA
Michigan	MI	Washington	WA
Minnesota	MN	West Virginia	WV
Mississippi	MS	Wisconsin	WI
Missouri	MO	Wyoming	WY

70d • Problem Typing

15 minutes

Problem—Report with Short Table

Full sheet
60-space line
Double spacing
Single-space
the table

Directions – Have a top margin of two inches (12 spaces). Allow eight spaces between the columns of the table.

• *In double-spaced copy, a triple space should precede the table and a triple space should follow it.*

AMERICAN ECONOMIC SYSTEM

Triple-space

An economic system is the method used by the people of a country to make a living. The system in our country tries to give the people as much freedom as possible to work for and use the things they need and want. It is sometimes referred to as the free-enterprise system. It gives us the desire to put forth the best we have in ability and energy. Listed here are some of the freedoms our people enjoy.

Triple-space

FREEDOMS WE ENJOY

Triple-space

Own property	Travel
Express opinions	Organize
Buy where we wish	Live where we wish
Choose a job	Protect our ideas

Triple-space

What about the American system? How well does it work? Our system makes it possible for us to have more of the things needed for a comfortable living than most people have in other countries. For example, Americans own six out of every ten automobiles, half the telephones and radios, and two of every three television sets in the world. About sixty percent of our families own their own homes. We have about five times as much living space per person as the Russians have, for example.

We are making progress all the time. A worker today can produce about six times as much in an hour as he did a century ago. Our free-enterprise system makes this possible.

70e • Extra-Credit Typing

Problem 1

Directions – Type the names of students in your typing class by rows. Provide main, subheadings, and columnar headings. Arrange the columns and center the table on a full sheet.

Problem 2

Directions – Type a summary of the report in 70d. Do not use a table, but use the ideas in it. Use the directions in 70d for typing your summary.

Problem 3

Directions – Use the first paragraph in 70c, page 121. Type as many errorless copies of this paragraph as you can in the time that remains.

• Lesson 68 • 60-space line

68a • Keyboard Review • Each line three times

5 minutes

All letters	SS	Randy Jay packed five more bags with a dozen boxes of quail.
Figure		St. Augustine, Florida, our first town, was founded in 1565.
Easy		Less talk and more work will result in rewards for them all.

| 1 | 2 | 3 | 4 | 5 | 6 | 7 | 8 | 9 | 10 | 11 | 12 |

Wrists and elbows still

68b • Skill Comparison • 1-minute writing on each sentence. Compare gwam.

5 minutes

Easy	SS	The first rule of writing good copy is knowing your subject.
Script		*When you write papers, be brief; there is no weight to wind.*
Rough draft		In the a free country ies there will all ways be a clash of of ideas.

| 1 | 2 | 3 | 4 | 5 | 6 | 7 | 8 | 9 | 10 | 11 | 12 |

Type without stopping

68c • Typing from Dictation and Spelling Checkup

5 minutes

Directions – Type 67b, page 117, from dictation. Check for correct spelling. Retype any words in which you made an error.

CENTERING COLUMNAR HEADINGS

Follow these steps to center headings over the columns of a table:

1. Set the carriage at the point a column is to begin.
2. Space forward 1 space for each 2 spaces in the longest line in that column.
3. From that point, backspace once for each 2 spaces in the columnar heading.
4. Type the heading. It will be centered over the column.

68d • Problem Typing

30 minutes

Problem 1—Practice Problem

Directions – 1. Insert a sheet of practice paper. The two entries below are the longest in each of two columns of a table.
2. Plan the tabulation, allowing 24 spaces between the columns. Type the two entries.

3. A double-space above the items type the columnar headings. Center the headings over the entries.

• *To center the headings, follow the steps in the foregoing explanation.*

Columnar headings ——————→Date

Longest entries ——————→November 14

Chairman

←——————Double-space

Lucille Washington

70b • Sentence Guided Writings

10 minutes

Directions – 1. Type each sentence for one minute. Try typing each at least four times in the minute.

2. Your teacher will call the return of the carriage each 15 seconds to guide you.

• *The rates at which you will be typing are given in the first column at the right.*

			GWAM 15" Guide	12" Guide
1	SS	Do you sit poised and erect as you type?	32	40
2		Do you type without pauses between the words?	36	45
3		Do you strike each key with a quick, sharp stroke?	40	50
4		Do you think and type the short, easy words as a whole?	44	55
5		Do you hold the wrists low and quiet as you strike the keys?	48	60

| 1 | 2 | 3 | 4 | 5 | 6 | 7 | 8 | 9 | 10 | 11 | 12 |

70c • Timed Writings

15 minutes

Directions – 1. Type two 1-minute writings on each ¶. Mark the one on which you made your best rate; then mark the one on which you made the fewest errors.

2. Type two 3-minute writings on the copy below. Circle errors. Compute *gwam*. Submit the better of the two writings.

		GWAM 1'	3'

¶ 1
50 words
1.3 si

DS   Do you know why many people fail in their jobs? Their   `11  4  54`
spelling, poor as it often is, is not the reason. They get   `23  8  58`
by in figuring, too. The reports of many studies show that   `35  12  62`
they fail because they do not work with one another as well   `47  16  66`
as they should.   `50  17  67`

¶ 2
50 words
1.2 si

We ask much of the other fellow, but give little in   `60  20  70`
return. We stress his mistakes with the same zest that we   `72  24  74`
use in hiding our own. We are not fair to him, nor are we   `84  28  78`
honest with ourselves. We simply fail to work together in   `96  32  82`
the office as a team.   `100  33  83`

¶ 3
50 words
1.3 si

Good teamwork comes, first of all, from handling our   `111  37  87`
duties well. It comes, too, from using kind words when we   `122  41  91`
refer to those with whom we work. Adopt the rule never to   `134  45  95`
say anything about someone else that you would not

All ¶'s
1.3 si

have said about you.

| 1' | 1 | 2 | 3 | 4 | 5 | 6 |
| 3' | | 1 | | |

Problem 2—Table with Columnar Headings

Directions – 1. Type this table in *exact vertical center* on a half sheet.

2. Single-space the columnar entries, as shown.
3. Leave 24 spaces between columns.

JEFFERSON CAMERA CLUB

Double-space ——————————————→

Program Chairmen Assignments

Triple-space ——————————————→

Date	Chairman

Double-space ——————————————→

Date	Chairman
October 3	Lucille Washington
October 17	Terry Tanida
November 14	Joseph Rodriguez
November 28	Melvin Goodman
December 12	Mike Ballou
January 9	Doris Musich
January 23	Donald Bruzek

• Lesson 69 • *60-space line*

69a • Keyboard Review • Each line three times

5 minutes

All letters   SS   Phil Singer wanted Jack to fly Liza to Quebec next November.

Figure-Symbol   Type market quotations in figures: Sell Lockhead at 27 3/8.

Easy   Talent is a gift; you can have it only when you work for it.

| 1 | 2 | 3 | 4 | 5 | 6 | 7 | 8 | 9 | 10 | 11 | 12 |

Quick carriage return

69b • Composing at the Typewriter

10 minutes

Directions – Type answers to as many of these questions as time permits. Use complete sentences.

1. By what name was William F. Códy generally known?

2. By what name was Samuel L. Clemens generally known?

3. What was the event that made Charles Lindbergh famous?

4. Which city is the world's largest? What is its approximate population?

5. Who was the first astronaut to step on the moon?

6. What event is celebrated on July 4?

7. If you start typing on the 13th line space from the top of your paper, how many inches are there in the top margin?

8. Name as many of the nine planets of the solar system as you can.

9. Who was the first United States astronaut to circle the globe in a spaceship?

10. What event made the Wright Brothers famous?

69c • Problem Typing

30 minutes

Problem 1—Table with Columnar Headings

Full sheet
Reading position
Single-space
6 spaces between
columns

THE HALL OF FAME

Elections Since 1950

Name	Calling	Elected
Susan B. Anthony	Reformer	1950
Alexander Graham Bell	Inventor	1950
Josiah Willard Gibbs	Physicist	1950
William Crawford Gorgas	Physician	1950
Theodore Roosevelt	Statesman	1950
Woodrow Wilson	Statesman	1950
Thomas "Stonewall" Jackson	Army Officer	1955
George Westinghouse	Inventor	1955
Wilbur Wright	Inventor	1955
Thomas A. Edison	Inventor	1960
Edward A. MacDowell	Composer	1960
Henry D. Thoreau	Writer	1960
Jane Addams	Social Worker	1965
Oliver Wendell Holmes, Jr.	Jurist	1965
Sylvanus Thayer	Army Officer	1965
Orville Wright	Inventor	1965

Problem 2—Table with Columnar Headings

Directions – 1. Type the table in Problem 1 in the *exact vertical center* of a half sheet. Include only the elections of 1960 and 1965.

2. Change the subheading to fit the table.
3. Double-space the column items.
4. Leave 6 spaces between columns.

• Lesson 70 • *60-space line*

70a • Keyboard Review • Each line three times

5 minutes

All letters   SS   We might require five dozen packing boxes for our July crop.

Figure   The average depth, in feet, of the Atlantic Ocean is 12,880.

Quick, crisp,
short strokes

Easy   Yet, the more you know, the more you know you ought to know.

| 1 | 2 | 3 | 4 | 5 | 6 | 7 | 8 | 9 | 10 | 11 | 12 |